Praise for Jeremy Reynalds' previous work

If anyone knows the ins-and-outs of homelessness and the solutions that will work, it is Jeremy Reynalds. I have grown to deeply respect his work and labor of love for the underprivileged and needy. I know this book will help keep a cause in the forefront of our national consciousness that needs our ongoing attention.

Once again I applaud Jeremy's willingness to champion the rights of those who rarely have such an impassioned advocate.

> Mike Shreve, B.Th., D.D. Cleveland, TN Director / Deeper Revelation Books Director / Triumphant Living Ministries Mike Shreve Ministries

"Now You See Me" is worth reading: it brought tears to my eyes! It is much more than a written book, it is lives completely sold out! Jeremy Reynalds and the team at Joy Junction show compassion, commitment for the homeless on a daily basis! Jeremy Reynalds pursuit of God's purpose has caused Him to breathe favor upon this ministry. Joy Junction have accepted and welcomed people from different backgrounds, races and cultures and lives are being transformed. As you being to read Joy Junction, I pray that you begin to see the wonderful plans that God has for you!

> Loriaan Smith-Taylor, housewife/missionary

Just like Dr. Reynalds' previous books in this series, "Now You See Me" gives us a continuing glimpse into the pain wracked and unbelievably difficult world of the homeless. As you read through these amazing stories of God's redemption, it is my prayer you will realize that in addition to ministry opportunities overseas, you have an entire mission field in your town and at your local mission.

> Dan Wooding, veteran journalist and founder of the ASSIST News service

"Dr. Jeremy Reynalds offers a practical solution to homelessness. He advocates a total restoration of those who are homeless and broken, often through no fault of their own. Joy Junction Homeless Shelter, with which I have been associated for many years, does more than simply feed and house its guests. It seeks to restore the entire person through retraining, healing and spiritual reorientation. "Now You See Me" brings both tragic and heartwarming stories of real people who are transformed through Jesus Christ during their stay at Joy Junction, and made whole, productive members of society. I hope these stories of hope will touch your heart as they have mine, and will encourage you that such miraculous transformations, and a ministry like Joy Junction, are also possible in your community."

> Chaplain Randy Wren, B.S., M.Div., Oklahoma City, Oklahoma

"When discussing homelessness in America, it's easy to get caught up in the numbers and statistics. Now You See Me lets us see the faces."

> Joel John Roberts, CEO of PATH Partners.

Jeremy Reynalds has a special combination of blunt realism and a relentless pursuit of sharing God's grace with those in need. I have no doubt that heaven is pleased by the work that Jeremy does, and this book is a reflection of his heart.

> Chip Lusko, Associate Pastor, Calvary of Albuquerque and General Manager, Connection Communications

"These stories put a face on the homeless"

> Ann Edenfield Sweet, founder/executive director, Wings Ministry

"This book will touch and impact your heart, changing your view of the homeless"

> Chaplain Johnny Probst, author, Strangers and Pilgrims book series

"We are so used to seeing the needy and homeless, that sometimes we don't 'see' them. While their often pleading eyes beg for a touch, smile, a simple hello or a cup of coffee, many times we just go on our way. In this book, veteran homeless advocate, Dr. Jeremy Reynalds gives us a glimpse into their pain wracked world and reasons why you need to respond with love to the many homeless people who live on the streets of your city. It is a book you won't put down."

> Dan Wooding, Journalist and founder of ASSIST Ministries and ASSIST News Service

"Jeremy has spent a lifetime of bringing joy to people who are struggling through some of the most difficult junctions in their lives. These stories put a face on the homeless, and show how sharing Christ's love and compassion brings about hope and renewal."

Ann Edenfield Sweet, Founder/Executive director, Wings Ministry, Albuquerque, N.M.

"I had the privilege of meeting with Jeremy Reynalds for coffee one morning In Huntington Beach, California. I was deeply moved by his compassion and sensitivity to several homeless persons near the coffee shop. He instantly recognized their plight and in thirty minutes observed and discerned more about them than many people would learn in a lifetime. That's because God has placed a call to the homeless on Jeremy's life and given an anointing and passion for those to whom he ministers. This dedication and love is presented throughout 'We All Need A Little Help'. Life drama stories in this book will touch and impact you heart, changing your view of the homeless."

Johnny Probst, Author and Chaplain

"Jeremy Reynalds' new book, 'We All Need A Little Help' is a collage of amazing stories and observations about people in need. Many of the stories are actually unbelievable. But the book is both insightful and helpful. It focuses on how God works through the lives of the destitute as well as in the lives of the Joy Junction leaders. Reynalds is both candid and transparent in sharing his life story and making life applications from the stories of those less fortunate."

Gifford Claiborne, Fundraising Consultant

"This book reads like a novel as Jeremy draws us into his life of care of the homeless with warm, personal stories. I've felt the trails of poverty, and seen how kindness and respect lifts people above them. The book is filled with hope and encouragement for me to get up and do what I can for others."

Ron Davis, President, Milwaukee Direct Marketing, Wisconsin

"With the increasing need for charity for homeless people, Jeremy Reynalds and Joy Junction stand out as a leader and a protector of many. Jeremy writes about what we all fear could happen to anyone. He brings reality to the forefront in hopes to make changes for many."

Larry Garrison, President of Silver Creek Entertainment

Homeless in the City II

A Mission of Love

Jeremy Reynalds, Ph.D.

WestBow
PRESS
A DIVISION OF THOMAS NELSON

WestBow Press books may be ordered through booksellers or by contacting:

WestBow Press
A Division of Thomas Nelson
1663 Liberty Drive
Bloomington, IN 47403
www.westbowpress.com
1-(866) 928-1240

Because of the dynamic nature of the Internet, any Web addresses or links contained in this book may have changed since publication and may no longer be valid. The views expressed in this work are solely those of the author and do not necessarily reflect the views of the publisher, and the publisher hereby disclaims any responsibility for them.

ISBN: 978-1-4497-0364-6 (sc)
ISBN: 978-1-4497-0365-3 (dj)
ISBN: 978-1-4497-0363-9 (e)

Library of Congress Control Number: 2010932294

This publication is designed to provide entry of an authoritative information with regard to the subject matter covered. It is sold with the understanding that the publisher is not engaged in rendering legal, accounting, or other professional advice. If legal advice or other expert assistance is required, the services as a competent professional person should be sought.

Printed in the United States of America
WestBow Press rev. date: 08/13/2010

CONTENTS

INTRODUCTION

What you are about to read has been harvested from years of practical ministry experience. When I began ministering to the homeless in Santa Fe, New Mexico, in 1982, I had no idea "ministry" included formulating budgets, keeping neighbors happy, and dealing with local government bodies such as the fire, health and zoning departments. I thought caring for homeless people meant sharing the love of Christ with them and giving them a hand up instead of a handout.

But such work is an integral part of any legitimate and successful ministry. In addition to dealing with local government, there is also the requirement of working with the Internal Revenue Service to establish a nonprofit tax-exempt corporation, and the successful maintaining of that status.

This book is written to encourage my readers to obey God's calling if he is leading them to full-time ministry. But it is also a personal story of how the Lord has worked in my life and how, in the midst of a very dark time, he personally reawakened his original calling in my life.

It is also designed to help us "do it right" and avoid bringing reproach on ourselves or the body of Christ. Of course, it is important to remember that while ministry is most definitely not glamorous, it is nonetheless the most rewarding thing one can do if doing it in response to God's call in one's life.

This book is dedicated to the Lord, without whom Joy Junction would not have come into existence, and to the many homeless men, women, and families who have met their Lord and Savior Jesus Christ and experienced his compassion while staying with us.

My thanks go also to Dr. Bob Gassaway, formerly of the University of New Mexico's Communication and Journalism Department who, in addition to being a wonderful mentor and a good friend, gave me a lifelong appreciation of the importance of correct grammar.

For more information about Joy Junction, please visit our Web site: www.joyjunction.org. I may be contacted at P.O. Box 27693, Albuquerque, NM 87125, or by telephone at (505) 877-6967. You may also e-mail me at jeremyreynalds@comcast.net

Jeremy Reynalds, Ph.D.
Albuquerque, New Mexico

Part 1

Preparing to Care for the Homeless

HOMELESS IN AMERICA

1

I was not on a mission for God, just a broke young Englishman stranded in the American Southwest.

I had made it to the New Mexico-Texas border but ended up standing in the blazing sun for hours. Cars sped by, but none stopped. As the hours passed, I was getting more and more tired, so I left the highway and walked to a store. I wearily looked through a telephone directory and called the first church I could find. I asked whoever answered the phone if he could help me find shelter. The man told me that I was welcome to sleep on the church floor, but I would have to walk there—a distance of about five miles. Needless to say, walking that far on an unknown Texas highway was more than my body or spirit could endure. I thanked him and dejectedly hung up.

Walking back a few yards, I saw a restaurant that was about to close for the night; it didn't matter, because I had no money for food. I saw that behind the restaurant there was a storage shed filled with odds and ends, and I looked for something to sleep on. The only thing that looked suitable was a piece of fiberglass, and that was my bed for the night.

I woke up early the next day and headed down the highway again. Soon, a trucker stopped and gave me a ride to Phoenix. By this time, I was starving. Without me asking, the kind trucker shared his sandwiches with me.

Looking back all these years later, I see the Lord's hand in my life. Back then, I was just another homeless person on the road, but today, I am founder and CEO of Joy Junction, New Mexico's largest emergency homeless shelter. The transformation came through God's grace in my life.

Growing Up in England

I lay in bed and listened to the muffled, angry voices coming from the living room. My heart began to pound. My mother and father were arguing again. About what, I did not know. I just knew they were fighting.

At the age of eleven, I hated my parents' almost nightly fights. I knew my mother was unhappy living with my wheelchair-bound father, diagnosed several years earlier with multiple sclerosis. On a number of occasions, she acidly told me that if my dad had not been sick, she would have left him. At other times, Mom informed me that I should be grateful she stuck around to take care of my older brother and me. Lots of parents would not have done that, she said. Mom succinctly explained to me that she only married my father because he told her he would apply for a commissioned officer's position in Britain's Royal Air Force. He failed to do so, and now, because of his disability, there was no chance of that. She felt cheated and angry.

As sharp tones filtered through the muffled voices, I focused on the one bright spot on the horizon: I would be leaving for boarding school in a few weeks. Initially, I looked forward to this as an escape, but later it became my own private nightmare.

At night, I was the routine victim of schoolboy pranks, such as having my bed short sheeted. Days were filled with dread, as I worried about being laughed at for my stammering when asked to give an impromptu answer. If that wasn't enough, there was also the necessity of faking a sickness to escape the perils of hockey games, rugby football, cricket, or cross-country running—all nightmares for my unathletic body and so much fun for others to laugh at. I was learning that I didn't seem to fit in anywhere, so I retreated into a world of books, where no one demanded anything from me. This traumatic time was perhaps the beginning of me emotionally shutting down. The pain of being continually taunted by a multitude of pampered and merciless British kids was too much for me to bear.

The school was in Bournemouth, only about an hour's bus ride from my home on England's south coast. Ironically, my escape was to go home many weekends to the home from which I had tried to escape. Looking back, perhaps I concluded that the tension at home was somewhat bearable compared to the abject misery I endured at school.

Admittedly, there were a few fun times. One early morning, all the kids in my dorm awoke at about two o'clock, buzzing with excitement. The chapel was on fire. Since a destroyed chapel meant no church services in the morning, and maybe for a long time, the kids were elated. In my pre-Christian days, these chapel services were extremely boring for me—just something else in my life to be endured rather than enjoyed.

The next morning, the fire and the circumstances surrounding it were the talk of the campus, and did we love what we found out! The word was that the school chaplain had gone for an evening of entertainment in a nearby town. Returning to school (where he lived) in the early hours of the morning, he found the chapel on fire. However, this hip spiritual adviser had not gone to the dance dressed in robe and cassock. He had been dressed in full sixties regalia, including a Beatles-style wig and high-heeled boots. Naturally, we all thought this was hilarious. No one talked about anything else for days afterward.

I scarcely remember anything about most of my classes and my professors. There was one very memorable class I attended, however, even though I hated it. It was math class and my professor, a born-again Christian, was someone I have never forgotten. The last few math lessons of each semester were different. For a treat at the end of each semester, this professor asked if we would like him to read to us. Naturally we agreed, even though his choice of books was not ours. (But then, anything beat math!) His readings of choice were evangelical Christian books, usually dramatic life stories about a hero of the Christian faith who had done exciting things for the Lord. While I did not know the Lord of the Good Book, the stories were very gripping and easily held my attention.

I took it on myself to argue with this teacher about Christianity's irrelevance to the culture. I was then a vegetarian, and I had read books that perverted Scripture to prove that Jesus didn't eat meat, either. I used those books as weapons to argue with him.

Instead of falling for my arguments, this godly man responded that the important thing not what Jesus ate but what he had done for me on the cross. I responded by letting my long-suffering instructor know that Christianity was a crutch for the intellectually feeble and for old women. How difficult it must have been for this professor to deal with my obstinacy. Still, those powerful, end-of-term stories remained with me, as did my memories of this faithful, patient man.

I wanted to study sociology, a subject not offered at my boarding school, so I finished the last couple of years of my education back in Bournemouth, living at home again. I still did not fit in. It was a different school, with different people, but I encountered the same misery. I was desperately lonely and felt like an outsider again.

I threw myself into my newfound studies of sociology and English literature and soon adopted all the latest sociological buzzwords and phrases into my vocabulary. One such phrase was Karl Marx's well-known saying, "Religion is the opiate of the people."

I remember scoffing at various religious posters I saw plastered around Bournemouth. I proudly declared, "I am not a Christian. I am an agnostic. You can't tell if there is a God." My mother was bitterly angry about this, but I reasoned that if the Bible was not true, and I had already made up my mind that it was not, then Christianity is false, since the Bible is its foundation.

Desperate for friends, I eagerly welcomed attention of any type. On day I was sitting in the student lounge, when an attractive young woman came up to me and started talking. I soon learned that her name was Jenny Griffith. There was a "hook" to the conversation, however. Jenny was a Christian, and she invited me to church. I did not relish the prospect, but I definitely liked the idea of seeing more of Jenny, so I went. Was I in for a shock! This was not like anything I had imagined. My idea of church was based on very formal, proper, incense-burning Anglican parishes. This church was not like that at all. It was very small, and it had no organ. There were seats instead of pews. The congregation sang lively, upbeat songs and sounded as if they actually enjoyed being there. Everyone was very friendly. Surprisingly, I liked it. This was definitely unlike any other type of church or religious organization I had ever encountered.

I continued returning to this small, friendly, informal little church— although not for the right reasons. I was hoping there might be the possibility of a relationship springing up between Jenny and me. The Lord, meanwhile, had other more significant things in mind, beginning with my salvation!

The Gospel Hits Home

Following one Sunday night service, the pastor approached me and asked if I wanted to do anything about "it." I asked him what "it" was, and he again responded by saying, "It." I told him I was not interested in "it," and that was the end of the conversation.

It was not until much later that I learned that Pastor Phillip Powell was really asking me if I wanted to commit my life to Jesus Christ. He did not want to be overly pushy and force the situation. Hence the mystery about "it." He did not want me to run out the door and never come back.

As the weeks went on, I continued attending church. Curiously, I even started listening to contemporary Christian music at home. I was also developing an interest in what the pastor was saying. It seemed the Lord's hook had caught another fish, and it was time to reel it in. While initially attending church to spend more time with Jenny and not to learn about Jesus, I heard the Word preached and taught, and now it was beginning to take effect.

One day, I purchased a copy of a modern translation of the Bible, *Good News for Modern Man*, and for the first time, I read it with an open mind. Instead of considering myself to be intellectually superior, I read the Bible with a sincere interest in knowing who God is. I picked up that book and said, "God, if you're real, please speak to me in a way I can understand." At that point, I can honestly say that I had a genuine, supernatural experience. The letters on the Bible page in front of me appeared to be about six feet tall.

From that point on, I read Scripture with a different set of eyes, the eyes an understanding God had given me. And I knew what I read was true. I asked God to intervene in my life in a way I could grasp, and he honored my request. He will do the same for anyone who asks him.

The Word says if we seek God, we will find him. That supernatural experience was over thirty years ago. It was a one-of-a-kind encounter, and God chose to meet me where I was at that time in my life. Although there have been other supernatural experiences, nothing quite like that one has occurred since. My relationship with the Lord has deepened over the years, and I suppose he no longer needs to communicate with me quite so dramatically.

Despite that extraordinary incident, I was still not on board with trusting Jesus as my Savior. I had not completely surrendered my life to his control, but the Lord was supernaturally preparing my heart to do so. I did not even know how to "get saved." A week later, however, I was reading a book by an Anglican clergyman named David Watson. He made a very simple, yet profoundly compelling statement to the effect that if you have never asked Jesus Christ to be your Lord and Savior, you are not a Christian, and you will be eternally lost.

My newfound understanding of the truth of the Bible swept away any reasons to hesitate. At that moment, I bowed my head and asked Jesus Christ to be the Lord of my life. There were no flashing lights and no further supernatural experiences; it was just a quiet act of obedience to God's Word. At that point, the future course and direction of my life became clear. I was a Christian, and God was getting ready to begin an exciting work in my life, a life God himself had ordained for me.

Becoming a Christian brought with it certain profound changes in my personality and behavior. My mother began noticing those transformations in me and became rather worried about my sudden religious "fanaticism." At first, she was not overly concerned about the changes she saw, because she thought it was just another phase I was going through and that I would get over it.

Then, as my faith began to increase rather than dissipate, she became very concerned. My mother even went so far as to make an appointment for me with a local Anglican parish priest. He asked me if I really thought that anyone who did not receive Jesus Christ as his Lord and Savior would go to hell. Assuring him that I most definitely believed just that, he terminated the interview, shaking his head in absolute disbelief (no pun intended). By the time I left his office, I thought for sure he had given up hope for me. What he didn't realize was that I had an eternal hope by the name of Jesus.

Bible School

I felt the need to receive some Bible college instruction, so I spent the 1976–1977 academic year at a Bible college in South Wales. It was a good experience for the most part, like being in a spiritual hothouse.

After finishing a year at Bible school, I returned home to Bournemouth, where the burning question became what I planned to do with my life. As I prayed, I began to feel that God might be calling me to full-time ministry. That was a challenge for me then. The church in England in which I was saved did not give young people the opportunity to make their own decision about obeying God's calling in their life. In other words, you could not decide individually to obey God; someone had to decide for you. Still, I followed the call, so I applied to a couple of universities and to London Bible College (LBC). I was accepted at LBC, but shortly thereafter,

I began sensing a call from God to go to the United States. I applied to Southeastern College in Lakeland, Florida, and was initially accepted, but that was only the beginning. There were still lots of other issues to be worked out, such as how I planned to pay for everything.

While England was very generous in student financial aid, that generosity only extended to those attending British colleges and universities. The British government was not willing to finance a student going to school in the United States. I was at a standstill. I was unemployed, with an acceptance at an American college valid only if I could come up with the funds to get there and subsequently support myself.

Meanwhile, things were a little rocky at church youth group meetings, where I soon became the object of humor—especially when there were guest speakers. When other young people introduced themselves to guests and said what they did for a living, they would laughingly say, "Oh, that's Jeremy Reynalds, and he's going to America!"

The months dragged on, and I was not any closer to getting over the pond. Had I missed God's calling in my life? Perhaps I should abandon the entire plan.

A few weeks later, though, when I was on the verge of giving up my idea to immigrate to the United States, something very interesting happened. I had been corresponding with a minister who had previously spent some time in the United States, and he invited me to meet him. Consequently, a few weeks later, I took the train from Bournemouth to London, a journey of about one hundred miles, to meet with this individual. I told him all my woes, hoping he might offer me some money. He did not. Instead, he told me, "Jeremy, you say that God has called you to America. But right now you have a lot of time on your hands. I wish I had the amount of time you do. Go home and make up your mind that you are going. If you say that God has told you, act on it." This man's sound advice began to cause a change in my thinking. God used his words to speak deeply to my heart, and I knew from then on that I would be going to America.

America, Here I Come!

Three days later, a lady who did not profess any relationship with Christ, but whom I knew through friends, asked me how my plans to go to the United States were going. A short while later, she gave me two hundred dollars for the airfare. Ten days later, I was offered a place to stay in

Orlando, Florida, by an English pastor and his wife, who opened their home to me without even knowing who I was.

Seventeen days later, I was on the plane. Even though I was actually flying across the Atlantic, it was still hard for me to believe it. I had dreamed, hoped, and prayed for so long. Now my dream was becoming a reality. I might not have been so keen to go had I known everything lying in store for me, including homelessness, near poverty, almost losing my ministry, and an eventual divorce. But one thing I learned quickly: it was time for me to grow up. I was on my own now.

For the previous twenty years, I had lived a relatively pampered life. I had been to private school, and even though I did not care for it, there was a guarantee of a roof over my head and three meals a day from my parents. Whether I worked really made no difference. Now it was just the Lord and me, and I knew I would have to take care of myself.

Just before I left for the States, my mother made it very clear that I was making my bed and would have to lie in it, meaning I would have to face all the consequences. There was not going to be any help from her at all. She felt she had done enough, and now, she said, I was denigrating all her assistance by going to the "Colonies" (as she and a number of other Brits dubbed the United States) on a "wild-goose chase," all because of that "fanatical religion."

She did have some excuse for the way she felt. My mother had taken wonderful care of both me and my older brother, Tony. We both benefited from English private school educations. Consequently, my mother felt she had prepared us properly, and I admit that I was less than gracious or wise in my comments to her since my conversion.

For example, one morning my mother and I were in a heated argument. I made the mistake of telling this good, upright, caring Englishwoman that she was both a heathen and a sinner. Now, from a scriptural point of view, this was perhaps true. But saying so in the way I did was both unkind and unwise. To my mother, a sinner was someone like a prostitute, and a heathen was a half-naked person running around a jungle. My newfound Christian zeal needed some refining! Thankfully, God would work in me to develop the wisdom and compassion I lacked.

In retrospect, I can see that some of the experiences ahead of me were the Lord's way of preparing me for my work of ministering to the poor and needy. How wonderful he is to weave into our lives the very circumstances he will use to enable us to serve him.

After an uneventful transatlantic flight, I arrived at Miami International Airport, clutching my used one-way ticket to America along with fifty dollars remaining in my pocket. In 1978, an Air Florida ticket from Miami to Orlando only cost twenty dollars. Haven't times changed! I was in the United States with thirty dollars in my pocket, which represented all my worldly wealth.

I disembarked from the plane and made my way to Immigration. There were numerous booths from which I could choose, so I prayed and made my selection. I think inherently I knew I needed to trust God and rely on him for everything, although I did not always do so—to my detriment. The official asked me what I planned to do while I was in the United States and how long I wanted to stay. When I told him I wanted to preach, he looked a little concerned and asked, "Oh, are you going to make a living at that? There are people who make a lot of money doing that."

Many years later, I realized how the Lord went before me during that experience. I was told that the immigration officer should have asked me if I had a return air ticket to England. If I could not produce one, he should have inquired if I had enough money to purchase one. That would have been protocol. But, fortunately for me, he did not ask those things. It was evident that the Lord was serious about taking a middle-class English boy, who had absolutely no personal experience of being poor, hungry, and homeless, and sending him to the United States to help care for America's needy.

Finally, I arrived at the pastor's house in Orlando. A lady answered the door, introduced herself as Kathy, and said her husband would be back shortly. She gave me tea (naturally, she was English). When her husband, David, arrived, they questioned me closely about my plans and then made a statement that chilled me. It impacted me so greatly that I still remember it as clearly today as the day it was spoken. Dave said, "Our faith has gotten us here, and if you want to get anywhere, it's going to have to be your faith that does it. You're not going to sponge off us, okay?"

With a mouth that went instantly dry, I gulped a quick response, assuring the couple I would not sponge off them. I mean, what else was I going to say? I was now in a foreign country, staying with strangers, and the U.S. immigration law prevented me from working while holding a visitor's visa. I had nothing. In fact, I was very much like the homeless people I would be helping some years down the road, totally dependent on others for my most basic needs.

11

Dave and Kathy's attitude was not quite what I had expected. All sorts of things went flooding through my mind during the next few minutes. Maybe I could go back to England without losing too much face and reapply to London Bible College. Maybe … maybe … maybe. I was still trying to determine just exactly what I had really gotten myself into when the couple said they were really tired and showed me my room. I went to bed.

I lay in bed for a long time that night, thinking and wondering. It was obvious that this couple was not going to give me a free ride just because I said God had called me to America. They were letting me know that if God really had called me, they wanted to see some proof. The next day, I could see trouble brewing on the horizon when, in an expanded version of what they had already told me, they said, "You say God has called you to America. Well, he has called us as well. You are in our house, which is a tangible example of God providing for us. It has a pool and orange trees, and we have plenty of food in our pantry. If God has called you, he will provide for you as well."

I was getting more fearful by the minute. It is one thing to tell your peers in England that God has called you to another country. It sounds sort of grand, even if they do not believe you. And while I was telling them, I was still being provided for by my parents. Now, God would have to be my provider. If he did not, starvation or deportation was imminent, and those things were all I could think of.

After a couple of days passed, I made my first visit to an American church. While I did not know it, and cannot even remember seeing her, sitting in that service was someone who would change my life completely—my future wife. The big event I remember from that first service was not the sermon or the church building. As odd as it may seem, it was learning that the church had a secretary. This was my first real sense that I was being exposed to the American culture without much preparation. It was culture shock. All the evangelical churches I had visited while in England were small and poor. In one, the church did not even have an office for the pastor; he worked out of his house. Having a secretary was truly a privilege and, it seemed, an extravagance.

A Different Side of the U.S.A.

A few days later, Dave and Kathy recommended what they thought was a wonderful idea to introduce me firsthand to the realities of American life. They suggested that I spend the summer with a high-spirited group of Christians who traveled the United States holding tent revivals. This seemed a very unusual thing to do for a proper English lad.

Nevertheless, I packed my suitcase and met with a group of other believers from the Orlando area who were planning to spend their summer in the same way. We arrived in Anderson, South Carolina, at about one o'clock in the morning. Everyone was asleep—in tents.

This was my introduction to a new way of living. We had long Bible studies in the morning and ate peanut butter and jelly sandwiches, or whatever else was available, for lunch. As a result, to this day I cannot stand peanut butter! In the afternoons, most of us went street witnessing. Following that, we returned to camp, took showers, and had about an hour's free time before participating in long, evening revival services. We didn't eat supper until after the evening evangelistic meeting, and by that time, we were pretty much starving.

Once more, I can now see how the Lord was forming me for my ministry to the needy, which was still some years on the horizon. While in England, I truly never knew what it was like to be poor. I had everything I physically needed, and as I said earlier, despite not enjoying my time in the English private school system, the experience is still one that is sought after and envied by many.

England has what is known as "council housing." Here in the United States, the equivalent would be the "projects." Back in the sixties and seventies, most of this type of housing was painted a uniform dull, drab gray. My image of poor people, their needs, hopes, and problems, was shaped by listening to my mother make derogatory comments about them. She felt that these individuals ended up in project-style housing because of some deficiency in their personality and motivation. She believed, as many did, that the poor could have something better if they only tried harder.

You can see that the Lord had to straighten out my thinking by leading me gradually into his chosen calling for me. Talk about a strange work for God to choose for me. I really cannot think of any more unlikely person to minister to the needs of the poor than myself. My background was completely prejudiced against it.

The Lord did many wonderful things for me my first summer in the United States, especially by giving me many opportunities to share his Word. Many of the circumstances surrounding those events were quite humorous. For example, the evangelist in charge of the young people that first summer was constantly being asked by one visitor to have me preach. After honoring the request a few times, he said to the lady, "You must sure like what Jeremy has to say." "Oh no," she responded. "I don't understand a word of what he says. I just like his British accent!"

The Lord continued to show me the wonders of his provision. He supplied my personal needs, as well as those of the group. Meals were provided by members of the local church attending the meetings.

At the end of the summer, I returned to Orlando and was invited by Dave and Kathy to stay with them. Plans for attending the Bible college in Lakeland did not work out, and I really did not know what I was going to do. A few weeks after returning to Orlando, I met Sylvia, my wife-to-be, and we started dating in September of 1978.

I did not have any money, so we did not really go out on dates; it was more like a "hanging out" situation. At twenty-one years old, I was still very immature. Sylvia had been married previously and had a child. At the time, she was working full time in a day-care center. I was scarcely on my own and did not have any idea how to support myself, let alone a wife and a family. Nevertheless, a few months later, we were married, April 14, 1979. Sylvia paid for everything, even the rings, because I still could not legally work.

Following the honeymoon, reality set in. I was anxious to be in full-time ministry, but I failed to see the Lord's dealings in my life. I was leaning on my own understanding and ability instead of relying on God. Obviously, he knew the significant step I had taken by getting married. He still had more to teach me.

I had also neglected to consider that there can be a significant time difference between receiving the call of God into ministry and actually being in ministry. The biblical example of this is when the psalmist David was called to be king. Although the prophet anointed him, it was not until sometime after that he actually took on the role of king. The waiting time did not invalidate God's calling; it was just God's way of doing things, because there is much to be learned in the waiting.

Someone who is in tune with what the Holy Spirit is saying to them holds that word—that call—in their heart and knows they have a special purpose set aside for them to perform in the future. Unfortunately, I was not in harmony with God's timing and wanted to be "God's little helper" to move him along a bit faster! I thought I could help God out by not waiting for his timing. Consequently, I caused a lot of grief for myself and everyone around me.

One of the things I did after I married Sylvia was to apply for my green card, which I subsequently obtained. Following the receipt of my card, I could work. The only problem was I was not trained to do anything in particular. I worked a variety of odd jobs and took some community college courses, all the time wanting to be in full-time ministry. I was not willing to wait.

Very foolishly, I launched myself into a full-time volunteer ministry position. Lack of income resulted in our family becoming homeless in late 1981. A kind family in central Florida agreed to shelter Sylvia, our eight year-old son, Ben, and our two-and-a-half-year-old son, Joshua. Because of my arrogant attitude, that offer did not extend to me.

On the Road

With my wife and family safe and being provided for, I set out on the road. I had enough money for a bus ticket to Dallas, and from then on my mode of transportation was hitchhiking. On a late, cold evening in January of 1982, I arrived in Dallas. I had about ten dollars in my pocket, and I carried a small suitcase, which seemed unbearably heavy.

I stuck out my thumb so much it got cold and sore and felt as if it was going to drop off. However, just when I was about to give up, an elderly couple stopped their car. They asked where I was headed. It turned out they were Christians who actually lived their faith. They were like angels sent from heaven. They taught me some incredible lessons. They took me to their home, fed me a delicious meal, gave me a comfortable bed, and took me back to the highway in the morning. Even though it was a dangerous thing for them to do, for me, it was a great blessing!

I have found, however, that trials often follow blessings. By the next evening, I had gotten to the New Mexico-Texas border, where I ended up standing out in the blazing sun for hours (as I recounted earlier).

As hard as the lessons were to learn, my homeless experiences helped shape the ministry of Joy Junction. For example, I insist that we provide transportation to pick up new residents. I have also instructed my staff to see that guests who come in after the normal dinner hour are fed something, no matter what time of the day or night it is.

While I definitely did not enjoy my experience of hunger and homelessness, I know that if I had not gone through them, I would not have appreciated how good a bologna sandwich could taste when you have not eaten for a long time. If that church had not offered me shelter five miles away, I would not have understood how hopelessly distant and unreachable five miles sounds when you are broke, exhausted, and homeless.

Later, I arrived in Phoenix, and friends bought me a bus ticket to Flagstaff, where they picked me up and took me to their home in Cameron, Arizona. For the next few weeks, I stayed in Cameron, a little village on an Indian reservation, about fifty miles north of Flagstaff. I spent a lot of time thinking about my life's direction.

A few weeks later, on a wing and a prayer—really more of a wing than a prayer—I traveled to Santa Fe, New Mexico, the site of a bloody prison riot a year or so earlier. I heard that the penitentiary was hiring prison guards, and the pay was good. I arrived in Santa Fe on a Saturday evening. That night, I stayed in a hotel, and the following morning I made my way to Christian Life Fellowship, at that time pastored by Carl Conley. He not only became my pastor but remained a good friend throughout the years.

Another amazing event was about to happen. Following the service, a church member offered me a place to stay for a week, and then I stayed in the basement of another church member's house, a local property owner named Rudy Rodriguez. Rudy put me to work painting apartments for him, which must have required continuing faith and patience on his part, as I ended up spilling more paint on the floors than I put on the walls. Consequently, even long-suffering Rudy decided it would be best if I looked for another job.

A local hotel hired me, and I worked there for a while, washing dishes and driving their van. During this time, Rudy and the members of the Santa Fe chapter of the Full Gospel Businessmen's Fellowship collected money for me to bring Sylvia and our boys from Florida to Santa Fe. By this time, she was about eight months pregnant.

Sylvia arrived a few weeks later. New Mexico provided a big climate change and a culture shock after living in Florida. While it was good having a job and a roof over our heads, it was not easy living on minimum wage in Santa Fe. Still, we were more blessed than many Americans.

Postscript. Twenty-eight years plus later, Rudy still helps us. Along with a colleague, I was blessed to have lunch with him recently and caught up on what's been going in both of our lives and families. What a blessing Rudy continues to be.

FALTERING FIRST STEPS

Change was in the air again. My boss came to me one day and said that the owner of the hotel had just paid a visit and had decided to make some staff reductions. I was one of those included in the reduction. Sylvia was less than thrilled when I arrived home and told her that I had been laid off. No job meant no money, and that could mean being homeless again.

Before the layoff, however, one of the managers approached me and said he thought it was a blessing that I had lost my job. Seeing my look of amazement, he explained that he felt the Lord was opening the way for me to go into full-time ministry. I was not really enthusiastic about this, thinking how easy it was for him to say this to me since he was still employed. I had a growing family, including a brand new baby, and no job.

But I quickly began reflecting about God's call on my life and wondered if this was indeed the time for me to go into full-time service for the Lord. But with what? Definitely not my good looks! I started thinking about a coffeehouse-type of ministry where I could preach the gospel. I started looking for a building.

While walking around Santa Fe one day, I ended up in an older section of town on Agua Fria. I found a strip mall comprised of three bright pink buildings. One was a barbershop, and the second was a doctor's office. The store that interested me the most, however, was closed and dark and had windows with holes stuffed full of newspapers to fill the cracks.

I went into the barbershop to see what I could find out. He told me that while the empty building was rented, it was only used a couple of days a week. The barber gave me the tenant's phone number.

The next week, I went with Pastor Carl Conley to meet this individual, who ran some sort of a private club on weekends. He agreed to sublet to us, and thinking he was being very helpful, said that if the project did not work out, it was all right; we could stop leasing any time we wanted. While I was appreciative of the man's kindness, there was no question in my mind that it would work. It had to.

His Place started as a coffeehouse, at first open only a few hours each evening. I did not really know at that time the specifics of what would occur there, other than that I wanted to tell people about Jesus. My prayer was quickly granted but not quite in the way I had envisioned. One night I sat alone in His Place for hours before anyone came by. About nine-thirty at night, a truck stopped by, and I heard some men saying to someone outside, "Here. Go in there. You're wasted. Get some coffee and sober up before you go home to the old lady." For the next couple of hours, I had a captive, albeit drunk, audience to tell about Jesus.

I was getting a taste for ministry and began enjoying it. We had potluck suppers every Tuesday, and for a while, it was almost as if we were the Christian revival center of Santa Fe. But then the word spread that we were giving away free food. Consequently, the poor, needy, and homeless started to come in. I didn't go out to try to find them; rather, they just found me. Tragically, as fast as the homeless started appearing, Christians who had been coming for the teaching and music ministry started leaving.

As the months sped by, I decided I would really like to turn His Place into an overnight shelter. But there was a problem. With the main tenant occupying the facility for a couple of evenings a week, it just was not possible. So I prayed, asked the Lord's help, and for once in my life, left things in his hands.

A Learning Time

When the main tenant moved, we eventually opened up as an overnight shelter, offering beds to homeless men. Back in those days, I was still very naive and thought that if you gave homeless people a place to stay and a meal, they would automatically be grateful. It never occurred to me that people would not be thankful for something free and that they might even take advantage of you. But my first phone bill showed that there were some homeless people who would not think twice about using you. That was my crash course in running a shelter.

As the months and years went on, His Place gradually assumed more and more responsibility for taking care of Santa Fe's homeless. The daily *Santa Fe New Mexican* published a wonderfully descriptive article about the shelter written in the mid-1980s by freelance writer Douglas Conwell.

> The aim of His Place Coffeehouse is more than physical fare. It also includes spiritual fare. The "His" is Jesus, and the message is that "He" can change lives and give hope to the lost and forlorn. Today, the bright pink building on Agua Fria Street is more than a coffeehouse, although that is how it got its start in July 1982. Now it is a residential shelter for eight men, with a companion women's residence nearby—one of the few resources of its kind in northern New Mexico.
>
> His Place was the idea of a transplanted Englishman named Jeremy Reynalds, who heard the "call of the Lord" to come to America. Reynalds arrived in Orlando, Florida, in 1978, with $50 in his pocket and a sense of mission in his heart. He worked a number of odd jobs, married, and then moved in with his wife, just cruising about looking for some place to happen.
>
> It happened in Santa Fe, where he was offered a place to live and found employment. It didn't take him long to recognize a "desperate need" for services to the homeless; but he also recognized that as a relative newcomer, there was also a need to establish his own credibility.
>
> Within a short six months, however, Reynalds was serving the ministry of his church, Christian Life Fellowship, through the ministry of the coffeehouse. Reynalds credits the help of several people, including Blackie Gonzales, president of KCHF-TV in Santa Fe, and owner of KDAZ Radio in Albuquerque. Gonzales offered Reynalds half a day's free air time on radio and all the income he could earn from selling advertising spots. Enthusiastic conviction made him a successful salesman. Meanwhile, moral (and later financial) support came from Pastor Carl Conley of Christian Life Fellowship.
>
> First only open for a few hours a day for coffee and doughnuts, His Place remodeled and opened as a shelter for homeless men in November 1983. A similar sized women's residence opened recently. Together, they accept a large number of referrals from police, social services, churches, mental health centers as well as city and state

offices. And with at least somewhere for the homeless to go, the possibility of their causing trouble is reduced. As Reynalds said, "Somebody cold and hungry is more likely to steal than somebody well fed."

Not just the homeless come to His Place. There are some area families who are faced with the choice of either eating or paying the rent. They come to His Place so they do not have to make that terrible decision. As Reynalds said, "We help anyone we can in any way we can. We figure if we're going to be in the neighborhood, we'd like to help out."

Being neighborly has been a priority, as some of the nearby residents were not sure about the location of a shelter in their area. Reynalds makes a special effort to communicate and cooperate with these neighbors, and keep the area clean and well organized.

His Place does much more than just feed and house people. Of course imparting the message of Jesus Christ is foremost, and residents are required to attend regular devotional services and other events. But religion is seen in context with a person's life in the community and the feeling of self-worth.

Reynalds said that His Place aims to "provide an uplifting atmosphere and to let people know the shelter staff loves and cares for them. Our whole aim is to make people responsible. We help them through a transition from feeling broken down, useless and feeling incapable of feeding themselves or working, to being a person who can put a few bucks away and put a down payment on an apartment."

All residents are expected to find work, but Reynalds tells them, "Hey, I don't expect you to work harder than I do." There is little chance of that—as Reynalds puts in sometimes more than 60 hours a week.

The hundreds who come to the door on Agua Fria have gone through many doors before—doors of divorce, broken homes, alcoholism and drug addiction and aimless wandering from halfway house to rescue mission. Many are in a cycle of poverty, dependent on public assistance that does not meet living expenses but is enough money not to give up. Frequently they have been told they are worthless; and most have come to believe it.

The coffeehouse tries to break that cycle with the force of love, but also with rigidly enforced structure. Each person must search daily for employment. "This is not a flop house," Reynalds emphasized. There are plenty of other places for people to flop.

Although the maximum stay is 14 days, Reynalds is flexible. If someone fails to try and improve their situation, they are asked to leave. On the other hand, if a person is making a genuine effort to succeed and just has not had any luck finding a place to stay, then he or she is allowed to stay longer.

This article was a great source of encouragement to me, as the author really captured our reasons for existing. His Place provided a training ground and cemented God's calling on my life to minister to the homeless. However, in almost four years of running the shelter, I had taken only four days off. In February of 1986, Sylvia and I took a couple of days rest in Phoenix. During that time, I felt God speaking to me about resigning my position at His Place. So I did just that and resigned effective May 31 1986. Unfortunately, I made a major mistake. I told the Lord I would do whatever he wanted except that I would never run a shelter. Never tell the Lord never!

The month of May came very quickly. I looked at the possibility of pastoring a church, but there were no churches available. My replacement for His Place arrived and expected me to be moving on quickly.

The "Almost-Homeless" Former Shelter Operator

By this time, I was really desperate and needed a place for our family to stay, as our house went with the job. How ironic that the home-giver was about to become homeless!

I called a longtime friend who lived in Taos, New Mexico, sixty-five miles north of where we were living, and he offered us a place to stay. The experience tested the friendship of both families, but we all survived the experience and that friend is now on the board of directors for Joy Junction.

After a few weeks, there were still no job offers. I was getting worried and began to sink into depression. While living in Santa Fe, I had made brief contact with an individual running a shelter located on Kirtland Air Force Base. The ministry was called the Reach Out to Jesus Family Chapel was and part of a program initiated by the Department of Defense. The program allowed nonprofit corporations to use vacant military buildings to help the homeless. The director of the program invited me to help him.

We stayed for a few weeks, but I knew that God had something else for me to do. While praying and considering my future one morning, the Lord called to my mind a vacant property in Albuquerque's South Valley. All I knew about the acreage was that it was large and formerly used by an area alcohol and drug rehabilitation program operated by Christians. It had been vacant for some months following the closure of the program.

I went down one morning to check out the property. I was impressed with what I saw and made contact with the board president of the group owning the property. I told him I wanted to open a shelter for homeless families, and I would like to use the available land and buildings. He said he would get back with me. I left, not really expecting him or the other board members to take me seriously, but I did not know that prior to my application, several board members had already expressed their thoughts that a homeless shelter would be a good use for this property. Isn't it amazing how God had given me favor with these men before I even approached them? This is exactly how he works.

A New Home

During the period between leaving His Place and where I was now, God dealt with my heart about the homeless. The Lord showed me through a variety of means that he still wanted me to house and feed homeless and hungry people. However much I might not have really wanted that calling, it was still what God wanted me to do.

A few weeks later, I received a call from the property owners, telling me that the board members had accepted my proposal. I was ecstatic! The terms were reasonable, including a week's free rent on a mobile home for my family and five weeks' free rent on a ministry building for the homeless. After that, the rent would be $650 a month. While that was not a lot of money, back then it seemed like a fortune. Anything is a great deal when you have next to nothing. But I have always thought the word "poor" can be a relative term. One can be materially poor and spiritually wealthy, or vice versa.

We moved onto the property, which I decided to call Joy Junction. I was extremely grateful that we all had a home again. The trailer was not much, but it was home, and we didn't have to share it with anyone.

I rapidly became busy. Looking back, I can see several indications God's hand was on the shelter right from the beginning. First, I had begun the work in response to what I believed was God's calling on my life. Second, the timing was right. Shortly after I left the shelter on Kirtland Air Force Base, it closed. A small shelter for families run by another local agency also closed, making Joy Junction the only family shelter in the entire Albuquerque area.

The Joy Junction ministry grew, and so did our income. Shelter income climbed from $11,000 the first year to about $300,000 in 1990. The Lord blessed my efforts, and the shelter quickly gained a good reputation. Joy Junction was often featured on the local television newscasts and in local newspaper articles. My God-given skill was definitely in the production of publicity to get attention for the ministry.

Although I had previously done everything from keeping the books to teaching many of the regular evening Bible studies, the day-to-day financial management of the shelter began to escape me and those I had entrusted to do the accounting. While I knew the shelter was getting in the hole financially, I did not know what to do about it. There were outstanding bills and staff salaries that could not be paid, and I saw no way to get out of the financial hole into which I was all too rapidly sinking.

Crisis!

The pressure quickly mounted, so much so that I felt I just could not take it anymore. I decided the only solution was to go public with the problems the shelter was facing. I announced a public ultimatum that if at least $20,000 was not raised by the end of the next month, I would close Joy Junction. This was not necessarily the best thing to do, but at the time, I was absolutely desperate and could not see any other way. I felt totally on my own and did not even know whom to ask for help. Various local television and radio stations publicized the need, and some additional finances started to come in. I thought perhaps things were beginning to look up. However, I had not even seen the beginning of where things were headed. A lot of troubles, trials, and trauma lay just a few weeks ahead of me.

A reporter from the *Albuquerque Journal*, Leah Lorber, called and wanted to do an in-depth story. It became apparent that she did not want to do a light, fluffy report detailing the shelter's need but rather a hard-nosed investigative piece about the problems we were having. It turned out to be the most frightening ordeal of my life.

The next week I spent long hours with Leah. She was going to tell the community why the shelter was in its financial bind, and I was going to be held accountable for everything that had happened. She wanted to see a budget to help explain how we got in such a financial bind. Budgets were foreign to me. I had been so busy raising money to pay bills and answering telephones and signing in homeless people, that the idea of a budget never even occurred to me. Obviously, I had a lot to learn about the financial aspects of running a shelter.

As a matter of fact, that is one of the reasons for this book. While I had the best of intentions, the road to hell is paved with good intentions (and that old expression is true). And good intentions just do not cut it when you are dealing with the public's money. You have to know what is expected of you. At that point, I honestly did not. I was naive in more ways than one.

The reporter concluded her first session by asking me if I had copies of the shelter's 990, an Internal Revenue Service form that nonprofit organizations are required to submit each year to the IRS. I referred her to the shelter's volunteer bookkeeper, never dreaming what the result might be. A few days later, Leah called me to request a second interview. The questions went something like this: "Jeremy, can you tell me about the bounced checks and the unpaid payroll taxes for the shelter?" My heart sank. How did she know? The volunteer accountant told her. After all, I never told him he should not, and my sending the reporter to see him made him think he was to answer any question he was asked.

I decided there was only one thing to do. As the reporter continued to reel though a list of problem areas, I looked her right in the eyes and said, "Leah, the public is tired of hearing excuses and seeing the blame put on someone else. As head of Joy Junction, I take the blame. Many of our problems and inefficiencies are due to an excessive workload on my part and an organization that has grown incredibly fast—maybe too fast."

The next few days, Leah contacted me numerous times as she added details to her story. Needless to say, I was growing increasingly apprehensive about exactly how the story would be worded. I rushed to get the newspaper each morning, wondering if that morning was going to be the day the story would appear.

One Saturday morning, I ran to get the paper and hastily opened it up. The story was worse than I thought. There, right at the top of the main section (above the fold), was a long article headlined, "Joy Junction Runs by Seat of the Pants Finances." To add insult to injury, there was the worst picture of me I had ever seen.

After letting the article sink in, I dragged myself to the office. The phone started ringing. Many calls were supportive; some were disgusted and angry. But one call summed up several others: "You've done too much for too many with too little for too long. It's time we came forward and helped you."

The article showed me many things. Some people I believed were real friends completely ignored me after that. Then there were those I never thought even cared who came forward and offered prayer and financial support. One of those who stuck with me through everything and encouraged me during this difficult time was Gino Geraci, then an associate pastor of Calvary Church of Albuquerque and now pastor of Calvary Chapel of South Denver. Carl Conley also made himself available to me immediately, as he had for many years, and agreed to step in for as long as I needed him. He also became board president for a while.

Many people told me afterward that the reason they continued to support the shelter was because I admitted full responsibility. While some of the things for which I was blamed were not directly attributable to me, in one sense they were, because I was leader of the ministry.

Months later, when the same reporter interviewed me again, she said she believed me, because I had not attempted to hide anything from her. I was open in all of my answers to her very probing questions. There was never any hint of financial impropriety or questionable actions. As I said before, the main problem was being too busy to oversee everything effectively.

According to Romans 8:28, the Lord turns everything to the good if we let him. The apostle Paul said, "And we know that in all things God works for the good of those who love him, who have been called according to his purpose." That has certainly been proven true in my life and the work of Joy Junction.

The result of Leah's article was the expansion of our ministry board and the Lord's gift of a business manager, something I had needed for a long time. The *Albuquerque Journal* later put it like this: "Joy Junction has bowed to the inevitable, and put its financial affairs under the watchful eyes of a business manager." For a while, I joked with our then business manager, calling him "The Inevitable."

One vision yet to be fulfilled was the purchase of our fifty-two-acre property in Albuquerque's South Valley. That blessing was yet to come.

THE PROMISED LAND

The Old Testament tells the story about how the patriarchs traveled through the wilderness to find the Promised Land. From the very beginning of Joy Junction in 1986, the Lord gave me a vision to claim land in the name of Christ for the homeless of Albuquerque.

Most of the other agencies and ministries in Albuquerque that deal with the homeless are downtown. They have absolutely no room to grow, and even when a possible opportunity presents itself, angry neighbors rise in a chorus of protest against any expansion.

We are in a somewhat different situation, because Joy Junction's nearest neighbor immediately to the north is the city of Albuquerque's sewage treatment facility. One day while speaking to the director of that facility, I told him that our two agencies really had a lot in common. A little surprised, he asked why I believed that to be so. I told him that while everyone was in agreement that we both provided important services for the city, nobody wanted either one of us as their next-door neighbor!

During the last few years, there has arisen an increasingly hostile climate to the homeless in downtown Albuquerque. Proponents of downtown revitalization have felt that for the downtown district to become an area where people want to spend their time, the homeless have to leave.

At one meeting some years ago, members of a group of individuals and businesses attempting to revamp Albuquerque's jaded downtown image handed out a report filled with recommendations on dealing with the "problem" of the area's homeless population.

Sadly, the homeless were no longer people to be helped, human beings with souls, minds, and bodies. Instead, they were labeled a "problem," standing in the way of business, and they needed to be moved out of the downtown area. No one quite knew where the homeless could be relocated. The only thing the neighborhood association spokespersons could tell the area media was that the homeless should not be moved into their area. How deplorable. Tragically, the situation hasn't gotten that much better.

Buying the Land

With this sort of attitude gaining ground in our area, it became important for us to secure our fifty-two-acre property. Let me explain what that entailed. While our landlords had generously offered to donate ten acres to us, we would have to pay the appraised price of $19,000 per acre if we wanted more.

We eventually managed to buy the remaining forty-two acres, where, in addition to housing the needy, we grow crops. I am unable to report any dazzling overnight miracles concerning the purchase of this acreage, such as a huge sum of money given to us at the eleventh hour that enabled us to buy the property without going into debt. Rather, it took us a long time to come to the place where we could buy that additional forty-two acres, and the process involved a lot of prayer and a capital campaign of sorts.

Fund-raising for capital projects is always difficult, and I pray that this account of how the Lord dealt with us will encourage you.

Having been involved in parachurch ministry to the homeless for over a quarter century, I have studied quite a lot of material about capital campaigns. Most of what one hears about capital fund drives run by agencies specializing in raising money suggests that they are all overwhelmingly successful. Maybe that is because they cost such a huge amount of money to finance. I remember one of the quotes we got from an agency to undertake a capital campaign for Joy Junction was for almost $100,000. This seemed to be a classic case of where, in order to raise money, you had to already have money. Where were we going to get $100,000? My thinking was that if we could get hold of that sort of money, we probably would not need to have a capital campaign in the first place. In any event, not having the money, we mostly went it alone.

With some help from a friend of the shelter, we came up with a nicely designed appeal letter to our donors, announcing our desire to purchase the property. Despite that letter, on which we pinned all of our hopes, we soon realized we had a problem. Although we prayed fervently, money for the capital campaign was not coming in nearly as fast or in the amount we needed. Therefore, we initially resigned ourselves to settling for the ten free acres our landlords were willing to donate to us.

Of course, I really should have been much more grateful. That ten-acre property donation from our landlords was a great blessing. Even though the additional funds we needed were not coming in, our landlords (another Christian ministry) told us to be encouraged and said they really believed in what we were doing. Their donation, they said, was prompted by a desire to ensure our successful continuance should we not be able to either raise enough money or convince a bank to give us a loan to secure the rest of the acreage.

We found a Texas-based company that specialized in church bonds to raise money for property acquisition. After reviewing our financial statements, company representatives said they would like to work with us on a program to allow us to buy about twenty-one of the available forty-two acres. A company representative came out to Albuquerque, and we had a series of meetings to try to generate enough interest in the program. After three such meetings, it looked like we had succeeded in our goal.

The Lord, however, who always has an incredible plan as well as a wonderful sense of humor, had something else in mind. I am unable to tell the story any better than *Albuquerque Journal* reporter Paul Logan in a September 1996 story. Here is his account:

> Joy Junction has scrapped plans to sell $330,000 in general obligation bonds and will use a bank loan to buy the land it leases.
>
> The Albuquerque homeless shelter and Bank of New Mexico have signed a letter of commitment for a 15-year mortgage on the 25-acre property and buildings at 4500 Second Street, shelter executive director Jeremy Reynalds said Friday.
>
> The bank became interested in loaning the money to Joy Junction after learning about the shelter's plan to hold a public bond offering, Reynalds said. Great Nation Investment Corp., a Texas investment-banking firm, had been working with the shelter on the bond deal.
>
> A Great Nation representative contacted Bank of New Mexico about investing in the bond deal, banker Steven Scholl said Friday. The bank decided not to invest, but Scholl said he told the representative the bank was "interested from a loan standpoint."

Great Nation passed along Bank of New Mexico's proposal to the shelter. Joy Junction's board decided last week to take the bank up on its offer instead of selling the bonds, Reynalds said.

"By giving us the tip," he said of Great Nation, "they basically did themselves out of business."

Until Bank of New Mexico's interest, Joy Junction and the Amarillo firm were planning to complete the bond deal, Reynalds said.

Earlier this month, Great Nation held three meetings in Albuquerque to answer prospective investors' questions about the bond offering. Reynalds said that about 38 people made bond inquiries and that it was enough investment interest to go ahead with the bond issuance.

Interestingly, by the time that everything had been worked out so that we could buy the land, our small, locally owned Bank of New Mexico had been acquired by one of the nation's then megabanks which had turned us down for a property acquisition loan a few years before.

The day before we were due to sign the final documents, on Labor Day of 1998, at about 10:00 PM, my pager vibrated. Looking at the small screen and recognizing the call-back number as the telephone number for our landlords, my heart sank. Being a pessimist by nature, I immediately began to think, "Oh well, I guess we won't buy the property after all. Something's gone wrong." After all, why else would there be a call at that time of night?

I called the number, which was answered by our attorney, who rather than telling me that the sale was off just asked me if it could be postponed a few hours. Both he and the attorney for our landlords were feverishly working on last-minute paperwork and trying to tie up loose ends. I breathed a big sigh of relief.

I slept restlessly that night, but finally the morning came. The big day had arrived, and after more than twelve years of renting property, Joy Junction was going to be a property owner. It was still hard for me to believe. I had prayed and dreamed about this day for so long that when it did come, I had a hard time convincing myself it was really happening.

Later that day, I excitedly met our business manager and our attorney over at the title company. Representatives for our landlords turned up a little later. After a three-hour marathon of signing more documents at one time than I had ever signed before, it was all over. We now owned thirty-one acres of property! That comprised the ten acres gifted to us by our landlords and the twenty-one we had purchased. During a break in the process, our attorney gravely reminded us that we were now legally and morally obligated to make a sizable mortgage payment each month. Even though I knew the Lord was faithful to allow us to make that monthly payment for the next fifteen years, I felt he had entrusted us with an awesome responsibility.

Even though I was thrilled that we now owned thirty-one acres, I still had my heart set on the additional twenty-one acres that were still available. And I felt very strongly that the Lord wanted us to buy that acreage.

More Land

I prayed, wracked my brains, sent lots of press releases to the media detailing my concern, and pleaded with God to make a way for us to buy this land. Yet nothing seemed to be happening. For a while, it seemed to me I was the only one who realized (or cared) the importance of this additional property purchase. My feeling was that unless we purchased the available land quickly, we might never get another opportunity. It would be sold to whomever made an offer, and then, I was convinced, the zoning could be changed to disallow a shelter for the homeless. If someone else bought the property, there would be absolutely no chance of ever seeing the land used for the ministry of Joy Junction.

The bank did not want to lend us any more money. Bank officials indicated they were open to talking more at some time in the future, but we did not have the luxury of waiting that long. Understandably, our landlords felt that they needed to sell the property as soon as possible. If we were able to come up with cash, or proof that a bank was willing to grant us a loan, they would be happy to sell us the property. But if not, they reminded me, the for sale sign would be posted. I kept on praying.

A few days later, a postcard miraculously arrived from a company offering church bonds, much like the company we dealt with previously. This company specialized in assisting churches, rather than ministries such as Joy Junction. After telephone calls and submission of some financial documents, I learned this group was willing to help us with a bond issuance large enough for us to pay back the debt on the twenty-one acres we bought in 1998—as well as allow us to buy the twenty-one additional acres.

What pleased me no end was that the company was willing to sell most of the bonds to their own investors. This meant it would not be necessary for us to conduct public meetings to sell these bonds to our donors, something that, I explained to company officials, I was far from enthusiastic about doing. On the surface of things, this seemed like the answer to our prayers, but as our business manager consistently reminded me in our weekly meetings, the fees this company charged for their services were very expensive. Consequently, we decided to continue looking for other avenues of funding, while keeping our options open with this company.

Sometime later, while listening to early morning talk radio, I heard an advertisement for a small local bank that had recently opened in Albuquerque. Since small local banks are usually thought of as being much more approachable and open to community needs than the national chains, I gave them a call.

Much to my excitement, bank officials expressed an initial interest and encouraged us to stay in touch. After sending the officials our audits and other financial data, two of the bank's officers came down to visit the property. The visit appeared to go smoothly, and I remained quite optimistic that this institution would be willing to provide sufficient financing for us not only to buy the additional acreage we wanted but to refinance (at a better rate) the property we already purchased and financed through another bank.

Everything went just as planned, with no last-minute disasters or even any hitches. Closing day arrived, and along with our business manager, I found myself back again at the title company, signing lots of documents. Joy Junction was now the proud owner of fifty-two acres of property—and responsible for a $7,400 monthly mortgage payment to the bank.

I was elated, as this acquisition allowed the shelter ministry a sense of permanency and stability that as renters we had never experienced. To me, it also meant an increased hope that however hostile downtown business owners grew toward the homeless, and however large the homeless situation grew in Albuquerque, we would be able, with the Lord's help, to be a part of the solution.

Renovation

Now that we owned the property, our next step was renovation, which we could do only as funds became available. On the fifty-two acres sits a beautiful but dilapidated adobe chapel. For a number of reasons, it had fallen into disrepair over the thirteen years Joy Junction occupied the other part of the property. Since we are a faith-based ministry, I felt it was important for us to make a statement about what was most important to us. With that in mind, I thought it would be appropriate to renovate the chapel first. At least those were my plans then. How our plans do change!

Let me tell you how the chapel came to be in such a neglected state. I woke up one morning in early 1987 and discovered that the entire chapel basement, which was about six feet high, was flooded. The property owners at the time bought a water pump and pumped out the basement, but mixing water with adobe can quickly produce a disastrous combination. The chapel was no exception, and that flood nearly became the straw that broke the camel's back. The building already suffered from structural problems, and the water damage combined with the lack of use eventually reduced it to a shadow of its former self. But help was on the way in the form of Robert Crawford, a former Joy Junction chaplain.

One day, shortly after buying the first twenty-one acres of our property, I was discussing with one of my staff what we could do to draw attention to the sad plight of the chapel. Without ever thinking he would agree, we came up with the idea of asking our chaplain if he would consider living on the roof of the chapel for a while. To our amazement, he agreed! We sent out press releases describing the plan. That was the beginning of a torrent of publicity documenting Robert Crawford's forty-day plus rooftop spiritual experience.

What was interesting to me was that this was not the first time I had attempted bringing the plight of the chapel to the attention of the media, but it was the first time I had personalized it. A few weeks prior to this, I sent a release to Albuquerque media outlets describing the sad condition of a "possibly historic" building. One local television station had responded, but that was it. Nobody else appeared to be interested. But what a difference occurred when we put a living, breathing person on the chapel roof. Here is what one reporter wrote in the *Albuquerque Journal*:

> On the grounds of Joy Junction, Albuquerque's largest emergency homeless shelter, sits the former, and now derelict, Our Lady of Lourdes Chapel. In an attempt to raise public awareness about the need for restoration of this once beautiful building, Joy Junction Chaplain Robert Crawford is forsaking a warm bed and the comforts of home to live on the chapel roof. With Crawford's "home away-from home," a tent, already in place, and a "port-a-john" at the base of the chapel (insurance regulations prevented

the "port-a-john" from being hoisted onto the roof), Crawford has begun his adventure.

Shelter director Jeremy Reynalds said he admires Crawford's commitment to seeing the chapel renovated. "Judging from comments I've heard here and there over the past decade, this chapel holds a lot of memories for quite a number of people. It's a beautiful building, possibly historically significant, and we'd like to see it restored to its former beauty. It would be a wonderful place to have services for our guests and also to hold some of our community events," said Reynalds.

Reynalds said that Crawford has told him that he plans to stay on the roof until enough funds have been raised for restoration.

"And that—very conservatively speaking—will be at least $100,000, and that's with a lot of volunteer labor," Reynalds added.

In addition to funds for the chapel renovation, Reynalds said that Crawford is open to donations of home cooked meals, hot cocoa and anything to help pass his time of "exile."

Crawford's wife has declined an offer by her husband to join him in this exciting adventure, saying that there'll be no fighting over the television remote while she and her husband are apart.

The media attention continued. In addition to coverage in the *Journal*, Crawford soon became quite familiar with reporters and photographers from the local CBS, ABC, and NBC affiliates. I am sure they provided some welcome relief from the monotony he experienced while spending so many hours, days, and weeks away from his wife and the comforts of home.

Although Crawford planned to stay on the chapel roof until all of the necessary funds were raised to renovate the chapel, the Lord had other plans. He had to cut short his ambitious plans and had to leave Joy Junction to go to Missouri and help care for his ailing father. By the end of his rooftop stay, he had raised about $11,000.

Even though we raised only 10 percent of our total goal, the project was not a failure. While I am admittedly disappointed about not reaching the $100,000, I look back at the project as a success—just not the sort of success I had originally envisioned. Why? We were able to bring the need of the chapel's restoration to a large number of Albuquerqueans, and out of the "rooftop reverend's" time at new heights, we had for a while some excellent help in restoring the chapel. Alas, community interest and funding waned, leaving the project unfinished. We were able to gather enough interest to do some structural work to keep the chapel from incurring any further damage. It is still on my heart, however, and we continue looking to the Lord for funding.

I was poignantly reminded one day that the chapel holds so many memories for people in the Albuquerque community. One quiet Sunday afternoon, I saw an elderly couple driving around our property. It turned out that the man had gone to school on our property back in the mid-1930s, when it was a Catholic boys school. He told me he helped build the chapel. I asked him if he would like to see inside, and he quickly agreed. He enthusiastically pointed to some of the beams on the chapel roof and proudly told me that those were the beams he put up there himself as the chapel was being built. It was evident that just being there brought back myriad boyhood memories. It is events like this that act as a constant reminder of the need to renovate this beautiful old building.

Education for Excellence

My vision for reaching the homeless led to obtaining a bachelor's degree with a focus in journalism and a master's degree in communication from the University of New Mexico (UNM). In 2006, after seven years of additional study, I earned a Ph.D. degree in intercultural education from Biola University in California.

The thought of obtaining an undergraduate degree, let alone graduate degrees, was the furthest thing from my mind when I began Joy Junction. After all, I was thirty-three when I commenced undergraduate studies at UNM, and I had a time-consuming position as director of Joy Junction. Beyond that, I had a wife and family of five children to care for. Yet, I definitely felt the Lord wanted me to refine my skills to do the best possible job for him, and so I embarked on university studies.

I obtained my undergraduate degree in 1996 and a master's degree in communication in 1998. By this time, I was "hooked" on school and wanted to continue. But a desire to study for a Ph.D. doesn't always mean that you will be able to do so.

So, I was thrilled when I was accepted into the doctoral program in intercultural education at Biola University, located just outside Los Angeles. Although I was busy directing the daily operations at the New Mexico–based ministry of Joy Junction, I also felt God wanted me at Biola. My only option was to commute. One day a week, I flew out to southern California to attend classes. Feeling that this was probably not how the typical shelter director spends his or her time, I thought the local media might be interested in featuring a story on my travels. Consequently, I sent them the following press release:

> Joy Junction Founder and Executive Director Jeremy Reynalds is planning on racking up a lot of frequent flyer miles over the next few years. Reynalds has begun taking classes toward his Ph.D. in intercultural education—at Biola University in Southern California. He's flying to Los Angeles every Thursday afternoon and returning to Albuquerque early Friday morning.
>
> Running New Mexico's largest emergency homeless shelter and doing six hours of classes toward an advanced degree would make some younger folk think twice, but Reynalds has never been one to be put off by a challenge. To finance the cost of four air trips a month to California, Reynalds will be teaching two public speaking classes as a part-time instructor at the University of New Mexico.
>
> Reynalds, 42, who has an undergraduate degree in journalism and a master's degree in communication from the University of New Mexico (in addition to being a published author), says he is looking forward to a new school, even if the schedule threatens to be somewhat punishing. "I'm used to hard work and will be in constant contact with Joy Junction for the few hours I'll be in California. I'm also very excited because my schooling thus far has been of tremendous benefit to the shelter."

This release produced much more attention than I originally anticipated. The *Albuquerque Journal* decided to write a personality profile on me, while at the same time try to dispel some rumors that were started about me and the shelter by a small number of disgruntled former residents.

The finished product by *Journal* staff writer Rick Nathanson appeared on Friday, November 12, 1999, and it was headlined with a quote from me reading, "'If hoping to get free news coverage to tell the plight of the homeless is shameless self-promotion, then I stand guilty as charged. In order for us to continue getting funds from the community, our name has to be kept before the public.'" Appropriately, it concludes with a shelter guest summing up her stay by telling the reporter, "'Joy Junction allowed the family to stay together, and that's the most important thing.'"

From 1999 through 2002, I commuted weekly from Albuquerque to Los Angeles. Believe me, this was some sort of feat for someone desperately afraid of flying! The Lord most definitely has ways of keeping us on our toes. He doesn't want us to be afraid of anything and will deal with us directly in the areas where we are fearful.

The Tide of Time

My weekly trips to Biola were punctuated by two dramatic events; one that touched only my life and the other that touched the whole nation. The first event was the death of my mother in 2000. My wife and then pastor encouraged me to visit her in late February of 2000, a few weeks before she died. I am so glad I made the trip to England when I did.

When there, I made my way slowly up the stairs to the second floor of the hospital in South England, where my mother was a "guest" of the country's nationalized health service. She was in the geriatric unit, and as I walked through the ward, I passed a number of elderly people in various states of mental and physical decay.

While I had been warned that my mother's health was rapidly deteriorating, I was still shocked when I saw her. She was sleeping, and her breathing was labored. Her hands were badly swollen, and her once immaculately coiffed hair fell untidily in all the wrong places. My mother was not fully aware of her surroundings or who was present. There was little I could do except express my love. After a second visit, I returned to New Mexico.

The following weekend, a nurse called to say my mother was getting steadily worse and that she probably would not live through the day. What else could we do except pray and commit the situation to the Lord? Later, the nurse called again to say Mum had passed on a couple of hours before. I believe one day I will join her around the throne of God, and we will praise and worship him together for all eternity.

The second dramatic event was the tragedy that touched the whole nation on September 11, 2001. I spent September 10 at Biola and was at the Los Angeles Airport early on September 11, expecting to get my regularly scheduled plane back to Albuquerque as I had each week for a couple of years. I intended to put in a full day's work at the office once I arrived back home. My plans changed that day, as did the lives of millions. Since all planes were grounded, I rented a car and began the long drive back to Albuquerque.

During the journey, I listened to whatever radio stations I could pick up. Listeners seemed glad talk radio was giving them an outlet for a collective chat around the "electronic fireside." Not surprisingly, many listeners were angry; at the same time, they were sharing their disbelief that with all of our sophisticated intelligence-gathering techniques, a tragedy of such cataclysmic proportions could occur in the United States of America.

Over the weeks and months that followed 9/11, we learned of many acts of heroism that occurred on that fateful day, as well as in the days following. God's name was mentioned often in previously forbidden public places, and there wasn't a peep heard from the ACLU, or Americans United for the Separation of Church and State, or other groups trying to strip all vestiges of Christianity from the public square.

Shortly after the tragic event, I wrote that only eternity will fully reveal what we as a nation learned from that fateful day. Sadly, it appears we haven't learned much; we have returned to our former ways of self-sufficiency and lack of dependence on God. I hope we learn that the Savior is the only source of all the blessings we continue to enjoy in this great country of ours.

Struggling with Depression

During my years of doctoral work, I struggled with depression. Working on a graduate degree is not an easy thing, and directing a ministry for the homeless on a long-term basis takes an emotional toll. I'm afraid the experience of my depression emerged in some of my writing and even in communications to our donors. At that time, I did not know that one battling depression should tell someone what he is feeling and seek professional help. I did not do that, and in late 2004, I was feeling very negative about my situation.

Feeling totally alone, deserted, and abandoned, I wracked my brains for a solution. It seemed as if things were falling to pieces around me, and I was powerless to do anything about it. I felt as if I was coming emotionally unglued. It seemed as if the weight of the shelter's then entire $1.2 million-dollar annual budget rested on my shoulders. There was the weekly payroll to be met, and late in the week, we had nowhere near the funds needed. I visualized the line of people trooping into the office in a couple of days, expecting their paychecks. After all, they had a right to do so. They worked for their money, and it was my responsibility to make sure funds were there to make what they earned a reality.

To make things worse, our business manager told me in a tense telephone call there were insurance payments and a laundry list of other bills demanding our immediate attention. As if that wasn't enough, I found out that a sizable bequest on which we had been counting to help us navigate through the stormy financial waters leading to the upcoming season of giving would not arrive until the end of the year.

As I worried about the financial needs of Joy Junction, I experienced chest pains and dark depression. Beyond this, I felt emotionally traumatized and unable to think. I would have liked nothing better than to jump in my car and drive and drive and drive—and forget about Joy Junction. I wondered if it would always be like this. Many years ago, a friend in Santa Fe gave me some wise advice I mostly dismissed at that time. He said running a nonprofit organization always means dealing with money woes. "You'll never have enough money," he told me.

The question now was how many more times I could deal with the ever-increasing financial strain. Because we were a faith-based ministry and not a social service agency, we did not receive money from any branch of the government (and that was the way I wanted to keep it). But it meant that when we ran short of funds, we could not go to the city council or another government agency, hat in hand, and ask for a financial bailout.

Some people wondered why we couldn't just cut back and live within our means. We did cut back, and we planned a more conservative budget than we might otherwise have done. But we did not even meet that, so we took emergency steps to deal with decreased revenue. We did not want to be examples of the old adage, "When your outgo exceeds your income, it will be your downfall."

But as I thought about where we could prune costs and provide fewer services, I also reflected over the prior months, which had been the busiest ever in my then eighteen years of running Joy Junction. On many nights during the height of summer, we had sheltered two hundred people, and sometimes many more. This was a sharp increase from other years, when even in the depth of winter, with temperatures plummeting to the forty-degree level and at times even lower, we had only sheltered about one hundred fifty people. Unfortunately, the increase did not result in a corresponding increase in income to the shelter. We saw one of the worst summer slumps ever in donations.

While nonprofits locally and nationwide anticipate declines in donations during the summer months, until 9/11, we had things pretty well figured out financially. During the last couple of months of the year, we always received more income than needed to run the shelter. For those months, we put the excess funds into a savings account we could draw from to help get through those traditionally difficult cash-shy summer months.

In addition, prior to 9/11, we had developed a small group of faithful donors who gave us gifts of stock in the summer to sell as needed. We would apply the funds to meet budget deficits. But the events of 9/11 changed the whole giving cycle, resulting in generating much less revenue than anticipated to carry into the coming year. On top of this, the crash of the dot-coms very effectively disposed of the formerly disposable funds given to us by generous donors.

The Iraq war served to further compound an already very difficult financial situation. Understandably, people were focused on the Middle East and international events. I understood and supported that different focus while significant international issues were being played out, but local needs continued. Homeless women and families with their children were still in desperate need of a safe place to stay, and while we were glad to be able to provide for those needs, we couldn't do so without community participation.

I issued a plea from the bottom of my heart, not only for Joy Junction, but for all the other rescue missions and faith-based ministries around the nation. More than ever, I said, we needed financial and prayer support from our friends to keep going. We knew God supplies, there was no question about that, but He also uses his children to do so.

The depression I felt did not go away, and I wrote this rather revealing letter to supporters:

> I don't feel a whole lot better about life than I did a couple of weeks ago.
>
> While I appreciate some heartfelt messages of prayerful support, lack of money continues to be a major problem at Joy Junction, New Mexico's largest emergency homeless shelter.
>
> As requests for emergency food and shelter have continued in torrents, the funds allowing us to provide those services have just trickled in. That's resulted in our laying off a number of staff and decreasing the number of hours the shelter van is available to provide emergency pick-up service for women and families on the streets. As you can imagine, these decisions weigh on me increasingly heavily—this year for some reason more so than ever. Maybe it's my upcoming 47th birthday and an impending mid-life crisis, or perhaps the stress is something I should expect as a normal part of running a growing ministry.

While some jobs require people to be temporarily on call 24/7, I feel that I'm permanently emotionally and physically tethered to Joy Junction. Whatever I'm doing or wherever I am, the welfare of the shelter and its guests is always on my mind. Whether it's waking up in the middle of the night wondering how to meet this week's bills, a concern about the welfare of a troubled staff member, or thinking of new and creative ways to share the gospel with our diverse population of homeless guests—Joy Junction is always there.

Now while I know being in that state of mind is not necessarily good, for me it is nonetheless a fact of life. So perhaps you're thinking, "Couldn't he leave Joy Junction? After all, no one is forcing him to stay there!" That's absolutely correct. I founded Joy Junction and remain as its executive director purely because I feel that I am where the Lord wants me to be. With that in mind, I ask for your fervent prayers both for me and this ministry as we continue in our nineteenth year of operation.

It is your prayers that will help determine our survival—or not. Because we are a faith-based ministry and not a social service agency we don't intend to ask the government for funds to bail us out. That leaves us with a couple of options. Either additional money has to come in or we have to make more cutbacks in service and while we'll do that if we have to, the prospect of doing so is very painful.

This was a true expression of my feelings at the time, and I could only pray the Lord would use my words to touch the hearts of our supporters.

Separation and Divorce

In retrospect, it was more than the financial difficulties plaguing Joy Junction causing me to feel depressed. For many years, my wife, Sylvia, and I had been having difficulties in our marriage. There were routine arguments and strained communication resulting, at least in part, from the lack of a shared vision.

The unhappy situation at home made me want to retreat into the peace and security of Joy Junction and my educational pursuits. Yet, the more I retreated, the worse things became. Of course, between Joy Junction and flying back and forth to school, my schedule was very demanding. As my studies progressed, there was more and more reading to do for my Ph.D. degree. For the three months before I took what are called, most appropriately, comprehensive examinations in June of 2002, it seemed that all I did was read and try to master the literature in my field. I read in bed, in the office, on the plane, and in the gym. Wherever I was, I read.

All the reading was partly a way of dealing with the painful reality that Sylvia and I were growing apart. While we had long discussions about what, if anything, was left of our relationship, they did not resolve anything and ended with arguing and the feeling we were only hurting each other. For the sake of the shelter, a possible divorce was something I always resisted.

Finally, in November of 2004, we agreed it would be best if I moved out of the ministry-provided house that had been our family home since the late 1980s. I moved into a very modest residence located on our fifty-two acre property. So modest, in fact, it did not have a working stove or microwave.

While my new living arrangements were lonely, they were at least peaceful. Basically, I buried myself in my office.

Although I was going through all of the motions of running the shelter, issuing news releases and the like, and trying to make sure the money kept coming in, I lost heart for what I was doing. I had shut down emotionally. I saw our guests as just people, not as hurting hearts and souls desperately needing the love and compassion the Lord wanted to minister to them through me. Who knows how long I could have gone on like that before having an emotional meltdown?

I kept a small number of close friends and colleagues apprised of my situation and asked them to pray about the situation. I am particularly thankful for the way the administrative team at Joy Junction supported me during those difficult days, especially a valued former staff member who helped me keep my priorities in order.

I believe it is important for Christians to "be there" to listen or offer some kind words to those both in the church and outside undergoing separation or divorce. Why do we seem to ignore their pain, or even treat them with contempt due to their problems, when they so desperately need our words of comfort and encouragement?

One day in February, a man appeared at my office door. He said, "Mr. Reynalds, I'm sorry, but I need to serve you these," and he apologetically gave me divorce papers. I shouldn't have been surprised. After all, Sylvia and I had been living apart for fifteen months, and any emotional bond we once shared had waned. We would soon add to an already unfortunate statistic and become one of the approximately 50 percent of evangelical Christians who have been divorced.

I had come to see that as a community leader and the longtime director of Joy Junction, I was supposed to be stoic and unmovable. During the months of my separation and subsequent divorce, a steady parade of people trickled in and out of my office throughout the day, seeking help with their needs, apparently not recognizing I had needs, too.

While my own marriage sadly had fallen apart, Joy Junction was and is all about keeping families together as well as just loving people and giving them hope. The Lord's prompting helped reawaken me to the needs of the hundreds of people and scores of families pouring through Joy Junction, and I realized the Lord's calling on my life had not changed. Only now, I was no longer shut down; I was completely aware of the needs of the downhearted people around me, and I was focused on doing everything I could to provide for them. Although I was unable to save my own marriage, I understand the mission God initially gave me—to keep families together and minister to them as a cohesive unit—is still the foundation of this ministry.

Since then, I have found myself going through a continuing metamorphosis (or maybe an "epiphany" would be a better word) in my life. I fell in love with the Lord again and with the people he had given to help me. I agonized with Joy Junction guests when they hurt and rejoiced with them when they had even small victories—like celebrating a month of being drug or alcohol free.

Our resident services manager at Joy Junction, Anita McCullough, recently asked whether it ever gets any easier to see the continuous stream of needy, precious humanity flow through our doors. My honest response was, "No, it doesn't get any easier. In fact, it gets harder. If you find yourself able to look at our guests without being touched, and their pain and plight doesn't gnaw at your soul, then it is time to start looking for another job."

The Lord prompted me through a former staff member to begin writing a series of books that tell the stories of broken individuals who had come to Joy Junction and gotten back on their feet again. These coincided with a burning passion to encourage people to quit judging the homeless and writing them off, but instead to reach out with the love of Jesus and minister to their deepest needs.

I never wanted to be guilty of doing what I heard the main character articulate in the movie *The Book of Eli*, "All those years I'd been carrying that book and reading it every day. I forgot to live by what it said: 'Do more for others more than you'd do for yourself!'"

I have also increased our outreach to the local community. While we have had a presence with the Albuquerque Chamber of Commerce and the Hispano Chamber of Commerce for the last four years, we have increased our attendance at their meetings and functions. I have also determined to share the story of the homeless and Joy Junction wherever there is an open door. I believe strongly that we have a biblical and societal responsibility to reach out to the less fortunate among us. That includes telling their story whenever we can.

A significant expansion in our ministry occurred last year. Just before Joy Junction's 2009 banquet with our friend, country singer Rockie Lynne, we published our inaugural issue of the *Joy Junction Gazette.* We reported our wish for a lunch wagon to, "go mobile," to feed those individuals who, for whatever reason, did not want to come inside Joy Junction or any other homeless facility in Albuquerque.

A few days later, longtime Joy Junction friend Victor Jury, Summit Electric CEO, e-mailed me and directed me to a link on eBay, where there was a lunch wagon for sale. He asked me if we would like it. I took a look and was thrilled with what I saw. Vic was gracious enough to buy it for us, and he flew me out to West Palm Beach, where the vehicle was located. Along with a fellow Joy Junction staff member, I drove what became the Lifeline of Hope back from Florida.

Through the lunch wagon, we have met and served many wonderful people. The Lifeline of Hope is a continuing part of my evolving life and spiritual journey. Along with Kathy Sotelo, the outreach coordinator for Joy Junction, a major portion of every Friday is now spent going all over town feeding hot chili, soups, and sack lunches prepared in the Joy Junction kitchen. Kathy and I also go out with a larger crew every Sunday afternoon. One of our staff members, along with an assistant, takes the Lifeline of Hope out for an additional three days a week.

It is a wonderful experience to see downcast faces take on smiles of delight, as they sample a good-sized bowl of chili or soup and receive other essential items, such as personal hygiene items or blankets, which many of us tend to take for granted.

While providing hundreds of nourishing meals to those outside the walls of Joy Junction, the ministry back at the shelter is still growing by leaps and bounds. We are feeding at least ten thousand meals per month and providing about nine thousand nights of shelter. Our Christ in Power

Life Recovery Program (CIPP) is active and growing. We have a number of graduations each year, which are wonderful occasions. At these ceremonies, we present graduates with certificates of completion and recognize their accomplishments. Graduating from the CIPP is no easy feat, and we want to make it an experience to remember. In addition, we have had a number of baptisms and marriages, which are always very exciting occasions.

What breaks my heart and the hearts of our collective staff is when our facility is filled to capacity, and we have to turn away people who have no other place to go. We know there is a good chance when we say we are full that these precious souls will have to spend the night on the streets. How can anyone possibly get a restful night's sleep on the ever-increasingly dangerous streets of Albuquerque? At the very least, they would have to sleep with one eye open.

With that in mind, we are launching some ambitious expansion plans at our South Valley property, which would take care of some of the growing number of people seeking help from us in this difficult economy.

What a ride the last twenty-four years have been at Joy Junction! I am sure as we continue trusting the Lord, the next quarter century and beyond will be even more exciting. I have no plans to retire. When the Lord gives someone a burden to care for hurting people of any kind, that burden must be acted upon. I hope sharing my experiences will help translate that calling into reality. Above all, we must be able to maintain the excitement we experienced when we initially received God's call on our lives.

If the Lord has given you a heart of compassion to care for hurting people, whoever they are, I pray this book will help you translate that passion into practical reality, whether you do it as a profession or as a lifestyle. And at the same time, I hope you will be able to maintain the excitement and passion you experienced when you initially received the Lord's call on your life.

A History 4 of Shelters

It is important to get some idea of why homeless shelters exist, what they are, where they come from, and who they serve. They have been around for so long that we sometimes take them for granted. Many of our neighbors might not want to be next door to a homeless shelter, but they still accept them as a normal part of American life.

In his book *Unto the Least of These: A Handbook of Specialized Ministries in the Rescue Mission* (International Union of Gospel Missions, 1974), William Seath wrote that many years ago there were groups of people commonly referred to as migrants or vagrants. These individuals were mostly runaway slaves, trying to make a new life for themselves in big cities and stay as far away from their former masters as possible. Rome was a great center of attraction for runaways.

There were also travelers, minstrels, traveling monks—maybe similar to the Methodist circuit riders of the last century—and also those who just had the traveling bug and wandered around the known world. These people earned a precarious living, entertaining or performing some sort of menial tasks along the way. Today, we would probably call it day labor. They stopped along the route to work just long enough to get some money together to take them on to the next city. Seath said that that outside the children of Israel, most nations took little or no interest in the poor and unfortunate, accepting their sorrow and misfortune as a fact of life. In Jesus' time, even many Jews did not pay much attention to the poor and needy beggars, as we clearly see in scenes like the pool of Bethesda (John 5).

Seath cited the story of the beggar Lazarus in Luke 16:19–31 as an example of this: "There was a rich man who was dressed in purple and fine linen and lived in luxury every day. At his gate was laid a beggar named Lazarus, covered with sores and longing to eat what fell from the rich man's table. Even the dogs came and licked his sores" (19–21).

The Growth of Christian Concern

Unto the Least of These reveals that years later in Europe, many monasteries opened their doors to wanderers, such as I have described above. Monasteries gave these individuals food, shelter, and other services, almost like a modern social service agency.

In England, poverty became so great that in the 1600s, eighty thousand people were classified as "vagrants." In 1602, King James I issued a proclamation ordering that vagrants be deported from the country. Shortly afterward, buildings known as workhouses were established to care for the indigent, handicapped, and aged. Conditions in these places were incredibly bad.

The United States' oldest rescue mission was founded by Jerry McAuley in 1872; however, even prior to that, the homeless population was growing rapidly. Following the Civil War, many men grew restless and began moving around the country. After having been uprooted from their homes at a young age, they saw new sights, sounds, and places. While they were subject to strict military discipline, they tamed the urge to wander. But on release from the military, they felt a great sense of freedom. Remembering all the new experiences they had while in uniform, they wanted to see all of these places on their own.

Often, this newfound freedom took hold of them and became a way of life. Shortly after 1865, the railroads signaled there would be future growth in the West, and they started expanding the amount of track. This resulted in the need for more temporary railroad laborers, men who were to form the nucleus of the transient seasonal labor movement. As large farms opened and road construction became a major industry, the need for transient workers was greater than ever before. Adding to the need for these temporary workers was the great increase in the lumber industry and ice harvesting. Transient laborers reached a three-and-a-half million peak in about 1926.

The majority of these temporary laborers were homeless; they had no permanent residence. Many came from poor families and had limited education. As with everything, there were notable exceptions. Among this huge army of people were alcoholics. All of these individuals were prime candidates for service and ministry by the rescue missions of the day.

Fighting Poverty

In his article in the Fall 1990 edition of *Policy Review* titled "Beyond the Stingy Welfare State," Marvin Olasky wrote that poverty fighters one hundred years ago were more compassionate in the literal sense of "suffering with" than many of us are now. Olasky wrote that these individuals opened their homes to deserted and abandoned women and children. They offered jobs to traveling men who had abandoned hope and most human contact.

Most important, Olasky wrote, these poverty fighters had moral requirements for those they helped. They did not allow those who received their kindness to just eat and run. They saw family, work, freedom, and faith as central to our being, not as lifestyle options. How times have changed. Joy Junction and other shelters, both in Albuquerque and nationwide, have been criticized many times for having mandatory church attendance. But if God calls one to start and run a homeless shelter ministry, that is what it is first—a ministry. While on many occasions Joy Junction is referred to as an "agency," in the sense that we perform social service functions, we are a ministry first and foremost and an agency second. Our primary aim is to see a hungry "sinner" come in and leave as a well-fed "saint." Our focus is to present the gospel of Jesus Christ, to let everyone who enters our doors know that Christ died for their sins and rose from the dead to give them new life. We teach that after one comes to faith, they are transformed and begin showing marked changes in behavior. They find new freedom from their former conduct and addictions and in so doing, experience new life in Christ. We have found that this includes a more helpful attitude toward others with whom they live at the shelter and renewed relationships with family and friends.

A major reason for including this brief overview of the work of rescue missions is so all will know the heritage of the work we do. In addition, many Christians today sometimes forget the works and lives of those who have gone before, which really is a shame, as we have so much to learn from them.

Marvin Olasky showed that the work of compassion about a century ago was carried on in scenes at least as squalid as we can imagine in today's worst barrios. Thousands of orphans roamed the streets, and infant mortality rates were ten times the present levels. New York Police Commissioner Thomas Byrnes estimated that there were about forty thousand prostitutes in the city of New York in 1890. A survey conducted about the same time found 6,576 New York slum families living in tenement "inside" rooms, or rooms that had no windows facing out. All these rooms had airshafts, which many tenants used as garbage dumps.

And yet, during this period, a successful war on poverty was being waged nationwide by many thousands of local charitable agencies and religious groups. These groups were often small and made up of volunteers, and they were led by poorly paid professional managers. Much was written by the journalists of that time on how effective these volunteers were. Olasky concluded the charity workers of a century ago were successful because they were inspired by seven ideas recent welfare practice has abandoned.

Olasky listed these concepts:

- Affiliation—emphasizing the restoration of broken ties to family and friends;
- Bonding—forging long-term, one-on-one contact between a volunteer and a needy person;
- Categorization—using "work tests" and background checks to distinguish between different types of applicants;
- Discernment—learning how to say *no* in the short run so as to produce better long-term results;
- Employment—requiring work from every able-bodied applicant;
- Freedom—helping the able needy resist enslavement to the charity of governmental or private masters; and,
- God—emphasizing the spiritual as well as the material.

I find it fascinating this very effective way of operating is now almost completely foreign to the way most social service agencies operate. During the last century, when individuals with real needs applied for material assistance, charity workers began by interviewing applicants and checking backgrounds with the goal of answering one question: Who is (morally) bound to help in this case?

For example, the case notes from files of the Associated Charities of Boston read that when an elderly widower applied for help, "The agent's investigation showed that there were relatives upon whom he might have a claim." A niece was unable to contribute, but a brother-in-law who had not seen the old man for twenty-five years promised to send regular financial support. The individual made good on his promise. The brother-in-law's contribution paid the man's living expenses and reunited him with his late wife's family.

The charity caseworker said that if there had not been a diligent investigation, all the man would have received would have been some food. His living situation would not have improved. But rather than having just his basic needs met, he was reunited with the family who loved him.

The last principle of the seven concepts used by last century's charity workers was an emphasis on God. A charity magazine of the time wrote that true philanthropy must take spiritual as well as physical needs into account. The magazine said, "Poverty will be dramatically reduced if the victims of appetite and lust and idleness... revere the precepts of the Bible and form habits of industry, frugality and self-restraint."

Bad Choices

Unwise use of resources is a great problem for homeless people. There is really so much to be learned from looking at how the great "rescuers" of yesteryear used to minister to the needy. Some time ago, I looked at a family walking through the door of our facility. This family was loaded down with sodas, chips, goodies, and disposable diapers. There would be nothing wrong with this—if the family was not homeless. But the objective of staying in a homeless shelter is to save as much money as possible, in as short a time as possible, so the homeless person can get back on his feet as soon as he can. That family did not make it and eventually left town. I cannot help but wonder if we had made them more aware of the principles of last century's rescuers, would they have made more of a success of their lives? We now incorporate financial concepts into our program to help residents understand the importance of personal money management.

We all make choices, and the homeless are no exception. As we think about policies for today's rescue operations, we need to keep the policies of last century's rescuers in mind. But remember also that we are faced with a much more complex world and way of living than families of a century ago. For example, today so many more homeless families are from broken and blended families.

Christian Compassion

Late nineteenth-century American Christians who read the Bible regularly did not see God as a sugar daddy, feeling sorry for people in distress. They saw God as showing compassion while requiring change, and they attempted to do the same.

St. Vincent de Paul, the Catholic charity, is a name probably familiar to most. In their magazine from about one hundred years ago, an author wrote, "The Vincentian must be prepared to discipline, admonish and encourage … [Most of the poor] must be disciplined into providence, for they are seldom provident for themselves. To be their true benefactor, the visitor must admonish them to know and appreciate their high destiny."

Groups like the Industrial Christian Alliance reminded the poor that God made them and had high expectations for them to, restore the fallen and helpless to self-respect and self-support.. That is why it is so important for Christians to know we really do have the edge on the world in helping the poor and needy.

While we can attempt to teach the importance of education, the need to be responsible, and the necessity to regularly get up and go to work, what is really going to help is a change of heart. That is, all the help we can give the poor is secondary to entering into a personal relationship with Jesus Christ. They have to learn godly responsibility, and Christ will give them the reason and the motivation to do so.

As the 1890s progressed, there emerged what is called the Social Gospel. Leaders of the movement were convinced that real charity must be both universal and unconditional. According to Olasky, part of this new thinking was based on a changed view of the nature of God and the nature of man. Whereas the previous view saw God as both holy and loving, the new view tended to mention love only. This new view saw humanity as naturally good and productive, unless put in a competitive environment that "warped finer sensibilities." In this new way of thinking, to put people to a work test (if a person does not want to work, they should not eat) was cruel, because someone who has faced a "crushing load of misfortune" should not be faulted if he or she does not choose to work.

These new thinkers believed that challenging people would not bring change, but change would only occur when they were placed in pleasant environments to bring out their "true, benevolent nature." This is in direct opposition to the biblical view, which describes human nature as being, "deceitful above all things and beyond cure" (Jer. 17:9).

It is very important to understand these views, because proponents of the Social Gospel tend to criticize evangelical shelter ministries. To require families staying at shelters to attend gospel services will definitely bring criticism for a variety of reasons, including charges of infringing on their rights. When one knows the history of charity work, however, where it came from and how it is used, one sees clearly the change in the current method of operation.

There should be a balance to both ways of thinking, and Joy Junction has been criticized outright by advocates of both approaches. Members of the Social Gospel movement have disagreed with Joy Junction for requiring attendance at religious services and for our thinking that human nature is depraved and sinful. But many of those who support our theological stance fail to understand the dynamics of homelessness when they come down to visit the shelter and observe many of our guests "sitting around." Perhaps they just finished working their shift. Perhaps they are new residents who have not yet been assigned a job. Or maybe they are recovering from many failed attempts to find work outside the shelter.

Another thing many visitors may fail to understand is the reality of clinical depression and how it renders someone totally unable to work. They do not see that homelessness and its associated problems did not happen overnight and, in all probability, will not be cured overnight. They do not see the working of the Holy Spirit in the lives of these people, as those of us close to them do. Visitors may not realize these precious individuals are in various stages of recovery, and although they have come very far, they still have a long way to go in order to become contributing members of society. With the Lord's help, we are assisting them to do so.

Families with children still represent relatively uncharted territory in the rescue movement, so there is no precedent or historical experience to offer help. The one thing that is sure is we need to be guided by the Holy Spirit on how to help in each situation. History can and will give some good underlying principles, and lots of common sense, but every person and every family must be treated as individuals. We should not be servants of convention, but instead, we should be creative in ministering to individuals in individual situations. And we would do well to let them assist us in making recommendations on how to minister to their needs.

Changing Viewpoints

Sometimes people go to extremes, and this is also true of those who exercise the ministry of compassion. I want to achieve a balance. So, while history's shelter ministries did many things right, I believe there were some things they did wrong. Nevertheless, we can certainly learn from them.

As the progression of the Social Gospel wore on, many began arguing that only the government could create an economic environment to rescue all. In effect, what they did was take away the necessity of trusting Jesus as Savior and substitute the government as a means to economic parity and personal salvation. The idea that compassionate people would rally around the creation of new programs became popular. Some even believed that the construction of government housing projects would bring about a kind of socialistic utopia. What they forgot was that before any real and lasting improvement can come about, the human heart has to change, and only a relationship with Jesus can bring about lasting, observable change. You can put a pig in a palace, but he is still a pig. And if a king is put in a pigsty, he is still a king. Changing the environment can help in human terms, but it cannot bring the long-lasting sort of social change humanistic advocates have so long believed it would.

Sadly, as the momentum of the new programs began gathering steam, people became embarrassed by the evangelical emphasis of the older philosophy. The *Encyclopedia of Social Reform* even suggested that evangelical underpinnings to charity work were wrong because university-educated experts now knew "social wrongs" caused individual problems, and these social ills would disappear once the poor were placed in a better living environment.

Motivation for Service

Those whose motivation for volunteering was seeing souls delivered from sin, as well as hungry bodies fed and clothed, found the new emphasis frustrating and unrewarding and often quit their charity work. Personal spiritual involvement was replaced by the secular approach of social work professionals. These professionals used psychological theories and behavior modification techniques to try to change attitudes and practices. These techniques offered no hope of long-term transformation, and the reason is, as evangelicals know full well, men and women cannot change themselves. The gospel of Jesus Christ, however, transforms lives by the Holy Spirit, and a life wholly committed to it and to him exhibits true and lasting visible changes.

In the mid-1920s, the transient worker's life was dramatically influenced by automation and the introduction of modern machinery. Thousands of jobs were eliminated almost overnight. The introduction of combine harvesting equipment eliminated thousands of manual farm jobs, and new techniques in road building caused road construction jobs to follow suit. Mechanical refrigeration almost eliminated the necessity to harvest ice, and there were rapid changes in the logging industry. About the only thing left for the temporary worker to do was lay track, maintain the railroads, and clear the railroad tracks in bad weather.

The years 1929 through 1933 brought the Great Depression, creating larger and vastly different problems for rescue missions. Entire families became homeless. Many of those looking for help sought it for the very first time. In addition, many families were unable to support their children, so a vast number of children as young as seven or eight years old left home to look for work on their own.

At about the same time, because of the migration of churches from the inner city to the suburbs, a new avenue of service arose for the rescue missions. When all these churches followed their congregations out of the city, the streets of the inner cities were vacated, leaving it to someone else to fill the void. It was often the rescue missions that stepped in. In many cases, those who moved to the suburbs were replaced by the aged, the unemployed or unemployable, and minorities.

During the Great Depression, when millions of people were unemployed and quite naturally jobs were not readily available, it made sense to have lots of government programs. Marvin Olasky contends that continuing some of the New Deal programs during the postwar return to prosperity set the stage for our modern welfare crisis. In the fifties, he writes, many poor families remained intact, and—very importantly—most people saw benefits not as rights but as supplemental income for use only during dire emergencies. The "entitlement revolution" of the sixties has not helped the poor, according to Olasky, who summed up the overall change in shelters as he saw it between the 1890s and the 1990s.

In his article published in the Fall 1990 edition of *Policy Review* titled "Beyond the Stingy Welfare State," Olasky wrote, "To see firsthand what homeless individuals could receive and were expected to do, I recently spent a couple of days dressed as a homeless person in Washington D.C. I was given or offered a great deal of material at shelters and agencies, both government supported and private. This included lots of food, lots of medicine, and lots of clothes (even a bathing suit so I could use a free swimming pool). But not once was I asked to do anything for these things, not even to carry away my tray after a meal."

Olasky said that an able-to-work homeless person in 1890 would have been asked to take some responsibility for his or her own life and to help others as well by chopping wood or cleaning up trash. Then, the homeless person would have had to make contact with other people, whether relatives or former colleagues, to see if they were in a position to be of help. But today none of that happens, and the homeless man or woman is free to be a "naked nomad," going from meal to meal. When anyone suggests personal responsibility might help this person, he is told very emphatically that would be infringing on rights.

The Necessity for Balance

Again, balance is the key word. It is true that some people come off the streets to stay at shelters are mentally and psychologically unable to work. They are almost shell-shocked; call it PTSS—posttraumatic "street" syndrome. Before this type of person can do anything, she needs to heal mentally and emotionally. There will come a time, and it could range from a few days to a few weeks, when the individual will need to work. The person may be self-motivated to work, if that is part of the background and training. If unwilling on her own to do so, she should be encouraged to work as part of the healing and growth process. Initially, the work might be around the shelter, perhaps as part of a therapy program to get people back on their feet again. Then, when ready, they may be able to accept full-time work as a shelter employee or work outside the shelter. Our responsibility is to treat every person as an individual and to be sensitive to the leading of the Holy Spirit.

PART 2

OPERATING A HOMELESS SHELTER

STARTING A SHELTER

I would now like to address those readers who want to start a shelter or get involved in the people-helping business. Whether starting a homeless shelter, a Christian school, an alcohol and drug rehabilitation program, or a crisis pregnancy center, there are some very similar principles that need to be followed, beginning with the call of God.

The Importance of a "Call"

The most important element required for any ministry is the call of God. This is more important than it sounds, because that call is what keeps you going through the hard times.

God speaks to his people in various ways. To some, he speaks through pastors, ministers, priests, or concerned laypeople. To others, it is through circumstances, and to others, he might highlight some particular aspect of his revealed Word.

When I resigned from my first shelter in Santa Fe in 1986, I made the mistake of telling God I would do anything he wanted me to do—except run a shelter. I figured I had paid my dues running the shelter in Santa Fe for four years, and now, I informed God, it was time to do something else. Not only did I tell the Lord I was unwilling to start another shelter, I told him I was unwilling to start another ministry of any sort—period. Some of the reasoning behind my fervent determination was that the hours worked often paralleled those required for the opening of a new business. Outrageous working hours are exchanged for small and often late paychecks.

For a ministry to succeed, you have to sell yourself and your vision to the community and the local pastors. Potential donors have to believe in the one starting the ministry before they will believe in what that person represents. It is easy to see from where donors and pastors are coming. They receive so much mail asking for money that it would be impossible to respond to every solicitation.

These were some of the thoughts going through my mind as I kept myself busy telling God what I would and would not do. Meanwhile, God's plans were not my plans. "For my thoughts are not your thoughts, neither are your ways my ways, declares the Lord" (Isa. 55:8). They were much better and infinitely higher. God had eased me into my calling in Santa Fe, but if I had been sensitive, I would have realized he orchestrated so many special events in my life to give me empathy for the homeless that he was not going to let me out of the calling. He made it clear he was going to use me in that particular way, and he was going to work in me to help me receive that calling.

As a matter of fact, I believe it is a positive sign to worry a bit about taking steps to begin a ministry. That way, we can use the questions in our minds to pray more, both individually and with those who offer us spiritual counsel. If we decide at this point not to go ahead, it is okay. It does not mean we are less spiritual than anyone else. Rather, it means that God has something else in mind for our lives. On the other hand, we need to make sure we are obeying God and not giving in to fear. Trying to wriggle our way out of God's calling, as I tried to do, is not the way to go.

During my last few months in Santa Fe, I applied at different churches looking for a pastor. During the trial sermon, I told the congregations what I thought the prerequisites for a good church were. A recurring theme in my messages was always ministering to the poor and needy. It was not really intentional, but the subject just kept coming up. Evidently what came through in my messages was that I was more interested in the poor and needy than the spiritual needs of the church members.

Needless to say, I was not offered the pastorate in any of those churches. I came to the end of my time in Santa Fe with no job offers. In desperation, I applied to a foreign missions agency for a job and was accepted. That should have been cause for rejoicing, except to take the appointment would have required relocating to Denver. Moreover, the job was a "faith position." In other words, I had to raise my own salary. I attempted to raise some money, but nothing happened to clearly move me in that direction. It seemed to be all my own doing, with no guidance from above. I felt like I was fighting my own battles, and life was getting very discouraging.

Yielding to God's Call

Feeling you are on your own is what happens when fighting God's will for your life and being reluctant to listen to the still, small voice of the Holy Spirit. Sometimes God has to hit us over the head with a spiritual two-by-four. On the other hand, it is wrong to run into ministry because it is "cool." Operating a shelter and ministering God's love is some of the hardest work we will ever do in life. It will certainly take everything out of us if we are not spiritually prepared for it. And in many cases, no one except God thanks you for all the hard work.

It is very hard to describe God's calling, because it is such an intangible and personal experience. In many cases, it almost defies written description. In my case, while my family was staying in Taos, New Mexico, on several occasions we visited good friends who formerly pastored a little church in Questa, a village community about twenty-five miles north of Taos. While visiting these friends, we also had several occasions to go with them to the mountains to pray. Talk about God orchestrating events.

My friend was at that time a pastor in the Assemblies of God denomination. Little did I know that four years later, I would meet him at a mutual friend's home in Santa Fe, and the Lord would use him to bail both me and the shelter out of a financial mess when we received unfavorable publicity in June 1990.

When I was seeking the Lord for his direction in my life, he brought Scriptures to my mind. God also gave my friend words of encouragement and direction for me. Those Scriptures and my friend's words confirmed what was already in my heart, but I was unwilling to face the fact God would not let me out of my calling.

God Works in an Orderly Way

I think it is rare that God uses others to speak to us about a situation or a calling, or a change in calling, about which he has not already spoken to us. I know of situations where people have received and acted on directions to quit a job, sell everything they own, and move to a far corner of the earth. But God had not been speaking to them directly, nor had he been preparing their hearts. Instead, they listened to others with erroneous advice masquerading as "word" from God. We can know God is working and speaking to us, because he orchestrates in an orderly fashion the course of events leading to his perfect will, including the people he sends to help us in that regard.

The Scriptures the Lord used to direct me that critical year included verses from the forty-first chapter of Isaiah:

> The poor and needy search for water, but there is none; their tongues are parched with thirst. But I the Lord will answer them; I, the God of Israel, will not forsake them. I will make rivers flow on barren heights, and springs within the valleys. I will turn the desert into pools of water, and the parched ground into springs. (17–18).

While the Lord spoke gently to other people in my life that serving the hungry and homeless was still where he wanted me to be, it really took something more drastic than a gentle nudge for me. God engineered the circumstances and took every other opportunity away from me before I finally gave in and said, "Yes, Lord. I'll do what you want." And that is the way God works. He will do whatever it takes to get our attention to listen and obey his calling. He will woo us and be very gentle initially, but if we are quite determined we are not going to obey, he will resort to other measures to get our attention.

The calling God has on our lives will also be confirmed by others in our fellowship or local church body. In all probability, if God has been dealing with someone about starting a shelter or entering some form of people ministry, it will be an extension of a call he has already placed on that person's life. What I mean is while a spiritual calling is somewhat intangible, it will in most cases coincide with tangible physical circumstances and visible actions. I will discuss that later.

There is probably not a reader of this book who does not have some concern for the poor, needy, and hurting people around us. Perhaps you have been encouraging your pastor and your church to do more for the hungry and homeless in your community. Maybe you have been taking into your home homeless families who call the church asking for help. (I would not recommend doing this, as it can be dangerous.) Or maybe you have been taking food and blankets to the homeless downtown. Perhaps you have had a real concern for the alcoholics you see wandering around town.

A real calling from God will transform our lives and allow us to keep our mental, emotional, and spiritual sanity when it looks like everything is crashing down. God's summons does not make us arrogant, but it does bring us peace.

Do not forget that if God has called you to do a job, while it is up to you to do everything you can to ensure success, ultimately the final responsibility for its achievement lies in God's hands. And remember, where God leads, he feeds, and where God guides, he provides. Keep praying while trying to work out your calling. God knows each person's heart and needs, and he is not impressed with the enormity of anyone's problems. He is Almighty God, and he is more impressed with our obedience.

Getting Your Spouse on Your Side

Spousal support is critical, since ministry will change your family life. Therefore, share your vision with your wife or husband. Ministry of most kinds, especially the start-up kind, will probably demand a dramatic change in schedule and quite possibly in the paycheck.

Think about these questions: Is your spouse willing to put up with the excessive hours you will initially be gone from home, quite possibly for some years into the future? Be realistic about this, not hopelessly optimistic. Spousal support is also an indication of the will of God, although this may not happen overnight. God may need to work in that person in order to bring them into the vision he has for you as a couple. Will you have to obtain outside employment for a while to meet even basic needs? Is your family not only willing but able to reduce its standard of living? If you are heavily in debt, this might be the time to stop right now. Rather than attempt to start a shelter, look for one already in existence and offer your prayerful and financial support.

If your spouse is not initially thrilled when you share what God has been speaking to you, do not give up. Do not write him or her off as being unconcerned or unspiritual. Do not make any rash moves, but do keep praying. After all, if the burden you have for the homeless comes from the Lord, and he managed to get through to you, he can also get through to your husband or wife and turn their heart in favor of the project. Remember, it is the Lord's responsibility to turn your calling into a reality.

Sharing with Your Pastor

Make an appointment to speak with your pastor. Tell him as honestly, simply, and clearly as you can about how God has been speaking to you. Ask him to tell you truthfully what he thinks. Be willing to listen to what he says, because he sees things about you and your family, both strengths and weaknesses, that you might not see yourself.

If you do not have this sort of relationship with your pastor, find someone godly you can trust who knows you and is willing to tell you both your strong and weak points. Ask them all to pray for you. Among other things, you will need prayer for wisdom, guidance, and God's favor.

Start to meet regularly with your pastor and/or those who have been praying for you. While there is a chance that God could deal with you in a manner similar to how he dealt with me—jobless and forcing your hand to get you to do what he wants—it is more likely you will be leaving a job where you have been relatively well established and may be earning a reasonable income. You will need all the prayer power you and your family can muster.

If you are thinking about leaving a good job, there are some people who will think you are crazy. And maybe you are. Could it all go wrong? It possibly could. If after receiving all the right signals you still decide not to go ahead, you will probably never be totally happy and fulfilled again. There will always be a nagging doubt at the back of your mind about what your life might have been like had you launched out in faith and obeyed God. God may approach you at another time in your life, but don't count on it. You must be willing to give your all to the Lord. If you do so, you will not regret it. Don't worry when the inevitable trials come; the Father is just forming your character into the beautiful image of his precious Son, Jesus.

Community need is also tied in with the will of God. Consider taking an informal community survey. For example, if you feel God has called you to start a Christian school and there is already one in the area, make sure you visit that school. Learn about the work they do there. Perhaps they are already doing the ministry you have in mind. Do not be a maverick, doing whatever you think is right. The best way to spread fear and rumor is to operate in secret and isolation.

Communication, the Essential Ingredient

Make appointments with the directors of already established agencies and ministries in your city, and let them know what you believe God is telling you to do. Make it clear to these individuals you are not planning to compete with them (that would be foolish anyway); rather, you are intending to complement what they do.

Allow me a word of caution. Sometimes Christians are very free in our use of evangelical jargon. And when we talk in "evangelicalese," no one else knows what we are talking about. If you are at the zoning office for an official appointment, do not talk spiritual lingo. Telling the zoning board you have "taken it to the Lord in prayer" is not going to get you very far. Be polite, official, courteous, and to the point. Then leave.

Is it always important for existing agencies to hear about your plans? Yes, it is very important. And they need to hear about your plans from you, not someone else. People have a tremendous fear of the unknown, and who knows what image your proposed homeless shelter (or whatever ministry you are starting) could take once it has traveled through a half-dozen people. Before you know it, someone will be claiming you intend to be the only shelter in town and that you plan to close down everyone else. Or you might be accused of planning to begin a cult! Gossip has never been based on common sense. Good communication with the community should result in less of that sort of thing.

Reassure any fearful agency heads. Unfortunately, even those in the people-helping business sometimes have a certain amount of territorialism. I suggest you use a soft approach as you tell existing agencies about your plans. Tell them you are concerned about the lack of family shelters, Christian schools, alcoholism rehabilitation centers, or whatever it is you are concerned about, available in your city. Ask them how they would feel about an additional agency in the city that targets the specific need that interests you. Hopefully, such a meeting will be a very positive experience, allaying any fears you are a maverick trying to sneak in the back door, steal their clients, or do something behind their backs. It could also serve as a good reference point for leads to attain adequate property for your proposed shelter, school, or other parachurch, faith-based ministry.

Location Is Critical

Finding adequate property that is correctly zoned could well turn out to be one of your most difficult tasks. In fact, there is a really good chance discouragement will set in during this process, which is another reason why it is so important to have a call of God you can stand on. With God, discouragement can turn into an opportunity to prove his awesomeness and power.

Joy Junction has been exceptionally fortunate in zoning issues. The property the shelter occupies is a fifty-two-acre farm in Albuquerque's South Valley that was formerly used as a Christian alcohol and drug rehabilitation center. When I began looking into this property, I did not realize how God went before us to prepare the way. It was about a year after the shelter opened when I found old press clippings from DARE (the name of the center that occupied the property). One story header stayed in my mind. It read something like this: "Angry Residents Protest Influx of Drug Addicts into the South Valley."

The property's former zoning status was A-1, an agricultural designation. Despite the protests of the concerned residents, the then county commission decided to grant a special use permit (S-U) for the life of the property. The S-U reads that permissible activities on the property are educational, rehabilitative, and religious. We were blessed with a zoning classification about which many mission directors only dream. God had given us exactly what we needed at that point.

Neighbors

During the years Joy Junction has been in operation, we have had only occasional neighbor problems. I guess our neighbors are more willing to have homeless families in their neighborhood than recovering drug addicts. Now, if you are sheltering, say, homeless families as opposed to homeless men, you will have the sympathy factor on your side. It is much easier to complain about a homeless man than a homeless woman and her child.

When there has been a problem with our neighbors, I have dealt with the situation quickly. I assure them we are as interested in their welfare, safety, and property values as we are in the care of the homeless.

Some time back, I invited our neighborhood association to meet on our site. I felt it would help alleviate any fears they might have about the shelter. The fear of the unknown is one of the best reasons for gossip, so I thought if I invited them to our property and they could actually see what we were doing, then they would realize the homeless are normal people just like us. My gambit paid good dividends.

Property and Prayer

Here is how to look for property: pray and look and keep praying. Ask your church to help in the search. Go to those who are praying for you, and consider joining one or maybe two civic support groups and service clubs like the Kiwanis or the Civitans. These groups are always looking for both worthy projects and good speakers.

Do not expect your search for suitable property to resemble mine. God works in an infinite variety of ways.

My experience in finding property in Santa Fe was very different from my Albuquerque experience. In Santa Fe, I quite literally had to tour the city on foot (I had no car back then) to find a suitable property. We also experienced frequent complaints from neighbors, who did not appreciate having a homeless shelter close by.

For Joy Junction here in Albuquerque, I thought about this property, did a quick tour of the facility, put a proposal in to the landlords, and awaited their response. A few weeks later, a favorable answer came, and we moved in. If you do not find a building at first, do not give up. If this is God's project, he will provide the means for you to accomplish it.

Your Personal Financial Support

While looking for a building, keep considering support, both to finance the ministry and to provide for yourself and your family. The apostle Paul warned us against becoming weary in doing good (Gal. 6:9). We will reap a harvest when the time is right, so do not ruin your family in your desire to help the homeless. We all need money to survive, and it is not unspiritual to admit it.

We need to enter ministry responsibly. Blaming God for half-baked ideas won't work. Yet, many Christians say God called them to a work without their being able to cover even basic needs. When I started Joy Junction, I had no reserves of money, but I did have part-time employment with a local Christian television station as a master-control operator. That put bread on the table and covered some basic needs.

The Bible says that if we do not take care of the needs of our family, or make no effort to do so, we are worse than unbelievers. Doing something silly and risky, like quitting our job and having no tangible means of support to fall back on, is not the way to enter ministry. That approach is very unwise and just brings reproach on the kingdom of God.

Some time ago, I was reading a story about a company expanding to the Albuquerque area. This was their fourth or fifth store, and their volume of business was now so large they were able to obtain outside financing for a start-up in Albuquerque. But it was not always like that. When the chain originally started, the couple who began the company maxed out the limits on their credit cards to self-finance their dream. They invested their own personal resources to turn their dream into reality, as well as put in many long hours. I am not advising anyone to use the cash allowance on their credit cards. What I am saying is what the world will do for business we must be willing to do for the kingdom of God.

A better way to enter ministry is to find a wonderful, loving pastor, or someone else in the community, who has a heart for seeing people move into ministry in a responsible way. When I started His Place in Santa Fe, I was a newcomer to the community, and I had no credibility. Pastor Carl Conley told me that as I contacted churches, people, and organizations in my attempt to solicit support, I could use both his name and the church name to gain credibility. His kindness was really an instant trust builder, as he was a well-respected community member.

If someone in the community is kind enough to do that sort of thing, we must not let them down. We must honor the promises we make, as this will be vitally important if we want to be credible witnesses for Christ.

How Do You Ask for Money Nicely?

Writing letters asking for money—nicely—is not always easy, but it is necessary in order to get your name and ministry into the minds and hearts of people in the community. Anyone who can write an acceptable fund-raising letter will be way ahead of many agency heads who have to hire outside consultants at high prices to perform that service. If you have never written such a letter, it may be a good time to get some experience in doing so by registering for a business writing, copywriting, or publicity writing course at your local community college or university. Back in 1986, I borrowed money for our first mailing. I wrote about three hundred letters and received one response of $300, enabling me to pay back our postage loan and write an additional letter, generating some more funds.

I also stayed on the phone a lot, calling everyone I could think of and telling them about the new homeless shelter in town. As word of our existence spread, people began referring needy clients to us. I also received a few invitations to speak, which generated a little more income.

Be prepared to work long hours with little expectation of reward, and keep your personal expenditures to a minimum. Ask your pastor for permission to share your dream with your own church. Maybe he will give you the opportunity to go before the congregation for a few minutes one morning. The church might take an offering for your proposed work and send you out with their blessing. They could even ultimately put your new work on their list of ministries regularly receiving money for missions.

How Much to Pay for Your Ministry Building

After finding a building that appears as if it might work, a call to the zoning inspector is in order. Let us imagine he or she says this just happens to be one of the few buildings located in an area of the city that would permit a homeless shelter, an alcoholism rehabilitation center, or maybe a homeless meal site. What is next? Make an appointment with the landlords to find out if they do mind the idea of their building being used for a homeless shelter. Be entirely honest with them, and do not forget to talk finances. Work out an affordable rental or lease agreement.

Just as credit card charges eventually have to be paid, so lease and rental agreements also have their day of reckoning. If you cannot afford the price of a building, do not rent it. The worst thing is to take on the responsibility for a building where there is no hope of bearing the cost and consistently being late paying the landlords. All that does is reflect badly on you, the ministry, and the body of Christ in general.

So Now You Have Your Building

I cannot emphasize strongly enough being prepared to do everything it takes, for as long as is necessary, to ensure the success of the shelter or chosen ministry. As Christians, we have God's blessing, but this does not preclude much long and hard work. There are no shortcuts, even if we are operating in his will. Here is how to do the math: God's will plus God's blessing plus hard work equal success. Leave out the hard work, and the success will not be there.

If one is interested in starting a homeless shelter ministry and has not already been in contact with those in the people-oriented ministry, that person is not ready to begin. Get together with these individuals; bring up the idea gently and courteously, in a nonthreatening manner, about the ministry you feel God has laid on your heart. Communication is essential.

Be prepared to start off small. Many want to start off big and grow even bigger, but God's way is usually for us to start off small and see what we do with what he gives us. As the parable of the talents in the twenty-fifth chapter of Matthew teaches, if God sees us being faithful with a little, he will reward us with more.

There is definitely no magic formula for starting out in ministry. The advice I would give for supporting yourself in the initial stages in ministry would be very different from person to person, depending on family size, whether there is some other means of outside support, and other factors. But there are some similar principles everyone can follow when getting involved in the people-helping ministry, regardless of one's personal situation. Those are what I have tried to cover in this chapter.

Starting and successfully maintaining a people-oriented ministry is very similar to starting and maintaining a successful small business. It is a time-consuming and emotionally draining process. Count on doing everything yourself until the income increases to the point where you can hire staff. Ministry can be very rewarding in a thousand ways, but it is definitely not glamorous. The only reason for wanting to be in full-time ministry should be to obey God's call and to share the love of Jesus Christ with hurting people. If you are thinking about ministry for any other reason, you are probably considering the wrong profession.

Nuts and Bolts of Ministry

I will use a homeless shelter as our example of a people-helping ministry in order to demonstrate the steps to follow in establishing and maintaining the ministry. If a reader is considering another type of agency, that agency can be substituted wherever I mention the shelter.

If God is calling us to be a part of meeting the need for a new shelter or another shelter in our community, what do we do? We have all heard the usual stories about people going off the deep end, quitting their jobs, and plunging their families into financial disaster. Please do not do that! Talk to your spouse first; if he or she is not in agreement with what you feel God is saying, maybe you should not follow through—at least right now. Consider the possibility God is speaking to you through your husband or wife. If taking care of the homeless has the potential to devastate your own family and leave you unable to care for them, the people-helping ministry is not for you.

After talking and praying over things with your spouse, and assuming you are in agreement, the next person to see is your pastor. Share with him what you feel God is saying. Hopefully, he will also bear witness to the work you feel God may be calling you. If your pastor thinks what you are proposing is a good idea, consider asking him to call a church meeting of those who might be interested in a shelter for homeless families.

Such a meeting might go something like this (adaptable to the way meetings are conducted at your particular church). First, communicate informally what you believe God has laid on your heart. Share your ideas about the dream you have to help provide physical and spiritual help for the suffering, hurting, hungry, and homeless women, children, and families of your community.

Then, remind those present of the scriptural obligation Christians have to take care of the poor and needy. Third, ask the people at the meeting if they think the time is right and whether you are the person to help alleviate some of the suffering in your town. Next, ask them to pray about their having any possible involvement in the ministry. Then, schedule another meeting. At that next meeting, it is time to ask for some level of commitment from those who have a call on their heart to join in this ministry.

For those who attend and appear committed, consider scheduling some luncheon meetings over the following few weeks. Ask individuals who appear to be sympathetic to your vision, as well as those you think you can work with, to be on your board of directors. Choosing an advisory board is a critical first step in realizing your vision.

A Board of Directors

A board? Yes, a board! I can almost hear some readers saying, "I wanted to help homeless people, not get involved with corporations and boards." But running a successful agency and having the public involved financially requires establishing a nonprofit corporation with a tax-deductible status. That means people who give to your organization can deduct the gift from their income taxes. And that is where a board comes in.

A nonprofit corporation needs a board, and before qualifying or even applying for tax exemption, the IRS requires a ministry be a state-approved, nonprofit corporation with a board of directors. How should a board be chosen?

The answer is, very carefully—and very prayerfully. In fact, rushing into selecting board members, or choosing them for the wrong reasons, could produce a disastrous situation. You could be terminated by the ministry you helped start and poured your life into. Sadly, I have seen this happen.

Make sure to be surrounded by a group of caring and loving people who are concerned for you and the ministry but who also will not hesitate to tell you if they see you acting inappropriately. Basically, this means that successful board members must be able to express their concerns about situations and circumstances that are harmful to the ministry from a strategic perspective. This is for your protection as well as theirs and the ministry. This must be done, however, as discreetly and confidentially as possible in order to protect the organization. Board members must have enough trust in the administration to allow it to run the everyday business of the ministry. Even if board members know a better way of doing things, if it is not a policy-related issue, they should leave those matters to the management.

Being careful about board members is of utmost importance. As you expand and grow more successful, there will be more people who want to get involved. Some may even want to buy their way onto your board. I would not recommend permitting anyone to serve on your board because of a large contribution. The ability to contribute financially does not mean someone possesses the savvy to run a business or ministry. Unfortunately, some people may think they can do the job better than you can. Even if that is true, it is not the point. If you started the shelter, you are the one God decided to entrust with the ministry. However, do not abuse the trust God has placed in you! Before going to your board with a proposal, I recommend getting initial confirmation for your decisions, at least the major ones that affect the shelter, by seeking the counsel of your executive-level employees.

Let me explain a little more about nonprofit corporations.

Nonprofits

There are a variety of not-for-profit corporations, but basically they all exist for the benefit of others. For example, there are nonprofits geared to the education of children. There are also those established to oversee the rehabilitation and care of developmentally disabled adults. Even some hospitals function as nonprofit corporations.

But to become a nonprofit agency recognized by your state, you must have articles of incorporation and bylaws. They are basically a statement about what you plan to do made to the state where you are located or where you want to be incorporated. The articles of incorporation are a written outworking of your internal organizational plans. They proclaim your reason for being and detail how you plan to carry out what you have outlined to the state. An example of the details in the bylaws might be how the ministry would consistently resolve disputes. This means you have an established policy that provides a uniform procedure for dealing with disputes. You do not deal arbitrarily with people depending on the time of day or the month of the year. You deal with everyone the same way, according to the bylaws.

To be granted tax-exempt status by the IRS means you are a church or a state-recognized, nonprofit corporation, organized and operated exclusively for religious or charitable purposes. If you are not willing to apply for this status, you need to ask yourself why. It is true you open yourself to possible inspection of your organization's books by the IRS as a nonprofit (unless you have been granted "church" status). But it also makes a public statement that you are willing to abide by the federal regulations.

Most corporations or corporate foundations to which you might turn when looking for a substantial gift demand the ministry be recognized as a 501(c) (3) by the IRS so they have the ability to designate that gift as tax-exempt.

Being a recognized nonprofit organization—also known as a 501(c) (3)—assures your donors they may deduct gifts to your organization (monetary or material) from their income tax.

Here are some specific details from *Christian Ministries and the Law,* by H. Wayne House (Grand Rapids: Kregel Publications, 1999).

> The nonprofit corporation is by definition a creature of the statutory law of the state in which the corporation is formed, and includes any corporation whereby no member, officer or director receives a profit ...
>
> Most states model their nonprofit corporation statutes after the Model Nonprofit Corporation Act ... The first step ... is to incorporate under this act. This usually consists of preparing articles of incorporation and filing them with the secretary of state, along with a filing fee ...
>
> Before sending the articles to the secretary of state, however, it is wise to check with the secretary's office to see if the proposed name of the corporation is available ...
>
> The act has certain significant requirements for the articles of incorporation ... They must include the name of the corporation, the period of duration, the address of the office of the corporation, the name and address of a registered agent for the corporation in the state, the names and addresses of the original board of directors and incorporators, as well as (its) ... purposes. ...
>
> ... If the organization is going to pursue federal tax-exempt status, the articles should include language indicating that upon (corporate) dissolution ... all of the assets will continue to be used for charitable purposes ...

> After the incorporation process is completed, the next step is to prepare and adopt bylaws ... (Once the byelaws are) ... adopted, the corporation may then begin officially functioning as a corporation ...
>
> ... The nonprofit corporation is the common form of legal entity for religious organizations ... in the United States today.

Once the state in which you are incorporating has approved your articles of incorporation and bylaws, you are able to apply for receipt of tax-exempt status from the IRS.

Seeking Tax-Exempt Status from the IRS

Gaining tax-exempt status is a completely different process from getting incorporated. What are the requirements to gain you this privilege? It is important to remember what I am outlining is only an overview of how to achieve tax-exempt status from the IRS. I am not in a position to provide step-by-step, formal, legal instructions.

To begin with, your organization must be a corporation operated and organized exclusively for religious, charitable, or educational purposes. The IRS further states that the net earnings of the corporation cannot benefit any individual. That does not mean you cannot get paid for working for your organization, but it does mean the agency you have helped create is now becoming publicly accountable, and the ministry bank account is not your private piggy bank.

As someone in the people-helping business, you definitely qualify for the intent aspect of the 501(c) (3) tax exemption. I suggest you check with someone knowledgeable every step of the way to make sure you are headed in the right direction. You could also call any of the IRS's toll-free numbers to obtain IRS Form 1023, the Application for Recognition of Tax Exemption.

Now a bit more on your salary situation. The IRS says your organization can pay you and your staff a salary as long as it is "reasonable." What is reasonable? What is reasonable to you and what is reasonable to the IRS might not be the same thing. Let me try and explain. If your organization is grossing an annual income of, say, $250,000 and your personal salary is set at $225,000, there is a strong possibility the IRS will define that as "unreasonable" should it be brought to their attention. If your organization has gross receipts of, say, $5,000,000 and your salary is set at $225,000, the IRS might well determine that as perfectly reasonable.

Why is the IRS is interested in your salary? It is because they consider tax exemption a tremendous privilege. It means you are not paying taxes on the monies coming into your organization, and you are also granted the ability to issue tax-deductible receipts to your donors. Having the advantage of tax exemption means playing by the IRS rules and going along with all the requisite paperwork.

Get appropriate advice from a certified public accountant (CPA) or tax attorney so the tax-exempt status is not risked. To the IRS, ignorance is absolutely no excuse for violating the law, and when it comes to facing the IRS in court, they usually win. They have a lot more money and resources to fight a dispute than we do. Be watchful, prudent, and cautious, and never hide information that will need to be disclosed later. If you do, it will likely be done at your own cost and to the possible detriment of the ministry.

I feel very strongly that anyone interested in starting a ministry should be fully educated about as many of the issues as possible involved with the realization of one's vision. One of the reasons for writing this book is to make sure God-given visions not only come to fruition but have lasting impact. Many well-intentioned people start ministries, but as good as the cause may be, they will not succeed if they are ignorant of how to incorporate as a not-for-profit organization and get tax-exempt status.

Once the application forms and all the appropriate paperwork, not forgetting the filing fee, are sent to the IRS, pray and leave it in the Lord's hands. During this time, your ministry can be in operation. You just do not have official tax-exempt status yet. Do not call the IRS to ask them what they are doing if you have not heard within a few weeks. I would give them at least several months before making any phone calls.

After patient waiting, the day comes when that all-important okay from the IRS finally arrives. The ministry is now a 501(c) (3) tax-exempt organization. Congratulations! But remember, there are now obligations to conform to all the rules imposed on nonprofit corporations.

Details Count

Payroll taxes are probably not the first thing on the mind when entering ministry. But if there are employees, they need to be paid, and we as ministry directors are responsible for payroll taxes. (Remember those deductions appearing on your paycheck for years before becoming the employer?)

Depending on the number of employees an organization has, payroll tax money can quickly accumulate into a large amount. Every time a payroll is issued, make sure to set aside the right amount of money to deposit to the IRS account at the bank. It might not seem like a lot at first, but if left unpaid, it quickly increases. Never borrow from this money if running into a cash flow problem.

I know how tight money can be for nonprofits, especially during the summer slump months. But the payroll taxes set aside for the IRS do not belong to you. It is employee money that has to be deposited into their account with the IRS. The IRS is never happy when people do not pay or are late in paying their taxes. IRS agents take an especially dim view if you steal (because the IRS regards it as stealing) the payroll tax deposits. The way to be safe is never to issue a payroll without the accompanying deposit to the IRS.

Not playing by the IRS rules is just not worth it. Always remember, payroll taxes belong to someone else, not you or the ministry, and if the IRS hears about questionable handling of payroll tax deposits, agents will be at your door. If the situation escalates, you could ultimately have your organizational funds levied, which means the IRS could go to the organization's bank accounts and order your bank to give them all the money they say you owe them.

In addition, if your shelter owns land and buildings, the IRS could put a lien on them. In a worst-case scenario, they could also come down and seize shelter vehicles, furniture, and anything else that can be sold to pay your debts to the IRS. In extraordinary cases, the IRS could also come after the personal assets of your board and financial manager. The resulting publicity would probably close you down, because there would be an immediate crisis of confidence among donors.

If I have not scared you so far, I do hope I have communicated what a serious matter it is to be a steward of public funds. Some ministries do not take any federal, state, county, or city funds, but in one sense, they are still guardians of public funds: they are being entrusted with donations by a concerned public to do a certain job. That is both a privilege and a responsibility, and it opens us to more scrutiny than someone working for a secular corporation. Taking public funds for the work of ministry means we are ambassadors of the body of Christ, and whatever we do reflects positively or negatively on the church and ultimately on God himself.

Probably the most important advice I can offer is this: do not try writing your own articles of incorporation and bylaws. Attorneys are expensive, that is true, but if you have to hire one to write all the necessary documents and get them done in a professional manner and the way you want, then do so. A few more dollars spent now could save you a lot more money and a whole lot of hassles later.

Do the payroll taxes and all the deductions correctly. If you cannot afford or do not now need a full-time business manager, think about having the payroll done by contracting with outside professionals. You will be glad you did. There are a multitude of regulations (and they are increasing every year) that relate to payroll, employer responsibilities, and so on, and it takes time to keep up with the changes in employer responsibilities.

This merely scratches the surface on the nuts and bolts of ministry. I have only managed to deal with generalities. For specific advice on your situation, contact the IRS, a CPA, or tax attorney. Deal with emerging problems quickly and professionally, and do not wait until there is a full-scale public relations disaster. Damage control after the event is more costly and time consuming than damage prevention. If you do not follow the steps outlined, you will have a lot of explaining to do later — probably before the public.

Working with Officials

Zoning! The very word strikes fear into the hearts of shelter directors, drug rehabilitation program operators, Christian schools, and even pastors. Let me share my experience with this pernicious thing called zoning.

Joy Junction is neighbor to the city of Albuquerque's wastewater treatment plant. Sometime ago, while on the phone to that facility's director, we both agreed that while our two organizations perform vital services, no one wants us as their next-door neighbor. Most people agree on the need for shelters, but it seems many feel somebody on the other side of town can take care of it.

Some years ago, I attended a city council meeting, where members dealt with another local mission's very legitimate attempt to expand its facilities. Neighbors of the Albuquerque Rescue Mission were upset and petitioned the council to deny the mission's request. Residents said their area of town was overloaded with services for the homeless and that additional space for this purpose would result in more homeless people being drawn to the downtown area.

There was as much discussion of the overcrowded homeless shelter situation downtown as there was on the addition of another building, which, it was feared, might serve to increase the existing homeless population. The individuals in this particular downtown neighborhood felt slighted by what they saw as a city unsympathetic to their problems.

The mission's contention was that rather than drawing more people to the downtown area, additional space would just enable them to service the existing homeless population more effectively. The mission's request was denied. Reporter Lesley Casias of the *Albuquerque Tribune* wrote the following article in 1992:

> The executive director of the Albuquerque Rescue Mission says he is disappointed by the City Council's refusal to approve the shelter's plan to expand, but he has not given up.
>
> "There are no dead ends with God," Mark Fairchild said Tuesday in response to Monday night's 7–1 decision that supported neighborhood protest to the expansion.
>
> The mission, 509 Second St. S.W. in the Barelas neighborhood, had requested an expansion that would increase the number of beds from 32 to 62.
>
> Currently, the mission's 32 beds are completely filled all year. The mission also often shelters between 15 and 30 people in sleeping bags on its dining room floor.
>
> Neighbors feared the shelter's expansion would decrease their property values and threaten their personal safety.
>
> Fairchild said in the five years he has worked at the mission, there has not been a complaint lodged by neighbors about the shelter's users.
>
> But Councilor Steve Gallegos, who voted against the expansion, said since his nine years as a representative for the area he has received many complaints about public drunkenness, drug abuse and indecent exposure.

The *Tribune* added that Gallegos said the complaints were not about all the homeless people, just a small percentage who ruin things for everyone.

Emotions, not reason, usually dominate discussions on the homeless, and it is very hard to strike a balance. Sadly, most of those who think they know the most about how to deal with the homeless population actually know the least. However, these same individuals may be influential in the community. As much as representatives from the Albuquerque Rescue Mission tried to explain calmly and rationally that additional assistance for the homeless would help and not hurt the neighborhood, it was all to no avail. All that can be done has been done at this point. What is left is to realize success or failure ultimately rests in the hand of God. If the Lord wants a new mission or an expansion of an existing facility, he will engineer the circumstances to achieve it.

Joy Junction has been exceptionally blessed with its zoning. The shelter is classified A-1, which is an agricultural zoning, with a special use permit for the life of the property. The special use designation is for educational, rehabilitative, and religious use. While we could not ask for better zoning, that original special use permit was not obtained easily. The alcohol and drug ministry using the property before us had to pray and fight for that zoning exemption way back in the early 1970s.

Our ministry has benefited from and continues to gain from someone else's fight to secure this zoning. How, then, is property that is correctly zoned, or has a chance of becoming so, to be found? All I can suggest is to pray and look diligently. When I was in Santa Fe, the situation was not quite as favorable as when I moved to Albuquerque. We occupied a storefront building in a residential area. The shelter was primarily for single men, who were sometimes not quite as compliant as they should have been.

I made a special effort to understand the concerns of neighbors who had been in the area for many years and saw a homeless shelter as something to be feared. My philosophy then was the same as it is now. We are not in a neighborhood to minister to the homeless and cause our neighbors misery. Rather, we are there to be a blessing to everyone. Look at it this way: if we take care of the homeless and win them to Christ, but at the same time make the lives of our neighbors miserable, what have we gained?

Keep a Pleasant Attitude

Everyone having anything to do with shelters must be willing to sympathize with neighbors' fears and concerns. That does not mean letting the neighbors automatically ride roughshod over you or giving in to their every demand. It just means making every possible effort to be a caring, respectful, and responsible neighbor. And remember that in many instances the neighbors were there before the shelter ministry.

Even if you have been behaving responsibly, that is not an automatic guarantee problems will go away or neighbors will think the idea for a shelter is just great. They still might not like the idea of a homeless shelter in their area. If you have a continuing problem in this regard, and all efforts seem to fail, do not get angry or discouraged and give up. Discussing situations agreeably over a cup of coffee tends to solve a lot more problems than adopting an unpleasant attitude and threatening to go to the press. Doing God's work does not warrant special treatment for you; it does, however, require you to treat others as Jesus would treat them. You are neither above the law (God's or man's) nor people's feelings.

It will make a big difference if the neighborhood, city zoning board, and the board of appeals see that you are reasonable and willing to work with them. You still may not get exactly what you want, but at the very least, you might arrange some sort of compromise.

Sometimes one comes to a place where there is absolutely nothing that can be done except to pray and wait. While that may seem like a troubling position to be in, it is often the best. Take the example of the Albuquerque Rescue Mission. I was at the meeting when council members denied permission for it to expand. The mission director tried his best to make the appropriate arguments in favor of expansion. But it was a fruitless cause. He told the council members that while they were seeking formal permission to expand from thirty-two beds to sixty-two, the increase was not as bad as it sounded. On many occasions, the mission official said, the shelter was already accommodating about thirty people beyond their bed capacity just to keep them out of the cold. But the additional people were on the floor, in sleeping bags.

The neighbors complained that the additional space would bring more homeless people to a downtown area already overburdened with social services. A number of community members testified they already had enough problems with homeless people urinating in public, hassling patrons, panhandling, and so on.

The mission's contention was that an expanded facility would not add to the downtown problem. Rather, it would help ease the present conditions. One exchange at the council debate went something like this:

> Mission: There is a problem with people urinating around your business, right?
>
> Neighbor: Yes, and a bigger shelter would just make it worse!
>
> Mission: Why? If these individuals had adequate bathrooms to take care of their personal needs, they might not have to urinate close to your business.

A reasonable argument, wouldn't you say? But it was not enough to convince some people, who had already made up their minds that more adequate shelter for the homeless would automatically bring more homeless people to the area.

Thank God for the Outcome—Either Way

In a situation such as the one with the Albuquerque Rescue Mission, all that could have been done was exactly what was done by the director. After that, all that is left is to thank the Lord for the outcome, whatever it is, and believe there are no dead ends with God. Running up against a brick wall in the search for a building does not mean it ends there. Keep praying and looking. If God is in the project, he will work something out. And if not, there is no need to be involved with it in any event. Sooner or later, in God's time, he will guide you to the right facility to meet your needs.

There are no magic answers to finding a building that is right for what you need. The only advice I have that will work well in every situation is pray, look, and keep trusting God.

Once You Have a Building

Let us assume that after months of prayer and searching you do find a building that fits the bill. It does not look like you are going to have any (or at least not too many) problems with the neighbors, so now it is time to start cleaning the new building and getting it ready.

While you are cleaning, do not be disappointed if not everyone thinks your vision is wonderful. People prefer to board a moving ship. I do not mean to be cynical here, but people might not support you until you become a winner, and when you experience problems, they may well desert you if the ship seems to be going down. That is a human characteristic and has nothing really to do with you as a person. Therefore, in all your dealings, you need to depend completely on the Lord.

But back to the cleanup phase. You find a building, the location and zoning of which appear to be just what the doctor ordered. You are excited. I know this because I have been there, and it is an exciting time. But there is a major problem: the building is a mess. At its best, it might be described as a "handyman's special" or a "facility with great potential." At its worst, well ... It does not worry you, because you can see it with the eye of faith. You can envision children running around a freshly painted nursery and families staying safely together with a roof over their heads and warm food on the table. You can visualize the counselor's office where, with the help of the Lord, broken families are being restored.

You take your best friend or your spouse to see what great potential the building has and what wonderful things the Lord is doing. But, for some strange reason, they look at you askance. Their only response is "Huh? Is

81

this all there is?" That kind of reaction is to be expected, at least to some extent. Do not get angry. After all, God gave you the vision, not anyone else. How does that all relate to cleanup? Well, you may end up doing the initial cleanup by yourself.

"Me do all the cleanup by myself?" Yes, you! If I could clean up the buildings out here before Joy Junction opened, and I am the most impractical person you could ever hope to set eyes on, there is hope for you. If you can corral any family members, friends from church, or others into helping you clean up or renovate, all the better!

Your life might not be so complicated if building cleanup and renovation was all you had to do. Remember, however, that building cleanup is only one of myriad tasks you will face.

Faith and Reality

Must you listen to the Doubting Thomases? You might hear something like, "I'm glad this building looks like it's going to be okay, but have you thought of all the expense involved? Where's all the money going to come from?" And it is at this point that you really have to be careful. While you do not necessarily have to listen to the Doubting Thomases, you do need to temper faith with a healthy blend of commonsense reality. In other words, do not be discouraged by those who say you will never accomplish your goal.

Still, do not run after that vision without using discretion. Avoid running up huge bills you are not and will not be able to pay. Remember that it is of no benefit for you to take care of the homeless at the expense of local merchants who are trying very hard to make an honest living. The idea is not to force local merchants into homelessness because the local homeless shelter is not paying its bills!

Be a person of your word, and pay your bills on time. If you run into some kind of emergency (an actual one, not a manufactured one), and it looks like you will be late in paying for something, let creditors know. Do not hide from them and say the check is in the mail, unless it is.

You also have to keep an eye on fund-raising, and right in the middle of one thing or another, you might have to dash off to speak to a group about the pressing financial need you face if your vision is ever to become a reality. This is why I emphasize the importance of being sure God has called you to this task. There are so many potential pitfalls and so many variables along the way, it is essential to know you are in God's will.

Being Christ-Like to Regulatory Agencies

You must maintain a good attitude when dealing with the various city and county departments that regulate your shelter. Even if you decide not to accept a dime of government money, you will still be regulated by various local government departments. Before you go any further, make up your mind that you will get along with the individuals who work for the government agencies. The way I look at it, these people have their jobs to do, just like I have mine, and both jobs will be so much easier if we can get along.

Most of these agencies will work with you if you act in a polite and respectful manner, showing you are willing to fulfill the requirements of the law. For example, the increased need for our services over the last few years has placed a tremendous strain on our old buildings. We have not always been able to keep pace with our building maintenance. In late 2005, I received a letter from the Bernalillo County Office of Environmental Health. It read, in part, "Bernalillo County Office of Environmental Health and the Bernalillo County Building Official have found insufficient plumbing fixtures (toilets, sinks and showers) to serve the rated occupancy load of the multi-purpose building of Joy Junction."

Right from the start, Bernalillo County officials understood what a huge undertaking this was and indicated their willingness to work with us as long as we demonstrated some progress was being made toward the goal.

Admittedly, the county told us we did not have to comply with the requirement for more bathrooms. But here was the catch. If we didn't, we would have to reduce the occupancy in our main building by about fifty people. Since the people we serve are like family, that was unthinkable, and so we immediately hired an architect to begin the process. But that, of course, involved the expenditure of a large amount of money the shelter did not have—as much as $450,000.

That really placed us in a financial squeeze, because this would be an unplanned, unbudgeted expenditure. Then the late Albuquerque philanthropist and Joy Junction friend Blake Chanslor stepped in with an initial surprise gift of $100,000. When funding continued to lag, Blake later gave an additional substantial gift that enabled us to complete the project. "I wanted to help," he told me, "as the work that Joy Junction does is indispensable to our community. I challenge others who are able to do the same."

Another example occurred some time before this. I returned from lunch one day, and the shelter receptionist smiled and said, "Guess who called?"

"No telling," I answered.

"The fire department," she said.

The receptionist and the majority of the shelter staff were surprised about the call, but they should not have been. The previous week I instructed all the staff to do fire safety checks.

"Why?" they had asked me.

"I don't know," I said. "I just have the feeling that something is going to happen, and we need to make especially sure that everything is okay."

I returned the fire inspector's call, and he said he had received a complaint about the shelter and would be down shortly. For emotional support and backup, I also called our then board president, who came down to wait with me for the inspector's visit.

As soon as the inspector arrived, we quickly made it clear to him we were going to cooperate with all of his recommendations. "Inspector," I said, "we've always cooperated with you. We always will." We did not claim any special church or religious privileges; we were just very polite and respectful.

Just like the health department officials, this inspector made it clear he was willing to work with us as long as we agreed to conform to the fire code and obey his instructions in the appropriate amount of time.

That visit cost us about $25,000. Even if what the county fire or health inspector says seems irrational, you are legally bound to obey their codes. Besides, in the end, your facility will be considerably safer. Now, in both of the cases I mentioned, we could have conceivably not cooperated with the county and created all sorts of havoc. If we had acted like that, everyone's life would have been miserable. And what would have been the point? We did not act that way, and we continue to have a very good relationship with all the officials in Bernalillo County.

Just because we are a Christian ministry does not mean we are above the law. With that in mind, be cooperative and do not try to claim any special privileges because you are doing God's work. Your ministry's facilities still need to be safe, and neither the fire nor health department officials are there to make your life difficult. These guidelines apply when dealing with every government agency, and they should govern your Christ-like interactions with everyone.

Being Christ-Like to Everyone

A well known Christian broadcaster has often encouraged his listeners to call legislators on matters relating to family values. I think it is appalling he has to remind Christians to be courteous and respectful when they call. We should not have to be reminded of those basic rules of civility that are valid even for those who are not Christians. Courtesy and respect never hurt anyone, and they pay tremendous dividends.

I hope you are encouraged about working with officials. What a tremendous privilege it is to serve God in a full-time capacity. Some people have romantic notions about the work of ministry, but while it is definitely rewarding, it is the hardest work there is. Go forward in faith, seek wise counsel, and obey God!

Developing Financial Support

It is time to consider the money needed to operate your ministry on an ongoing basis. Yes, I know God supplies, and I would be the first to tell you that. But there is also nothing wrong with a good mailing list. While there is always the possibility God can and does supernaturally supply money, in my experience, he usually does it through donors. All you have to do is your part. And part of that is to prepare letters to send to potential donors, so the Lord can put it into their hearts to give to your ministry. Perhaps you are thinking, *But I can't do that.* Well, think again. As the founder or potential founder of a parachurch ministry, you are probably going to have to spend a lot more time and money raising money than you might initially have thought.

Seeking Open Doors

When I began Joy Junction in 1986, I took every opportunity to speak to any civic group, church—really, anyone—who would allow me the opportunity to tell them our story. That was a good way to start getting names and addresses of people interested in donating to the shelter. Nearly a quarter of a century later, I have returned to that initial practice. Along with my assistant, we now spend as much time at community functions as we can. That contact is helping us build upon the strong media presence the Lord has helped us establish over the years. We have also joined local chambers of commerce to make more contacts and establish even stronger community ties.

The Meaning of Gifts

Whenever anyone brings a donation of food, furniture, clothing, or absolutely anything to the shelter, we give them a receipt with duplicate copies for both the donor's records and ours. That also means we can add the person's name to our mailing list.

People love to give clothing to shelters. You will probably be given so much clothing you will not know what to do with all of it. But before you start turning away clothing, and quite possibly offending some of your donors, think about this scenario:

You are in a financial bind. It has been a terrible week for donations, and the payroll, which at this time might include you as the only employee, is a couple of weeks late. You have been praying, "Lord, please send some money in …" Money is the only thing on your mind. You are still trying to believe God, but you are working long hours and not seeing your family as much as you would like. Not only is there no money for extras, there is no money for essentials, either. On top of that, you have perhaps overheard a few kindhearted but shallow-pocketed Christian friends say under their breath that if you had real faith, you would not be going through your current financial crisis.

The telephone rings. You answer, hoping that this could be *the* phone call. But instead of it being a donor asking if you can use a large cash donation, it is a call from a donor saying she has a three-quarter-ton pickup full of clothing. Will you be there this morning to receive it?

What do you do? Well, if you are a shortsighted mission executive, you will turn down the clothing. If you do and that person ever comes into some money, your ministry will probably not see it.

Hopefully, you will soon be in a position where you can hire some office staff. Make certain your reception staff treats every person as though they are a donor or potential donor. Of course, they need to treat everyone with respect and courtesy, especially the guests and residents. However, they need to be mindful of the potentiality of every person calling or coming into the office. Those individuals may be future donors, volunteers, or even employees.

I took a long way around to say this: I suspect your storage room will be filled to the ceiling within two weeks of your opening the shelter doors and allowing the first homeless family to sleep there. I know that the last thing you want now in the middle of hard financial times is to smile sweetly at a donor who merely wants a tax receipt for some clothes, which in all probability, he or she should take to the garbage dump. But you cannot afford to be ungracious.

With that in mind, you need to grin and bear it. Cheerfully help unload all those clothes, and make sure you get the donor's name and address. Before you write the next letter asking for contributions of money for the shelter, make sure that donor is on the mailing list.

I cannot emphasize strongly enough the need to use every available opportunity to get names and addresses. Yes, you are a faith ministry, and you are going to trust God for all of your needs. But many faith ministries live or die by their mailing list, and I believe God uses mailing lists as one of the tools by which he can supply our needs. Keep the list current, because the typical attrition rate for a mailing list is 20 percent each year. That means it will only take five years to lose an entire donor base.

This is not pie-in-the-sky theory from someone who does not know what he is talking about. You are learning the nuts-and-bolts reality of what it takes to get a ministry on its feet, stay on its feet, and be a good reflection of the name of Jesus Christ in your community.

Let's recap the ways to start and build a mailing list. Before you take any names, you have to sell yourself and what you stand for (you as a person; your principles) before you can sell what you are doing. Take every opportunity you can to speak anywhere, and get the names of everyone in your audience for your mailing list. When people ask you what you need, do not be afraid to tell them that you are looking for places to share your message. These speaking engagements can be far-reaching in their ability to help you in your networking efforts.

An additional tip: when you speak and when you write, share the needs of your clients, not the budgetary needs of the agency. As a rule, no one wants to hear about the needs of the agency that the budget should cover.

On the Public Relations Trail

I suggest you carry a notebook with you and get a supply of inexpensive business cards. Organize some special events that cost you nothing or next to nothing. Here is an example of something we did some years ago. Joy Junction was given over three thousand ears of corn. While thinking about what to do with them, I had an idea. It was getting close to Labor Day, and while we had never done anything special on Labor Day before, there was no reason why we should not start. So, we organized a corn-eating contest, which we opened to the general public as well as the shelter guests. Some local churches got involved, and some area Christian media provided free advertising for the event.

As an incentive for people to come, I called a local hotel chain and asked them if they would like to provide us with a free room and breakfast in exchange for being mentioned on all the advertising connected with the event. I also contacted Pepsi and asked for free sodas in exchange for advertising. I faxed press releases to all the local media, which really paid off. The four local television stations covered the event, and we were featured briefly on the evening newscast. One of the local newspapers ran a small article, and a local talk radio station called me for an interview.

The event was a great success. Some people from whom we had not heard for a long time brought donations to the shelter. (Yes, earlier we had taken down their names.) We were also the only shelter in town with any special event on Labor Day. The television crews told me that they routinely look for news to cover on Monday, especially a holiday Monday.

I have said that many faith ministries live or die by their mailing list, and that is true. Unfortunately, thanks to the dubious activity of some televangelists and others, with their hard-pitched, personalized, "send-me-all-you-can and God-will-bless-you" letters, mail solicitation has gotten a bad reputation in some circles. But, if you make up your mind in advance that you are going to adhere to a high moral standard, direct mail (letters soliciting contributions and mailed directly to individuals) is a highly valuable and legitimate tool to help you fund the ministry God has given you.

Mailing and Marketing

There is a balance to be struck in direct mail. Before you can mail, you need to have people to mail to, and that is why I have spent all this time talking about ways to capture names for your mailing list.

Now you can put the list to good use. You have been gathering names, and now you have to write a letter. You have called some marketing companies, and they asked you the size of the mailing list. When you told them it was five hundred, seven hundred fifty, or maybe even fifteen hundred, they just laughed at you. You still asked them the fees for their services, but when you found out, you nearly fell off your chair. You conclude the obvious: marketing companies are very expensive.

So, you are back to your own resources, staring at a blank computer screen with no idea what to say. Did you honestly expect it would be like this when you started in ministry? You had a wonderful idea, and you are doing God's work, but do not forget this ministry still needs to be administered just like a business.

You also need to get a bulk mailing permit as soon as you possibly can. There are various types of bulk mail permits, but the cheapest is for a 501(c)(3) nonprofit organization. At the time of this writing, the first-class mail rate is forty-four cents. The cost for mailing a single piece of bulk-rate mail is about one-third of that, so you can see the savings. I have discovered that the delivery time for bulk rate is usually very good. In fact, most of the in-town bulk-rate letters I mail get to their destination the next day.

Telling Your Guests' Stories to Your Donors

Take a questionnaire similar to the one I use (which I will mention in a later chapter) and hand it out to guests staying at your shelter or the clients of your particular ministry. As you have no doubt found by now, they are unique individuals with a variety of stories.

Tell your clients what you want the information for and obtain a signed release. Let them know you will be happy to change their names to protect their privacy. If you do that, when you write the fund-raising letter, be sure to tell your donors that everything is exactly as told, with the exception of the individual's name, which was changed for confidentiality.

Once you have the basic information, put it in a form your donors are able to read quickly. You have to grab someone's attention and make the individual want to go on reading. You also have to show how your shelter (ministry) played a big part in seeing that guest's needs met. Don't forget to make it clear you could not help people without your donor's help. It is a cooperative effort.

Remember that people donate for a variety of reasons. Some give out of a feeling of guilt, while others contribute from what they believe is a response to a command from God to take care of the needy. Donors give out of genuine concern for the needy, hungry, hurting, and underprivileged. But one thing all have in common is they want to feel their gift (of whatever size) counts and that they are playing a vital role in meeting the needs of your shelter or other faith-based ministry. Always remember the importance of your donors. You would not be able to continue with any sort of people-oriented work without their generosity. They are your lifeblood.

Anyway, back to the blank computer screen. You feel bad about asking for money, but somehow you must write a two-page letter (or thereabouts) that is going to make sense and touch people's hearts. What to do next?

Some Fundamentals of Writing Donor Appeals

The information you gathered from client questionnaires now comes into play. Take the most dramatic statement. Let us say it goes something like this: "I had nowhere to stay. I could not stay with my relatives, parents, or friends. There was absolutely nowhere for me to go. Then I found [the name of your agency]. They took me in; they gave me a safe place to stay. The people at that agency are really neat people."

Use that as your opening one or two paragraphs and then add words like these: "While it's true that our agency helped [insert the person's name] get back on his feet again, we just couldn't have done it without your gift. You made the difference."

I hope this kind of letter writing is a skill you will grow into. Even if you are not the best writer in the world, it is still probably going to be something you will have to do yourself for a while. Just remember that whatever you do, be scrupulously honest. Relate the story, tell the need, state clearly what your agency is doing to help, and then ask for money to help meet the need. Do not make any false "faith promises" in the letter, such as, "If you give to this ministry, God will bless you and heal you, and your gift will be returned to you a hundred times over." Do not be discouraged if you feel you cannot write donor appeal letters. I have been doing it for many years now, and I still have a long way to go.

Personalized letters, such as those that begin "Dear Jeremy," are not bad. But you are probably going to need some basic computer programming instruction if you want to do that. Otherwise, you will need to find a marketing company you can afford.

If you are fortunate enough to be able to use personalized letters, stay away from direct messages from God. I have had letters from evangelists, claiming God told them to write to me. I am told their justification is that I am on their mailing list. God told them to write to their mailing list, and so, in that sense, God told them to write to me. This is deceitful. I believe tactics like that are grossly deceptive and ungodly.

Action and Prayer Go Together

Do not skimp on your appeal letters. Make them look and sound professional, courteous, conscientious, and businesslike. Professionalism will pay back dividends many times greater than the amount of money and energy expended on making them so. You do not have to produce full-color, glossy appeal letters. If you attempt to do that, you could be accused of wasting your donor's money. But on the other hand, if you produce something that looks sloppy or is of poor print quality and does not follow any of the rules used in marketing and fund-raising appeals, you will probably not experience much success. Your potential donors will not want to support something that looks like an amateur production, and neither would you. Balance is the key word.

In talking about developing financial support, I do not want to suggest even for a second to neglect prayer. But my point here is that no one should ever think they can pray all their resources in. That is not the way to ensure the success of your ministry. The way to do that is to work long hours, write good letters, and call everyone you can think of. Do whatever it takes and then pray and pray again. Once you have done everything in your power (with God's wisdom) to make the ministry work, remember that the final result is in God's hands.

I have given some basic information about direct mailing and marketing to help keep you out of trouble. There is also another thing that is very important to remember. If you make false statements and mail them as a letter through the U.S. Postal Service, you could be convicted of mail fraud. Sometimes it is easy to get carried away in the heat of the moment and embellish or invent things said in conversation. But if we do this in writing and send it through the U.S. Postal Service, it is another matter. A few years ago, in my capacity as a freelance writer, a magazine asked me to write an investigative piece on a ministry that had allegedly been making false claims and promises in its mailings. As a result of the mailings, investigations were launched by a variety of federal agencies. Believe me, that kind of attention is not something you want for your ministry.

Fund-Raising Insights

There are definite standards in fund-raising, even though some people have no standards at all when it comes to raising money, while others believe that any form of fund-raising is sinful. This second group is the one you will more often encounter. As the director of a new ministry, or one about to launch soon, you will run across pastors and people in the pews who believe that it is wrong to ask for money. You need to know how to deal with this mistaken concept.

I would not recommend trying to convince these individuals that your request for funds is legitimate. You won't get very far, and there are enough churches willing to get behind and support a ministry like yours. You would do well to spend your time seeking them.

When you have found one, ask the pastor if you could speak to the congregation about the vision you have for ministry. Let them know that although the church does not have the facility or people-power to minister to the homeless, they can do exactly that by financially supporting what you are doing or preparing to do.

Invite those interested to form a group to meet with you personally or to view the site. You can give them a tour of the property while discussing your plans. Once they get hold of your vision, they will get excited and want to join you in establishing your ministry by providing the necessary financial support.

Although most people in the church would probably not work in a homeless ministry setting, they will feel good about themselves if they can help you and your staff do so. They want to get behind something they can feel good about and share with their friends. Speaking to churches is a form of networking you will not be able to do without.

There have been numerous examples in recent years of people who have abused the privilege of asking for financial support. I believe they have taken advantage of their donors' trust. When people intend to deceive by making untrue statements, especially if these people are involved in some form of ministry, it makes life harder for everyone. Make sure you are trustworthy and honest when handling funds and fund-raising. Maintain financial records that could be made public, because that could occur in the future.

How Do You Ask?

You have probably gathered by now that I have no problems at all asking for donations. The question is *how* to ask. The following is a reprint of a dated but still excellent article by Russ Reid, the former chairman of a large marketing company. It was printed in *Rescue Magazine*, published by the then International Union of Gospel Missions, and now known as the Association of Gospel Rescue Missions. It is used with permission.

What does it mean to have a faith ministry? Does it mean that your role is simply to pray and let God provide?

Or, do you show that faith by actively seeking resources to fund the vision God has given you?

This is a critical issue in raising funds for ministry, but it is not new. Two of the most important leaders in Christian ministry—D.L. Moody and George Mueller—were good friends on opposite sides of the debate.

Moody's attitude was that the Lord owned the cattle on a thousand hills, and all resources belonged to Him. He saw it as his challenge and opportunity to ask giants of industry to share their resources in Kingdom building. He chided his friend Mueller, however, for always explaining to potential supporters that he would not ask them for money, since God would supply all of his needs.

Moody insisted, "By telling them you're not asking for money, you're asking for money." And of course, he was right.

The interesting thing is that Mueller's orphanage, although a very important ministry in its day has since closed its doors. On the other hand, D.L. Moody began a ministry that has outlived him by over 100 years. Literally, millions of people around the world hear the Gospel today because of the financial foundation that he built to launch and sustain his ministries.

It seems to me that Scripture is very clear that the type of active fund-raising demonstrated by Dwight L. Moody has been a part of the work of God's people from Old Testament times through the development of the Christian church in the first century.

In Exodus 25, for example, God tells Moses to launch a "Capital Campaign" to build the Tabernacle. Moses is instructed to "Speak unto the children of Israel, that they bring Me an offering."

When it was time for the wall in Jerusalem to be rebuilt, Nehemiah solicited a major gift from the king of Babylon. "And the king granted me," the prophet wrote, "according to the good hand of my God."

Jesus' own ministry was financially supported by many disciples who gave financial contributions "out of their means." (Luke 8:3)

But it is the apostle Paul who outlines biblical fund-raising principles most clearly. Burning with enthusiasm to build new churches, he initiates a New Testament pledge plan: "Each one of you should set aside a sum of money in keeping with his income." (1 Corinthians 16:2)

Paul also writes two chapters, 2 Corinthians 8 and 9, which are filled with tips for fund-raisers. He not only uses all his persuasive powers to make the new church members enthusiastic givers, but he heaps praise and recognition on them for their previous generosity.

Paul also understands the importance of follow-up. "I thought it necessary," he explains to the Corinthians, "to urge the brothers to visit you in advance and finish the arrangements for the generous gift you promised." (2 Corinthians. 9:5)

The Bible is certainly not silent on the fact that all we have comes from God, and that our task is to challenge people with the opportunity to have significance in their lives by giving their resources to God.

So the real question is the most effective way to get that message out.

In today's world, technology has provided exciting new opportunities to find the thousands of people who may want to be a part of your ministry. Using new computer techniques, however, worries those who see technology as "worldly."

In fact, any kind of technology can raise this kind of anxiety. Some of you are old enough to remember when evangelists repudiated and denounced radio as an instrument of the devil, only to have them change their mind and see its potential to be a vehicle to tell the world of the saving love of Jesus.

Not many of us would discredit or disallow the work of a CPA to do an audit on our books, or an attorney to help us sort out the ramifications of a property purchase. Or in more recent times, to accept the help of a computer in making information available to us.

Should we be any less hesitant to utilize space advertising, direct mail, television, planned giving and major gift campaigns to provide the resources to fund all that God has called us to do? I think not.

Does this mean that trusting God is unnecessary? Of course not. Rich or poor, we have to trust God for every breath we take. But there are some clear distinctions between which responsibilities are God's and which belong to us.

I am often reminded of that when people ask me "Isn't it a miracle that thousands of people always come to Billy Graham's crusades?"

I have to say "No. That is not a miracle. Billy Graham's organization uses every resource available to ensure there will be a crowd."

The miracle happens at the invitation, when thousands walk the aisle to profess Christ as Lord.

In the same way, when money is raised for your mission, it takes hard work and solid know-how in the field of fundraising.

That is not the miracle. But after you have in faith spent the money to reach out to people in need, God begins to transform their lives. That is the miracle!

I believe that rescue mission work deserves the kind of fund-raising base that will allow each of you to do more of what God is calling you to do.

Isn't it time we set aside forever the idea that being a faith ministry requires us to ignore resources which can help us reach more people more effectively?

I totally endorse what Russ Reid writes. His organization has helped raise millions of dollars for missions around the United States.

Speaking from a longtime shelter operator's vantage point, there is something about running a faith-based homeless shelter that helps keep your feet on the ground. Maybe it is because we, as shelter operators, have to deal with such "earthly" or "worldly" needs as well as spiritual requirements. Each week, I have the opportunity to speak for a few minutes about Joy Junction on a local radio station. While I frequently talk about some of the wonderful ways in which the Lord is blessing the shelter, I also ask listeners for donations of various food and nonfood items we need, such as, toothbrushes, toilet paper, bleach, diapers, and other staples. While these are necessities for the shelter, they do not address spiritual things, which is the most fundamentally important aspect of need that exists.

To balance this out a little, while I am always asking for donations, I am reminded of something I heard someone say many years ago. The person said he usually has to tell Christians not to be so heavenly minded that they are no earthly good. He said that advice does not apply to shelter operators, however. This is because they have their feet on the ground to such an extent that he has to remind them God still works miracles. Keep this in mind as you ponder what has been said in this chapter. I do not want to give anyone the idea that God does not work miracles. He does.

But, just as God still heals supernaturally today, he also heals through medical science. Just so, God still provides supernaturally for homeless shelters and other parachurch ministries today. That is not in question. What I want to emphasize is that he also provides for homeless shelters by using mailing lists, marketing directors, and the latest in technology.

Should a Christian or secular company be used to help in raising funds? You and your board will need to seek the wisdom of the Lord on which one you choose and why. But let me ask a question. If you suddenly discovered you had almost certain terminal cancer, but there was a chance your life could be saved by new technological advances and some special form of new surgery, would you want to avail yourself of that opportunity? If you had the choice of two surgeons, one who was Christian but a second-rate surgeon and the other who was an atheist but a first-rate surgeon, what would you do? I hope that you would choose the more competent surgeon and pray for your operation and his salvation. Better yet, lead him to salvation so he can do the same for his patients.

When you go out to eat, do you ask for a Christian waiter? When you get your hair cut, do you ask for a Christian hairdresser? Probably not. As you consider which sort of marketing company to select for the fund-raising, do not forget to pray. Then consult your board. You do not need to ask your potential marketing company if they are Christians, but do request a list of their clients. Ask for permission to call them and get some sort of reference. Ask the company for references on in-town work as well as out-of-town jobs. You are entitled to this information, because you are considering the outlay of a large expense.

One year, Joy Junction undertook a large acquisition mailing. The job cost a considerable amount of money, plus a lot more in postage. (And the postage was the most economical form of bulk-rate mailing available.) A lot of money went into that mailing, but no ministry in my opinion can afford to ignore acquisition letters. If you do not do them, someone else will. Christian or not, they will end up gaining donors who, if they had been informed by an acquisition letter, very possibly would have been willing to help finance your vision.

Before you think that spending such a large amount of money is totally ridiculous, remember that Joy Junction gained thousands of dollars from that acquisition mailing and thousands of new donors. Think what the additional revenue from thousands of new donors could do for your ministry! Remember, it may take years to realize the ultimate potential of a mass mailing and the positive effects that will result over time.

As Russ Reid pointed out, there are tremendous skills involved in marketing. It is not just writing and mailing the letter. There is also the selection of the specialized areas of town in which to send it. This is called "target marketing." Effective marketing is adequately keeping track of the responses, as well as a large number of other variables that will determine the proper strategy for your ministry.

As complicated as fund-raising is, you might have to do your own marketing for a while. If there is no way you can afford a professional marketing company, consider finding one, explaining your plight to them, and asking them for some helpful insight and advice. Ask appropriately, and do not beg or use manipulative tactics. I would also be glad to help you.

Remember what the apostle Paul said: "And my God will meet all your needs according to his glorious riches in Christ Jesus" (Phil. 4:19).

Making Time for the Media

It is important to make time for both the print and electronic media. Yes, make yourself available to the media. I know some Christians feel the media represent a conspiracy against them. But with prayer and God's blessing, they can be a benefit to you. Here are some guidelines for communicating with the media.

Know what information to send to the media. There is a good chance that if it is something you would be interested in reading, it is probably news. Examples include additional services you are offering to your clients or a new location, building, or project. Other examples include the receipt of a large donation or a human interest story involving someone staying at your shelter. I have done extensive research on the topic of how the media portray the homeless in print and television. The results are available in my book, *Homeless Culture and the Media* (www.cambriapress.com).

I also recommend you do everything you can to help the media by providing them information about the shelter. If you send public service announcements, tell the station how many seconds your announcement runs. If you are sending a press release, keep it short and to the point. Make sure the thrust of what you want to say is communicated in the first sentence. Busy editors do not have the time to wade through a whole lot of information to get to what they need. Less is best!

Know when to send information and news items and when not to send them. In other words, try and get some sense of what is newsworthy and what is not. You might even consider enrolling in some basic journalism courses at your local university or community college to help you relate to the media. Do not forget to present all the information about your agency in a short and timely fashion. This will help get their respect and save you excessive typing and eyestrain.

Do not inflate stories to make you look better. Make sure everything you send the media is accurate; they do not want to publish or broadcast errors. If you have to use quotes, make sure you attribute properly by clearly indicating who said what. Neither the print nor the broadcast media want to spend time checking. The more time the media have to spend on your story or announcement, unless it is a really "hot" news item, the less chance there is of it being published or read. Always include a callback number. If the media are working under great pressure the day they deal with your story, the more time you can save them the better.

Indulge the media. I do not say that to sound facetious. I really mean it, and let me explain why. Some time ago, while covering then vice-presidential candidate Al Gore's visit to Albuquerque, I was very impressed with the way campaign organizers went out of their way to help the press. The media were provided with a complete text of Gore's speech as well as a complete schedule of his upcoming activities. Anything the press wanted, they appeared to get.

What a difference it makes to a busy reporter, struggling to make accurate notes of a complex speech, to have a complete copy of the text handed to him. He can then actually listen to, enjoy, and assimilate the speech, all the time knowing that he has a copy of the complete text at his fingertips. During that election, the Democrats took care of the press, and it paid off.

You may not like what I am going to tell you next. If you want to succeed in your relationship with the media and maintain a positive relationship with them, be available to them twenty-four hours a day, seven days a week. Give the media every telephone number you have. Always be polite, respectful, and appreciative when reporters call you. Never avoid them, and no matter what time they call, answer questions truthfully and briefly. Remember that reporters need quotes and information when they need it. Their schedule might not necessarily fit in with yours, so get whatever equipment you need to make sure you are always accessible.

Make sure your staff knows who is allowed to talk to the press. If you are the only one, inform them that they must call you if reporters show up unannounced.

Be scrupulously honest. Reporters are trained to uncover things you might want to keep hidden. If they ask you about a problem that exists, do not pretend it does not exist or that you do not know anything about it. Obviously, give your side of the story, but be honest and accept responsibility. Remember that if there is a problem, even if you are not necessarily at fault, the buck stops with you if you are the head of the organization, and you ultimately shoulder at least some of the accountability.

Dealing with the Media During a Crisis

In 1992, the *Albuquerque Journal* printed an excellent article by staff writer Paul Legau about how companies can deal with the media in a crisis:

> Whether Americans like to admit it or not, they are interested and titillated by the coverage of crises by the nation's media. That is why *60 Minutes* and *20/20* are popular television shows, according to a management-crisis expert. They satisfy the public's voyeuristic side, he said, except when the crisis is in your own business.
>
> "God gave us two ends," said Marvin "Swede" Johnson, "one to sit on and one to think with. Success in a crisis situation depends upon which end you use the most."
>
> Johnson is Coors Brewing Company's vice president for corporate affairs. Before joining the Golden, Colorado–based firm, Johnson served as the University of New Mexico's administrative vice-president for student affairs.
>
> With each organization, Johnson helped in handling potentially disastrous situations—the Coors mouse-in-a-can controversy, and Lobogate, UNM's basketball scandal.
>
> Although most national media coverage involves crises at larger companies, Johnson said New Mexico small businesses are just as susceptible to a crisis and the aftermath-media scrutiny.
>
> Johnson recently told an audience of business and community leaders "how to handle the media during a crisis" and how to avoid responding to the press "with throat-clearing, stammering gibberish."
>
> The media drive a crisis, Johnson said. "If they don't like you, they can prolong coverage of your disaster an interminable, excruciatingly long time. They make the difference in what kind of image is presented to the public."
>
> Johnson used the example of how United Airlines handled the cart-wheeling crash-landing of one of its aircraft at Sioux City,

Iowa, three years ago. The fiery crash killed 111 of the jet's 296 passengers.

However, the story was not about the mechanical defects that caused the plane's hydraulic system to fail, said Johnson, but rather the heroic flying ability of Al Haynes, the jetliner's captain.

The media reported the event as the story of a corporate hero, not a corporate mistake, he said.

"Much of this had to do with the way United's communications people handled the press immediately following the crash," Johnson said.

Every business faces a multitude of disaster possibilities, he said, including fires, accidents, market shifts, product failures and environmental problems.

Johnson said that Coors has an issues-management team that monitors potential crises, such as responding to a reporter who calls and says: "We'd like to know why one of your consumers in Florida found a mouse in a can of Coors beer."

Johnson said Coors was fully exonerated in the "mouse crisis of 1988." The person who put the mouse in the can went to jail.

However, the controversy surrounding the mouse "turned into a three-month media circus complete with law suits, declining sales and falling consumer confidence in our product," said Johnson.

In the mouse case, Coors had several short-term and long-term problems—determining how the rodent got into the can and turning around the lack of consumer confidence, he said.

Once the problem is identified, businesses should conduct their best case, he said. No matter how terrible the event, a company still has its own story to tell the media.

Johnson said a crisis-management plan should contain favorable, pertinent facts about the business to guarantee a quick response to media questions. He used a hypothetical example—prior to the company's mishap, it had not lost one hour of work in the last five years.

"I know most small-business people barely have time to manage employees, seek new customers and keep the old ones happy," said Johnson, "let alone put together a crisis plan that lists important facts about the organization."

If a small business can't compile information ahead of time, he said, the owner must spend a few minutes pulling it together when the crisis occurs, because it makes telling the company's side of the story much easier.

Taking some ideas from former American Motors chairman Gerald Meyers' book, *When It Hits the Fan*, Johnson suggested the following steps in managing any crisis:

The business owner or manager should let everybody inside the organization know you are in charge of handling media inquiries.

Pinpoint the problem.

Construct your best case. Tell your own story about the crisis.

Accommodate the media. Develop a rapport with the journalists covering the event. Tell the whole story and get it over with quickly to minimize the length of time that headlines stay on the front page.

Be honest and ethical. In this way, you will not have to worry about being caught in lies, which will be discovered anyway.

Speak with a clear voice—avoiding industry jargon or double speak.

Be available 24 hours a day—reporters want information when they want information.

Consider telling your story through advertising as well. Demonstrate your company's concerns, showing real human information.

In his seminars, Dr. Martin Stoler, a crisis-communication consultant, uses the case of the Exxon-Valdez oil spill to demonstrate the importance of a company in crisis showing concern, Johnson said.

Johnson asked those attending the luncheon the same thing Stoler asks his audiences: "How long was it before Lawrence Rawl, Exxon's chief executive officer, went to Alaska after the oil tanker hit the reef?

"A week maybe?" Johnson asked. "A month? No, it was one year before Rawl made the trip to the site of the spill because he was trying to distance himself from the event."

Johnson said Rawl should have met the problem head-on— flown to Alaska, knelt on the beach and picked up an oil-soaked duck, held it up to the news cameras and said: "This is a tragedy of major proportions. I will not rest until this situation is rectified."

If a corporate executive demonstrates legitimate concern, Johnson said, he or she eliminates the justification for the press constantly being on the company's case. Johnson listed the following no-no's when a company in crisis deals with the media:

Do not speculate publicly about what you do not know. Do not minimize the problem to the press. If it is serious, the media will find out.

Do not let the story dribble out, because each new fact will bring a new headline. Do not blame anyone for anything.

Do not play favorites among television, radio and print reporters. Media rivalry is alive and well without your influence.

Do not say "no comment"—it makes you look guilty.

"When have you ever believed the innocence of a person who sits across from Mike Wallace (of *60 Minutes*) and says "No comment?" Johnson asked.

"Instead, explain why you can't—that you are still investigating the problem, for example; or, that a lawsuit is pending."

Johnson recommends one final step after the crisis subsides— follow up. The head of a company should ask himself or herself: "Where are we now, and where do we have to go from here?"

Despite our best efforts, shelter ministry can be very crisis-prone. The article above applies to all of us who run people-helping ministries, and it contains advice that could save our ministry in a time of crisis.

Dealing with a Crisis

There have been times when I left the shelter in an absolutely peaceful state. You would not think anyone had a care in the world. Then, a few minutes later, my BlackBerry would start vibrating, and it is a phone call or an e-mail from someone on my staff, asking how to handle a crisis that has arisen without any warning.

Here is an example of a "crisis" that occurred many years ago; it could only happen within a homeless shelter. I firmly think that it was averted because of my good relationship with the press and many of the other agencies in town.

It started off like any other Friday—letters to write, the phone to answer, and general run-of-the-mill business to attend to. Then my secretary came in with a worried look on her face.

"Jeremy, it's [name omitted], and he says he's got to speak to you immediately. It's urgent."

"Hello, this is Jeremy."

"Yeah, Jeremy. What is going on at the shelter? You guys serving rotten water?"

"What?"

"We just had this couple down here complaining about your water. They brought this vial of water that has stuff that looks like toilet paper floating in it, and the water's yellow. They are saying that this is the sort of water that you are serving at the shelter, and this is a sample out of the bathroom sink. Oh, and they are also saying that they got tuberculosis at the shelter. Don't want to scare you, but I just thought you should know."

The man wished me a good day and hung up. I quickly ascertained the situation, but I had no idea what a day it was going to be!

Crisis and Vacation?

Some weeks prior to this troubling call, I had scheduled a couple of days out of town with my wife and family. We were to stay with some friends in El Paso. I did not feel comfortable telling my wife and sons that the whole trip was off because one of our guests appeared to have a grudge against us.

So, we left Albuquerque, and I thought I was gradually beginning to unwind and enjoy myself. Then, about one hundred or so miles south of Albuquerque, I felt that familiar vibration on my hip that meant someone was trying to reach me on my pager (that was in the days before BlackBerrys). I looked and read the message from my answering service saying to call a local motel.

Reaching for my cellular phone with some resignation, I dialed the number. The desk clerk said she felt she should call me, because there were some bad things being said about the shelter. She wanted to make sure I was aware of everything that was going on.

"Jeremy, this is what's been happening. I just got a call from a clerk at another motel, who is a good friend of mine. She told me that there are some people running around the city who claim to have tuberculosis, and they are saying they got it from dirty water at your facility. Those same people just called me, as well, and asked for a free room. I know you and the work you do and didn't believe it, but I thought I should call you."

I thanked my kind informant and filled her in on what I thought was happening.

"Those people want a motel room, and what's evolved in Albuquerque with Joy Junction being the only family shelter is that everyone gets referred to us. If they don't want to stay at Joy Junction, and if they don't have a legitimate reason not to stay, they have a real problem.

"I think they dredged the potty for urine, put some toilet paper in it, took it down to a local agency, and said, 'Look! This is the sort of stuff that

Joy Junction's doing. They are unsanitary, so do not send us there. In fact, we've been there and we've gotten tuberculosis.'"

The clerk understood the situation very well, which made things at least a little bit easier.

I figured I should call some of the other Albuquerque agencies to see who else heard about our special brand of water. Calling a number of agencies, I found that many had, but one or two smart ones had already taken steps to defuse the situation and said, "Look, that stuff about Joy Junction needs to stop immediately, and anyone who wants to keep on with it can see me and spend the night elsewhere."

Do not forget that while all this was happening, I was in the van with my wife and children, headed for a happy weekend's break in El Paso.

I called the shelter's operations manager and alerted him to the situation. Then I told all the staff to notify me immediately if any media should happen to call. I didn't think they would run with one side of the story without talking to me first, but there was always that possibility.

Meanwhile, I was asking myself if I should call the media and inform them about the situation, or if to do so would draw unnecessary attention to something that might resolve itself. As we were getting closer to El Paso, I decided not to do anything for that night and to call a few stations in the morning.

Whether to call the media in the hope of fending off a potential crisis will depend on your particular situation. If you have established a good rapport with the press, and they know you are for real, it might not be a bad idea to call them.

But, if you are still a brand-new ministry or you have gotten off to a rocky start with the media, it might be a good idea to leave things alone and pray they do not hear about what is going on. If they do, respond promptly, courteously, and truthfully. As Paul Legau says his article, in the end, the media will always find out.

So, on Saturday morning, I called the television stations and told them what was going on. They were not overly concerned, which I believe was a reflection of the positive relationship I had built up with the assignment editors at these stations.

I reported to the press what I had found the day before, when I called the analyst who tests our water monthly (we operate from a well). We had taken him five samples to test.

On returning to Albuquerque, I called the state environmental health department and asked them to send its representative down to take another four samples. He had already been alerted to what was going on. If you do not know how fast gossip and rumor travels in homeless circles, you will find out very soon!

The uproar began to die down when I received the second set of test results from our chemist. All the water samples were clean, as I had expected. A few days after that, the state notified me with the same results. I called the *Albuquerque Journal* and asked them if they would publish something to say that Joy Junction's water is clean and healthy. They agreed to do so, if I would send them the test results from the state and the analyst.

I guess the lesson is this: anyone can have a crisis. How one handles it will play a major part in determining how the media will respond. In dealing with the water situation, I drew upon years of honest communication with Albuquerque's media. Still, years of the media's perception of me as a person of integrity, followed by just one incident of dishonesty or being less than forthcoming, would have been a detriment to the shelter.

Build relationships with the press, be available, and ne honest. Above all, pray whenever you talk to reporters. You have an agenda (doing the Lord's work and feeding and sheltering people), and the press has an agenda (a story). If the two agendas are going to successfully mesh, you need the Lord's blessing and favor.

Always Take Media Calls

I take calls from the media any time of the day or night. Media deadlines do not wait until we feel like dealing with them, and so I encourage you to accommodate the media's schedule. Do not try to make them fit into your schedule, for they will not.

Here is one press release I wrote just after President Bill Clinton's victory that got after-hours attention and made the interruptions worthwhile:

> While Democrats cheered and rejoiced Tuesday, and Republicans wept, there were homeless people looking for a place to stay.
> And Joy Junction was there!
> It was cold last night. Thank God that Joy Junction was there. If the need continues to grow at the current alarming rate, Joy Junction will soon run out of space for all the people who are looking to us for help. Women, children, families! No place to go without Joy Junction.

But a shelter director's worst nightmare is beginning to unfold before his eyes! Outside my office are two beautiful buildings, almost ready for habitation by needy people. Combined, these two buildings comprise fourteen rooms and eight bathrooms. Once they are completed, Joy Junction will be able to house more people in dignity.

However, we face going through winter looking at two empty buildings and having to turn away needy, hurting people because of an inability to satisfy the Bernalillo County Fire Marshall's (very reasonable) requirements of installing two fire hydrants and a sprinkler system.

While many Americans are basking in what they feel is the warm afterglow of what they feel is a new and positive direction for America, many of their fellow Americans are cold and homeless, and many more face that possibility if the project is not completed in time.

And will Bill Clinton's ascendancy to the presidency result in any benefits for the homeless? I seriously doubt it.

There are no quick economic fixes in store for this country!

The result of that press release was a story in the afternoon Albuquerque newspaper, two stories on the local CBS affiliate, and one story on the local ABC affiliate. And that story in the afternoon paper resulted in a $25,000 gift, allowing us to finish this project so that fifty-six more people could be housed. What a blessing! The article appeared on a Friday, and the next morning a man called, asking if $25,000 would help us. I very quickly assured him it would be, so he asked if I had time to come and get it. Taking one of our board members, we made our way to this gentleman's house as quickly as we could. This was just one of many ways that God has used the media to allow us to meet the needs of the homeless more effectively.

Having a flexible schedule to accommodate the needs and deadlines of the media is very important. The two stories on the CBS affiliate were filmed on a Sunday afternoon, just after I came home from church. Do not tell the media that Sunday is your day off and ask if they could come back when you are "on the clock." The media will not call you back, and you will jeopardize, if not totally destroy, a great resource for publicity for your ministry.

The ABC affiliate interview was filmed live, outside in the freezing cold, again after my "workday" had ended. There really are potentially limitless possibilities if you are willing to work with the media.

Here is another press release that attracted a lot of attention. Because of the media's help, what began initially as a disaster was turned into an abundance of food to help the needy. This release resulted in coverage on television, local and national radio news, and a short article in the newspaper.

When a local cold storage freezer site went under, so did Joy Junction's plans for its annual Thanksgiving dinners—that is unless concerned community members can come through with generous donations of turkeys.

Joy Junction Founder and Executive Director Jeremy Reynalds explained. "We didn't have enough freezer space here so we contracted with a local cold storage site to store the turkeys for us. When we tried to call them the telephone was disconnected. When we sent a staff member up there to visit we were told that the turkeys had thawed."

Reynalds said this year should be the 14th year that Joy Junction has served hundreds of delicious Thanksgiving dinners. "We're supposed to be serving on Saturday 20th November and Thanksgiving Day. But there's a problem—no turkeys."

Reynalds said the shelter will serve something on those days, but it may not be a traditional Thanksgiving dinner. "And that would be so sad. I really hope that people will come through for us. I emphasize, we don't have one single turkey," he said.

Anyone wishing to donate turkeys should bring them to the shelter's location, or call (505) 877-6967.

Wow! Talk about an abundance of turkeys from concerned citizens. For a number of days after that story was featured, wherever I went, people would ask me if we had enough turkeys to feed the homeless for our Thanksgiving dinner.

Never exaggerate and never invent crises. By all means, inform local media about a crisis and what it will mean to those you serve, just as I did with the release on the ruined turkeys. But make sure what you are telling the media is exactly what happened. Members of the media have long memories, and if they suspect that you are not being truthful with them, you will probably live to regret it.

If you decide you are going to be the official media spokesperson for your organization, you need to equip yourself with a cell phone or a BlackBerry. Remember, they are dealing with deadlines, and they often need information within a few minutes of calling you. They just cannot be told that someone will call them back the next business day. Whatever number you give out to the media, be sure you always answer it.

Believe me, all of this is very important. I have had the privilege of actually working for the media and have seen firsthand what they need and how they can affect my ministry. My undergraduate degree is focused in journalism, and while studying at the University of New Mexico, I had the opportunity to intern for about three years for a local newspaper, two television stations, and two radio stations. While I observed a real willingness by both the print and the broadcast media to work with social service providers, that willingness seemed to be tempered by a frustration that agency officials did not know about, and apparently did not seem to really care about, the constraints faced by local media.

Terribly complex stories are not good material for television news. Because the typical television news sound bite runs between eight and twelve seconds, and the usual length of an entire story is maybe a minute and twenty seconds or less, there is just not enough time to explain complex issues. Our turkey crisis story is an example of good "meat" for television news, as is another crisis we encountered with a shortage of donated food to serve the homeless during the summer months. When we ran out of food, we used the following release and others like it to draw attention to our need.

> Vulnerable men, women and children are seeking shelter from the summer heat at Joy Junction and other shelters across the country. With many regions around the United States declaring a state of emergency, the poor are turning to members of the nation's sixth-largest charity, the Association of Gospel Rescue Missions, of which Joy Junction is a part, for protection from the elements. While many people associate the emergency service provided by Joy Junction with the dangers posed by the cold of winter, the summer heat can be as deadly for those who have no place to turn.
>
> Rising temperatures outside also produce rising temperatures inside. When two or three families share living quarters, which can be typical among the poor, disagreements can lead to homelessness. Often this includes children, who cannot turn to school for shelter in the daytime.
>
> Joy Junction Executive Director Jeremy Reynalds said that the shelter has been very busy the last few weeks. "As a result, we've run very short of food, including milk and meat," he said.
>
> Rev. Stephen Burger, the executive director of the Association of Gospel Rescue Missions, said many people do not think about how the homeless are affected by the summer heat. "Without the ability to go indoors, many people perish. It's no surprise that Joy Junction and other shelters are filled to capacity at this time.

If you think all of this sounds like a lot of hard work, you are right. But cultivating a successful relationship with the media will result in unbelievable blessings for your ministry.

Of course, it is important to remember that while successful relationships with the media begin by putting in a lot of hard work and continue with a willingness to be responsive to the media's needs, these relationships are really only successfully maintained by asking for the Lord's blessings in all of your dealings with the press.

PART 3

MEETING NEEDS ON A DAILY BASIS

When Vision Becomes Reality

Finally, your vision becomes a reality, and the long-awaited ministry is open. You should be excited, as this day is the culmination of months of prayer, strategizing, and planning.

When Joy Junction started in 1986, I spent long hours on the phone, calling various Albuquerque social service agencies and telling them that we would soon be open. This did a couple of very important things. First, the other agencies heard about the opening of the shelter from me and not from someone else. Hearing something directly from the person concerned is one of the best ways to fight off any fear and resulting gossip. Second, it was a way to spread the word around town about us and give other agencies the opportunity to refer guests, if they so wished.

Perhaps because of all that time spent on the telephone, a few days before our official opening, Joy Junction welcomed its first family. The man had just been paroled from prison. Along with him were his wife and two children. I was happy. They were delighted. Joy Junction was up and running!

I had received a call from the adult probation and parole people. Officials there had heard about our upcoming opening and wondered if we might be able to take in a family prior to opening day. I agreed, on the condition that the family indicated a willingness to help out with building cleanup. The parole officer said the only way that this gentleman could get out of prison was if he had a place to stay in a shelter like ours. So, the family came, and soon after, another family called. We had guests and were not even open! What a wonderful way to begin our work.

Time passed, and I was kept busy answering phones, making sure the evening meal was cooked, and teaching the evening Bible study. Every day, it got very late before I knew it, and I had not yet thought about going home.

An article by then staff writer David Morrissey appeared in a September 1986, edition of the *Albuquerque Journal* a couple of days after we opened. It was the start of what was to be a very fruitful relationship with all of the Albuquerque media. Here is the beginning of it.

> The Friday dedication of the Joy Junction emergency shelter underscores one of Albuquerque's contradictions—in the midst of a citywide housing boom, a growing number of people have no place to live.
>
> The Department of Housing and Urban Development says more than 8,000 housing units were built during the last two years in Albuquerque. Another 2,000 units are now under construction.
>
> There are so many apartments in the city, 15 percent are vacant—a rate twice the national average. At the same time, there are many with no place to call home.
>
> Workers at Albuquerque missions and emergency shelters say the need is growing.
>
> A potluck supper at 6 p.m. Friday will show off one effort to meet the needs of the homeless, said the Rev. Jeremy Reynalds, director of the shelter.
>
> Scheduled to open Oct. 1 [1986], the facility at 4500 2nd St. SW, is located at what was the dormitory of the now-closed Our Lady of Lourdes High School. The building, which is owned by DARE (Drug Alcohol Rehabilitation Enterprises), has been leased to serve as a shelter, said Reynalds.
>
> Joy Junction will provide both emergency and long-term shelter for single women and families, Reynalds said. The need for shelter for these people in Albuquerque is greatest, he added.
>
> Prior to the opening of Joy Junction, which will be able to house a maximum of seven families and 10 women, there were only three emergency shelters in the city with facilities to house families. Those shelters, serving Albuquerque's metropolitan area of more than 400,000 people, could handle a maximum of 14 families.
>
> Joy Junction, a non-denominational ministry, as well as, a shelter, will be funded by donations, Reynalds said. It will not seek

or accept federal, state, or city funds. The shelter especially needs food and bedding, he said.

Reynalds said he expects the shelter to help out those who are "temporarily economically disadvantaged"—people who can be helped to find new jobs and housing.

"Because of the current economic climate there are people using shelters today who never imagined they would need emergency housing," Reynalds said.

Doing Everything at Once

The first month passed quickly, and sometimes I wondered who and what I was. For the first month or so, I was doing everything. I was the shelter's executive director, but I was also working with private donors and the local food bank to make sure there was always something good to feed those] the Lord brought our way. I answered the phone and typed all of my own letters. In addition, I prepared the evening Bible studies—and occasionally left to go home to my family.

Who are you? The answer is that all you can be is yourself, someone very ordinary but still very special, because you are obeying God's calling on your life. You have been chosen to fulfill a very special function. The reality is that like the apostle Paul, you need to be all things to all people that, by so being, some might come to a saving knowledge of the Lord Jesus Christ.

You need to be very wise and discerning about how you share the gospel and with whom. Everyone is called to hear the gospel, and every evangelical Christian is charged with the responsibility of delivering that message to others. There will be times when you will be called to speak at gatherings that are secular in nature. You can still share the gospel message, but be mindful of your audience. Always ask what would be appropriate to share, and be respectful of the guidelines the person who invited you has set.

Don't try to push the envelope and preach, because you may not be invited again. You can share Jesus wherever you go, and sometimes this is done better through actions and the treatment of others than by words.

To some, you will be an administrator; to others, you will be an agency head. To still others, you will be a minister and a pastor. You can literally be all things to all men. I urge you to make good use of all of your opportunities.

As you launch forth on this exciting new venture, pastors, businesspeople, donors, vendors, and a whole variety of other people in the community will be watching you very carefully to see how you conduct yourself. For example, do you pay your bills on time? And if not, do you adequately communicate with people to whom you owe money to let them know what is going on? To be able to preach the gospel, you have to operate in a manner that is above reproach, because it will need to hold up under an incredible amount of scrutiny.

Sometimes you are also a cook. Have you thought what your emotional reaction will be when you have labored long and hard to cook a good meal (the sort of food that you would not hesitate to feed your own family), and you open up the serving hatches and hear a couple of guests look disparagingly at the food and say in a loud voice, "You know what? I wouldn't serve that to my dog!" Believe me, this has actually happened more times than I care to mention. That is when you need to know that you are in this work to obey the call of the Lord. If you do not realize this, you will quickly become biter and disillusioned.

David Morrissey of the *Albuquerque Journal* wrote another piece about Joy Junction on November 27, 1986, shortly after we opened. This time the article profiled one of the first families helped by our shelter. Here is what he wrote:

> Pilgrims at the first Thanksgiving gratefully thanked God for bringing them through a difficult and uncertain year.
>
> Ted and Judy Kotoff will offer much the same prayer as they sit down today for their Thanksgiving dinner in Albuquerque.
>
> The Kotoffs, both 32, are in many ways a typical family. They work hard, try to save their money and want the best for their four-year-old son Jesse.
>
> Thanksgiving is a day they reflect on their blessings. But this year Ted and Judy Kotoff are homeless.
>
> Their Thanksgiving table is at Joy Junction, an Albuquerque shelter for homeless families and single women, where they now live in one small bedroom.
>
> They arrived in Albuquerque three weeks ago from South Carolina. They lived in a trailer there—sometimes employed, sometimes looking for work. When jobs proved scarce, they headed west.
>
> It was not so much they intended to stop in Albuquerque, Ted Kotoff explained. It was just that here their meager savings ran out.

By chance they heard of Joy Junction, a shelter in the dormitory of the now-closed Our Lady of Lourdes High School at 4500 Second SW, run by the Rev. Jeremy Reynalds.

"We called Jeremy and he took us in," said Ted. "It's been like an oasis in the storm."

"We're both painters," said Judy Kotoff, adding that she was also an electronics technician while Ted had worked as a mechanic and a musician. "We want to work. We're not afraid of hard work." They followed the construction jobs in South Carolina and other states, trying to make enough to settle down, Ted said. But work was infrequent. Stories of high-paying jobs the next state over proved to be wistful thinking.

When construction went bust, the Kotoffs got on with a carnival in South Carolina, operating rides. But when the carnival operator failed to pay them wages they thought they had earned, they decided to make a new start.

In Albuquerque they found temporary jobs as telephone solicitors, earning $4 an hour, 20 hours a week. While staying at Joy Junction, they hope to save enough for an apartment, and find better-paying jobs.

While the homeless are difficult to count and categorize, the federal Department of Housing and Urban Development says they fall into three categories: people with chronic alcohol and drug problems, people with personal crises, such as battered women and runaway children, and people who have suffered severe economic setbacks, such as losing a job.

City officials across the nation report an increase in the number of middle-class Americans forced into emergency shelters through job loss or sudden catastrophic expenses.

Many of these new poor "are just like you and me," Reynalds said. "They're not street people, but people temporarily down on their luck."

Ted and Judy Kotoff are thankful today, but they are not satisfied.

If they have their way, the nation's homeless population will be cut by at least one family.

There were a lot of things on my mind when we came to the end of our first month. We had some discontented guests and some disgruntled donors. After having run a shelter in Santa Fe for four years, I was prepared for both. Yet, I had not thought the dissatisfaction would manifest itself this quickly. Why did it?

I am going to spend some time on what might appear to be some very small and insignificant things, but these little things can cause the shelter operator, or the head of any parachurch or people-ministry, much grief.

As I have mentioned previously, do not open a shelter for homeless people (in fact, do not get involved with any sort of ministry) expecting the homeless or anyone else to be grateful. Some may be, but most will not. Never forget, you do what you do for the Lord.

Try and empathize with those you are dealing with, as well as with their situation. Remember that the homeless or any of the individuals you are in a position to help are going through one of the worst experiences they have ever had in their lives. They do not want to stay in a shelter—and probably not in rehab either—and in all likelihood, anything that goes wrong is going to be blamed on you and not on their own inadequacies or choices. This is very typical behavior, so you should not blame yourself if this is the reaction you get.

Look to the Lord and him only for thanks. He will keep you from getting burned out.

Hazards of the Job

You will learn very quickly that as a homeless shelter operator and caregiver (whether you are dealing with the homeless, or hurting people in any shape, form, or variety), you have to work with two entirely different sets of expectations when dealing with your clients and your donors.

Take cleanliness of the facility grounds as an example. As the agency grows, there is no way that you will be able to clean up after all of the people staying at the facility. You should not have to. You will need to implement a chore system, and you will have to check up on residents after they have completed their chore duties.

To many people staying with you, it is quite natural for them to leave a trail of messes. If the Dumpster is overflowing and you say empty it, you mean empty it—now. There is a good reason it has to be emptied. A full or overflowing Dumpster is an eyesore as well as a health hazard. So, you tell a particular resident to clean up around the Dumpster, but the result is not what you had hoped. You failed to check up on the guest to make sure that he or she has completed the task. They do a sloppy job, and everything is a mess. Donors come down and see the mess, but they do not complain to you. Instead, they start criticizing the facility and making comments about the place always being dirty.

To add insult to injury, the same donors bring some food down and, walking in the door, they see what they believe to be lazy guests sitting around. Again, you do not hear about it firsthand. The perceived issue does not surface until some weeks later.

You have been invited to speak before a group, and after you make your presentation, there is time for a question-and-answer session. Someone stands up and sarcastically says, "I thought you had a work ethic or some sort of work policy at the shelter for the guests." You assure her that you do and ask her specifically what she means. She says, "Well, when a group of us came down a few weeks ago, we brought a lot of food from a drive that the club had." She tells you how heavy the cans were and how hard the group had worked. And then the punch line: "We walked through the door, and there were all those people just sitting around. I really resent that. Can't they help?"

You try to explain some of the dynamics of running a helping agency, including things like depression being so bad it can physically immobilize someone. You tell her about the increasing number of addicted and mentally ill people staying at the shelter. They may look normal, you say, but in reality, they are totally dysfunctional and suffering. You continue explaining about the guests working the nightshift, who just want some rest before going to sleep. You try telling her how being homeless is a demoralizing and dehumanizing experience. But all your efforts are to no avail. She is not satisfied, so you say no more. It would not be helpful to say anything more at this point.

Why Do so Few People Understand?

How do you handle situations like that? Incidents like the one I have described occur every day in shelters, drug rehabs, and other faith-based ministries all across the United States.

You must realize that such assumptions (such as seeing "lazy guests" sitting around) are an inherent hazard of doing anything for the Lord. Those who "do" generally get criticized by those who "do not do" (but think they know all the answers). After trying to educate the community about homelessness, alcohol and drug abuse, and mental illness, all one can do is leave the results in the Lord's hands. I have found that very few people are adequately informed about what being homeless actually does to a person. It positively destroys self-esteem, reinforces negative attitudes, and inflicts serious damage on an already strained marital relationship.

In many cases, people have become homeless by making inappropriate choices. (Joy Junction focuses on the underlying reasons why people makes those choices and in so doing, has discovered amazing stories of the crises many of our guests have endured.) They did not become that way overnight, and it will take a considerable amount of time and effort to change those behaviors that got them to that point in the first place. God will do some amazing things in their lives if they allow him.

Try to help donors understand what it means to be homeless. When you get the opportunity, respectfully ask people how they would feel if they had no kitchen in which to cook. Ask them how they would feel if they had no job, and their next meal and night's shelter were dependent on someone else's charity (or lack of it). It is difficult to comprehend that homelessness can happen to someone living in the wealthiest nation in the world, but sadly, it can and does. Everyone needs to find a way to contribute to solving this problem either financially, prayerfully, or by volunteering. We each need to give what we can to make a difference in our own community.

Stress Comes in Many Forms

Here is an example of one stressful situation and how we handled it. At about 2:00 one morning, we heard this when the phone rang: "This is the sheriff's department. We have just had a 911 call from the shelter, and someone claims they have had stuff stolen. What's going on?"

It turned out a resident who suffered from a mental illness had called 911 from the public phone at the shelter to complain about the treatment she had received from a local hospital. She believed the hospital had stolen her belongings and was keeping them from her in an upper room somewhere. The police responded, and when the woman would not settle down, the officers had to handcuff her and take her away.

Should we have tried to settle her down? Possibly. Would it have worked? Probably not. Did we like sending her to a hopelessly overworked county mental health facility, knowing that in all probability she would be out on the streets in a few hours? No, but we had a responsibility to all the other residents to ensure them a good night's sleep. And we had a responsibility to the sheriff's department to help prevent any more illegitimate 911 calls from residents. Our residents know they need to go through proper channels to address these matters.

We handle stressful situations by realizing we are running a shelter for the Lord and that we can only do what we can with the resources God allows us to have. We also have to commit all of our residents to his care. As much as we can, we must try to help them see that the Lord can do so much more, and their destiny ultimately lies in his hands.

For sharing and networking, and for getting some advice and feedback on frustrating experiences, I encourage you to consider joining the Association of Gospel Rescue Missions (AGRM). The AGRM is a loose-knit association of rescue ministries that gather together for conferences and fellowship and that provides resource materials that are helpful to shelter directors and their staff. It also has an excellent online discussion list for its members. The AGRM Web site can be accessed at www.agrm. org. If you are not considering opening a shelter, find out if there is a networking group for the particular people-ministry where the Lord has directed you.

It is helpful to have a supportive church and pastor where you fellowship on a regular basis. It is important to have other colleagues you can share experiences with, especially someone who has been there. Last but not least, your board is there to help you, so use them as a resource.

SHELTER POLICIES

Some people become homeless because they have not been socialized to obey the normal rules of society. Nevertheless, they must observe certain rules as guests in a shelter.

I remember some years ago, when I was running my first shelter in Santa Fe, I had managed to obtain temporary employment for a few weeks for one of the shelter guests. The company representative who called in for a worker wanted someone for about three weeks for at least sixty hours a week. They were willing to pay overtime.

I thought it looked like a good opportunity and gave the information to someone I believed would be grateful for the job and would handle himself professionally.

At about 11:30 AM, the shelter door opened and in walked "Joe." Surprised to see him back so soon, I asked what he was doing home so early. Wanting to believe the best, I even asked him if he had come home for lunch!

"Oh no," he replied. "That place you sent me to works you too hard. They had me lifting packing crates and a whole bunch of other stuff. I wasn't going to do that for anybody, so I just left."

Joe turned out to be an unmotivated individual who quickly wore out his welcome at the shelter. His biggest problem was his reluctance to admit he was not willing to work for food!

There was another man at the shelter, who I will call "the prophet." His response when I asked him why he was still at the shelter at midday was

124

that he was a prophet of God. "You should be glad I'm here!" he exclaimed. Needless to say, he did not last very long, either. My basic prerequisite for helping someone is that they actually want help and are willing to lend a hand at the shelter. They should be willing to do what is asked of them, while showing some humility and thankfulness to God for protecting and providing for them.

You will quickly find many heartrending cases as you become more involved in people ministry. Treat people as individuals, be compassionate, and be aware that everyone you are assisting is unique, as is their situation. Do not ever forget that they are hurting. They do not need you to feel sorry for them, but neither do they need you to lord your authority over them. Your guests need to know you are sincerely concerned and that you care. Be creative in your approaches to helping the different people God sets before you.

Clients' Length of Stay

How long should guests stay? While I would encourage you to seek advice from other established missions, do not feel that their advice is your only option. Some missions can be bound by their traditions and may not be flexible to the current needs of those they serve.

Nationwide, many shelters have a maximum number of days or weeks people can stay. It is easier to set a limit to the number of days guests may stay with you. You and your staff should be actively involved in evaluating each guest's situation and needs on a regular basis.

Take as an example a family of five (husband, wife, and their three children), to whom you give a three-week time limit. Shortly thereafter, the husband obtains employment as a dishwasher at a local hotel. The hotel pays its employees every two weeks, and "Jim" joins the staff in the middle of the pay period. This means he has to wait three weeks before receiving his first paycheck.

Applying the three-week time limit, this family will have to leave the shelter the day before the husband gets his first check. Even if you stretch their stay another day, there is no way a family can get back on its feet again with the money one wage earner will earn from a week's salary washing dishes.

What, then, is Jim to do? He has shown initiative in getting out there and getting a job. He has done everything possible, but "the system" has let him down. In all probability, unless there is another family shelter in town, Jim will become completely discouraged and possibly pack up his bags and family and leave town.

What will happen then? Maybe Jim and his family move on to another town, where there is a really good chance of the whole cycle repeating itself. If that happens, try and imagine the negative impact on Jim. The situation has the potential to damage his relationship with his wife and family, as economic tensions and pressures are already straining all the family relationships. As this continues, Jim is beginning to get more and more depressed, until ultimately, he does not even care if he gets a job. In the worst-case scenario, he could lapse into some sort of clinical depression, where all he wants to do is sit and stare into space. He may even return to his previous addictions to escape the stress of these life circumstances. The system that should have helped Jim and his family has ultimately failed them.

Some years ago, ABC television aired a docudrama about the plight of two homeless people. It featured a woman and her child, who lived in a tenement building in New York. Mom was employed as a maid at a local hotel. While the family was making ends meet, it was a tight struggle.

Things were going relatively well until the landlord announced he would be bulldozing the apartment complex to make way for a parking lot. That meant Mom and child would be without a place to stay. She looked and looked, but it was all in vain. On her minimum wage job, she could not afford any of New York's outrageously high apartment rents and security deposits.

This lady and her child ended up homeless. The only choice left for her was to go to a shelter. At the shelter, she faced a stoic woman, staring at her over pince-nez glasses in a demeaning fashion. The lady was quickly told that all residents had to be in by the shelter's curfew.

The homeless woman desperately tried to explain that she had a job that required her to work past the shelter curfew. The shelter operator was unrelenting, and consequently the lady had to make a choice between the shelter and a job. And why? Because that was how the shelter had always done it. We need rules, but we must always remember that people have hearts and needs, and they are all different.

Never continue a practice because, "That is the way it has always been done." On the other hand, never change a rule, policy, practice, or procedure just for the sake of change, without first determining its effect on others and on the shelter itself.

I attended a meeting some time ago where there was a discussion about whether shelter guests should be fed before Bible studies, or whether they should have to attend the Bible study and then be able to eat. A couple of individuals said they believed people responded to the gospel much better after a meal than they would on an empty stomach. That is also my opinion.

Put yourself in the place of those you are trying to help. You come to a shelter, and you are cold, tired, lonely, hungry, and afraid. Maybe you had not even thought of God at all. It is not that you do not believe in him; it is more that he does not seem have relevance in your life. But one thing you do know is that you are hungry. It is five o'clock in the evening, and after asking when the meal will be served, you are told that you and your family will be served after the evening service, which starts in an hour.

The hour prior to church, you are all getting hungrier and hungrier. The children are becoming restless. During the service, you pay no attention, and the message of God's love for you in Jesus Christ falls on deaf ears. That is because all you can think about is the growling pain in your stomach, which is getting worse and worse; that, and the sounds of crying children. The message and the deep meaning of the words of the pastor arc not heard by you or your family, because physical nourishment is neglected. Jesus showed his understanding of the importance of providing for one's physical needs as a precursor to spiritual nourishment when he had compassion on the crowd of five thousand and fed them (Matt. 14; John 6).

At that meeting, when some of those attending were asked why they made people sit through a gospel service before feeding them, their answer was, "Because that's how we've always done it!" This is not an appropriate answer. There is nothing wrong with tradition, as long as it is helpful. But tradition for its own sake is worthless and may sometimes even be damaging to the delicate emotions of those we are trying to help.

Rules for People or People for Rules?

You have to have rules, no question about that, but make certain those rules are relevant. Obviously, as much as you want to provide a family-type atmosphere and environment, you are still running an institution.

Joy Junction's rule of thumb for the length of stay is based on the need and motivation of the family, as was discussed previously. We try to be discerning and flexible. For example, take a family of dad, mom, and three kids. You notice that despite your best efforts, dad just sits around and does not appear to be in the least bit motivated to find work, preferring to let the shelter provide basic necessities for his wife and children. The shelter staff is beginning to get frustrated, so you decide it is time for you to get more involved.

You begin to build a relationship with the man, and several issues quickly begin to emerge. You learn that the reason for his lack of willingness to go out and look for work is simple but profound: the man just freezes when he goes to apply for work. In the unlikely event he will get past that first hurdle, he has no confidence about his ability to keep a job anyway.

Without telling the staff the details of a confidential counseling relationship, you tell them that this man is not lazy but has some issues to overcome in his life. You encourage them to go the extra mile to offer him encouragement and support. They are told to love him, to be very patient, and to tell him that with his effort and God's help, he will get and keep a job and will be able to move his family out of homelessness.

You and the rest of the shelter staff start by giving him small jobs around the shelter, which you know he can do, and verbally encourage him. Pretty soon, the man's whole demeanor and attitude begin to change, and his sense of worth and confidence improves.

Then the big day finally comes, and he goes out and gets a job that he is able to keep. Yes, you could have told him to go out and work months ago, and maybe told him that he should pull himself up by his bootstraps and get out of his financial hole. But at that time, he would have been emotionally incapable of coming through. The Lord, you, and your staff gave him the ability to get back on his feet and support his family again. You have just witnessed a great miracle!

In this case, a family of three boys might need more time at the shelter than a family of six children. Perhaps the father of six has been laid off from a job because of purely economic reasons, and within a few short weeks, he will have located suitable employment and be back on his feet again.

The only way you will ever discover this essential information is by taking time to talk with your guests. Cultivate relationships with them, because it is only then that they will be able to trust you enough to tell you some of the things that may have been bothering them for years. Once you understand where they have been, you can, with God's direction, help them get where they are going.

To Preach or Not to Preach?

Shelters for the homeless have been traditionally started and run by evangelical Christians. The chapter on the history of shelters in America will give you more information on that very important subject.

Should you, as an evangelical Christian, have mandatory Bible studies, and if so, how many? If you do not have any, will you be missing out on a golden opportunity to minister the gospel to those most in need? If you have mandatory Bible study, do you run the risk of making homeless people gospel-hardened, especially if they have been "mission-hopping," going from mission to mission, hearing the gospel with the ear but not with the heart?

When I started Joy Junction back in 1986, I immediately started Bible studies on six nights of the week, with Saturday being a night off. We continued like that for three or four years. Then I began sensing it was time for a change, when the Lord began nudging me about changing our Bible study schedule.

I was thinking of cutting the number of Bible studies we had, making them all voluntary, or going to some other system. One night, Rez Band was in town. They are a very successful Christian heavy metal band based out of Jesus People USA in Chicago. Rez Band is part of a Christian community that does a number of things, including shelter homeless people, direct an active jail ministry, and operate a home for the elderly.

Glenn Kaiser is the lead singer of Rez Band. Prior to that night's concert, I was talking with his wife, Wendi. She was interested in our work, as those who attended the concert that night had been asked to bring a can of food to give to Joy Junction. The question of mandatory church came up, and I asked Wendi what she thought. She is a lady who says exactly what she thinks.

Wendi said she was opposed to mandatory church services and did not think it was something Jesus would have done. So, I listened carefully, prayed, talked to some people, and arrived at a place I felt was right for Joy Junction.

After several variations, starting with services every evening, two of them mandatory, we now have three services—Wednesday, Friday, and Saturday. "We're not going to shove the gospel down their throats anymore," I told our staff back then. "So now, the life of faith you live out before our guests will make them curious about Jesus."

I am not criticizing shelters or agencies that choose to have Bible studies or services every day. That is their prerogative (Although I would strongly recommend that you always provide a meal before preaching the gospel). But we all need to be open and obedient to the leading of the Holy Spirit. Again, this is one of those cases where, as the founder and director of a shelter, you have the ability to set a new standard. In our case, we decided we were not required to have nightly services just because others did it.

Staffing Issues

Staff will make or break you. Before you think, *Staff? Jeremy must be out of his mind! I can't even come up with enough money to make a livable salary for myself each week. How does he think I'm going to pay staff?*

Money is tight for every new start-up ministry or business. We need to be willing and able to do everything in the beginning, but we will not be able to grow without bringing in additional staff to increase the talent pool of the ministry. And people will judge the success of our ministry to a large extent by the professional manner and caring nature of our staff.

Where do you find good staff? The first thing to do is pray and ask God to send you the right individuals who will be able to catch a vision for what God has called you to do. Ask God to bring people who will realize their role in the ministry and who feel divinely called to help empower you to carry out your work effectively.

Having prayed and believed that God has heard and will answer your prayer, there is nothing wrong with going ahead and believing you are moving according to God's plan and direction. Here are some practical pointers to help you. Obviously, all of my suggestions are only hypothetical until you can produce the income to make them a reality. To begin with, advertise with the publications of the AGRM. Also, consider signing up with Christian employment services.

I do not recommend that you have your staff raise their own support for their salary, because it diminishes their accountability to you. They begin thinking they are working for themselves instead of you.

Another thing to remember is that people are not automatically good workers just because they call themselves Christians. They should be, but my experience in many cases has been that some will justify their lackluster work ethic by saying they are accountable to God and not you. This is totally incorrect, as they are biblically accountable to you as their employer.

On salaries, you will usually get what you pay for. There is an occasional exception to this rule but very occasional. It is appropriate in some instances to pay minimum wage, but be aware that professional personnel usually come with professional prices. A shelter can get by with many unskilled staff people, but you still need some skilled professionals for key positions.

Hire a good business manager. You need a skilled individual to prepare budgets, monitor expenses, and ensure that the ministry is operating within the IRS guidelines governing 501(c) (3)s. As I have shared, I learned by very painful personal experience that a good business manager is the key to success.

Former Residents as Staff

Should you employ former homeless residents of your facility to staff the shelter? From what I have gathered, this seems to be a pretty common practice. But let me suggest something a little more workable.

Joy Junction formed a life recovery program for our residents. We named it the CIPP—Christ in Power Program. The Tyndale House Life Recovery Bible is used as a basis.

Several additional aspects comprise the program. Through a variety of classes and hands-on experiences, it offers training in basic life skills, financial management, cooking, and resident supervision. Many of the residents who come to us have some basic work skills, but they lack the social ability to allow effective functioning in the workplace. That, combined with some of the feelings of inadequacy I spoke about earlier, naturally renders people rather ineffective.

For that reason, we take people who have, for example, some basic cooking skills but maybe have a problem relating to their boss' position of authority. In a regular work setting, their boss might tell them to perform a specific duty, which is well within their ability to perform. Instead of cheerfully obeying, they get angry and tell their boss they have no intention of doing anything he says. Consequently, they get fired. The CIPP training teaches them their role and the role of their boss in God's economy, and that they are required to obey and respect their employer. The CIPP also teaches basic skills, like clocking in and clocking out of work, coming to work on time, and communicating and not reacting.

Some of the residents enrolled in the CIPP also get assigned to what we call floor duties. Basically, what that means is that they help staff check in residents, talk with other homeless people in crisis situations, and learn some basic people-coping skills. They also assist in caring for basic needs, like distributing shampoo, deodorant, and diapers, and helping to ensure general order. If any problems occur, the individual's instructions are to immediately find a staff member and not to try to solve it on his or her own. We also hope CIPP participants will use a watchful eye and some preventative skills so problems are averted whenever possible.

Our life recovery program helps us assist the homeless more effectively than just hiring former residents to staff the shelter. If you develop a training program, make sure there is plenty of Bible study and classroom training—the theoretical as well as the practical. Make sure you do not take advantage of those you are trying to help. Remember, you are conducting a training program, not attempting to staff the shelter with unpaid workers.

Allowing homeless people to serve in any supervisory capacity over other homeless people is something that has to be monitored very carefully. You might be surprised, but some homeless people, given a measure of authority, tend to be harsh in their dealings with their homeless peers. It may be a means for them to manifest the way they were treated at some point.

Keep in mind that if you do appoint formerly homeless people to staff positions, thus removing them from homeless status, it does not mean that the homelessness has been taken out of them. Homelessness is a state of mind as well as a state of being.

Even though they may have a roof over their heads now, unless those behaviors that caused the person to become homeless are addressed, they may become homeless again at some point.

When Do You Ask Rule Breakers to Leave?

When do you ask someone to leave? Let us look at a situation where someone violates the no-drinking policy. Do you automatically ask them to leave?

Again, I would suggest you treat everyone individually and consistently and not uniformly. Let me explain. I am sure that your shelter will have a no-drinking policy. In many cases, it is alcohol consumption that has resulted in people becoming homeless. But say you have an alcoholic staying at the shelter. A twenty-year alcoholic, while not necessarily drinking right now, is still someone with a twenty-year history of drinking. He may be able to stay clean for a few months, and he might be someone who impresses you so much that you put him in a position of responsibility.

Then he blows it and does not check into the shelter for a few days. The next thing you hear about him is a report from the police that says he is now incarcerated for driving drunk.

It is seemingly an easy decision to ask him to leave the property, since he has violated your no-alcohol policy. Even then (and I would suspect some of you will probably disagree with me on this point), I do not necessarily think someone should be asked to leave for one violation. I am not trying to encourage drinking. Absolutely not.

What I want to encourage is for one to act like Christ and show his love and compassion. I want to encourage us to act in such a way that we will not make people gospel-hardened. It took a twenty-year veteran alcoholic a long time to get where he is. While he might change instantaneously, in all probability that is not going to happen. It will take a while for him to be completely rid of his compulsive need to drink. Jesus is patient with all of us, so why can't we be patient with an overt alcoholic?

Now, let us consider a husband, wife, and children. Mom is trying really hard to fulfill all the requirements necessary to help her family get back on its feet. Dad, however, seems completely unaware that he also needs to play a major role in the process. In fact, it even seems he is trying to sabotage his family's success. He yells at the children and occasionally is abusive to his wife. As a result, you ask him to leave, but following the tragic pattern of an abused spouse, Mom lets him back in through the window that night.

What do you do? Do you ask everyone to leave and thus put a couple of innocent children on the street? If you allow the family to stay, are you encouraging Dad in his abuse? It is a hard situation without any easy answers.

Let me tell you what we do at Joy Junction. If Mom wants Dad to return, we would consider that request. We would need a written agreement from the husband, outlining what he is to do on his return. He will need to work at the shelter in some volunteer capacity, and he will be told that any drinking on his part, or any abusive behavior toward his wife, will result in his leaving for good. He will also have to agree to receive counseling on how to communicate more effectively with his wife and children. He may also be asked to see our staff chaplain or assigned a mentor to help him, a kind of accountability partner he can meet with on a regular basis and whenever he feels tempted to drink.

Above all, on the question of asking someone to leave the shelter, make your decision prayerfully and fairly based on what you believe is

Jeremy Reynalds, Ph.D.

an appropriate and just response to their situation. Obviously, you must have a no-alcohol policy, and that policy and all other policies should be enforced. The point I am trying to make here is that the policies must be open enough to allow people to be treated as individuals.

Remember, policies are established to facilitate healing and wholeness, so rely on intuition, common sense, and, most important, the leading of the Holy Spirit when establishing and enforcing rules.

THE HOMELESS SPEAK

Homeless families are the fastest-growing segment of the homeless population. Sadly, shelters that meet the needs of homeless families are not keeping up with the ever-increasing need for their services.

There is no typical homeless family, because all families are made up of different individuals. During my almost quarter century of running Joy Junction, however, I have seen a number of characteristics common to many homeless families. What follows is a composite picture of a typical homeless family. That means the "Wilson" family does not exist. I have taken many of the most common features I have found in homeless families and woven them into the Wilsons.

A Common Scenario

Let's visit the home of the Wilson family—Robert, Cindy, and their three children. Matthew is seven, Rebecca is five, and JoAnn is two months. The Wilsons live in Southfield, Michigan, and they have no idea that they will soon be living in Albuquerque, New Mexico. In fact, if you asked them where Albuquerque was, they would probably guess it was in Mexico.

It had been a worrisome day for Cindy. Only three months before, the plant cut Robert back to twenty-five hours a week, and there were rumors he might be laid off, along with one hundred others. Twenty-five-hour paychecks had quickly wreaked havoc with the family budget, so much so that, although it was only 11:00 AM on this particular day, three calls from creditors had already come in, each asking when they could expect payment on long-overdue accounts. Cindy began experiencing that panicky feeling; she was getting overwhelmed. She had no idea what they were going to do.

The door opened, and footsteps along the hallway interrupted her thoughts.

"Robert! What are you—"

"Honey, I've been laid off."

"Oh no, what are we going to do?"

"I'll file for unemployment and look for another job. I know we'll make it. We've got to. We've got each other."

The next three months flew by. While the unemployment checks kept the wolf away from the door, that was about all they were doing. There were no frills in the Wilson household, just barely enough to pay the rent and the utilities. Robert and Cindy had always paid their bills promptly and had once enjoyed good credit. But that was no more. The creditors continued calling, and the pressures continued mounting. The once free-and-easy relationship between Robert and Cindy became tense and bitter. Cindy began blaming Robert for the family's financial problems.

One day, Robert was overcome by deep depression. Slumping into his favorite easy chair, drinking a beer and other stronger beverages, he turned on the television. The phone rang, and Cindy answered.

"Robert or Cindy Wilson, please. This is Bill from the NCI Mortgage Company."

"This is Cindy."

"Cindy, we know you're going through a hard time, but we are a bank and not a welfare agency. Unless you can come up with two of your three outstanding mortgage payments, we'll be forced to foreclose in thirty days. I'm sorry."

Cindy hung up the phone in a daze and rushed back into the living room, where Robert was still sprawled before the television. She spewed out a flood of words she really didn't mean.

"Robert, how can you sit there, slugging down beers this early in the morning, when we're about to become homeless? If you really loved me and the kids, you would be out there looking for work. Why haven't you found a job yet?"

The torrent of words continued. Robert got up slowly, scowled at Cindy, and left the house, slamming the door behind him. He walked angrily down the street, resenting Cindy's words all the way. Why didn't she understand that despite every one of his attempts to find a job, the work he needed to provide for the family just wasn't there? Since the crash, the economy stank. Sure, he could possibly get a job at a convenience store, but it would pay less than a third of what he had been making at the plant. Why bother? A dark depression began to envelop him. A few minutes later, Robert walked into a local bar and began spending money he didn't have and should not have spent.

Cindy ran to her bedroom, flung herself down on her bed, held the pillow for comfort, and wept bitterly. What had she said?

The hours dragged by with no sign of Robert's return. At dinner, Rebecca innocently said, "Mommy, where's Daddy? I heard you yelling at him."

"Sweetheart," Cindy's could feel her emotions begin to rise, and she struggled to control herself, "he'll be back soon." With each word, Cindy lost more of her emotions, and her voice rose higher and higher. Rebecca burst into tears and was quickly joined by her brother and sister. Cindy ran to her bedroom, grabbing Joann on the way and leaving the other two bewildered and scared children in the living room.

At 1:00 AM Cindy woke to a crying baby. She comforted JoAnn as best as she could and ran to check on the other children. They were huddled on the couch with tear-stained faces—fast asleep. Cindy gently placed her children in bed and returned to an uneasy sleep. She was awakened two hours later by a sheepish Robert, crawling into bed. She reached for him and managed to say between sobs, "Honey, I'm so sorry." They fell asleep in each other's arms, weeping in the midst of a situation over which they had no control.

Robert and Cindy woke early after a restless night. They prepared breakfast and sent Matthew to school. Rebecca was still sleeping, and JoAnn was gurgling happily. There was time to talk, drink coffee, and get a head start on the day.

Robert spoke first. "Honey, this just isn't working. I've tried, you know I've tried." He started weeping, and Cindy put her arm around him for comfort.

"We could ask my mom and dad," Cindy said.

"No way!" Robert broke in. "They were always against us getting married anyway, and they'd love for us to break up. Anyway, they live in public housing and can't have anyone stay with them for more than a few days." Robert suddenly had an idea. "Honey, a few weeks ago, when I was out with the guys, we were just shooting the breeze, and they said there's welding work in Albuquerque, New Mexico. We could—"

"I'm not going to Mexico," Cindy said.

"No, silly," Robert said. "New Mexico, not Mexico. New Mexico's in the United States, stuck between Arizona and Texas. Let's check into it."

The next few days brought a continued barrage of calls from creditors. Robert and Cindy did not even bother answering the phone anymore. What was the point? There was no money to pay the bills. And then a few days later, they did not have to think about the telephone anymore. It was turned off.

One evening, a friend of Robert's came to visit. The conversation quickly shifted to money, or the lack of it.

"Rob, I know there's work in Albuquerque. Welders are getting paid $25 an hour. The housing's cheap, and there's plenty of it. Why don't you guys just pack up and go? What've you got to lose?"

A determined look came over Robert's face. "Man, I can't stand this anymore. Cindy, let's do it."

Cindy suddenly recalled something that filled her with more hope than she had experienced in the last few months. "Honey, one of the girls I graduated with from high school moved to Albuquerque. I haven't heard from her in years, but she lives somewhere close to downtown there. I know we could stay with her."

Over the next few days, the Wilsons sold most of their belongings, packed the rest in the dilapidated family station wagon, and set out for Albuquerque. They left Southfield with $350 in their pockets.

About an hour after they started, the radiator began to boil. A few miles later, there was a loud pop, and the car sputtered to a noisy halt.

Robert got out of the car and groaned. There were two flat tires, the radiator was still boiling, and the tailpipe had fallen off. He gave Cindy the bad news.

"I'd better hitch to the nearest gas station," Robert said wearily. "We didn't allow money for car repairs, though."

Five-and-a-half hours and a tow truck later, the Wilson's were on their way again, $250 poorer. Robert said glumly, "There's no way we'll make it to Albuquerque on the money we have left. But let's fill up the tank, get as far as we can, stop at the cheapest motel we can find, and think."

By nightfall, they had covered another two hundred miles, including a brief stop for bologna, mayonnaise, and bread. After checking into a motel, they talked.

Robert said, "Honey, we'll have to stop along the way. I'll work, and we can stay in the missions."

"Missions!" Cindy said, half-frightened and half-angry. "No way! We're not staying in any missions."

"Honey, we might have to, just for a little while, until we can get a few dollars together," said Robert.

The conversation continued on how the family could best make their way to Albuquerque.

The following morning, after more bologna sandwiches, the Wilson family was on the road again, with $32 and a full tank of gas. Nothing was resolved in the motel room discussion, because nothing could be agreed on. The family expedition lasted three weeks, and there were several arguments on the way. Robert and Cindy said many hurtful things to each other in the heat of the moment, and the scars from those hastily spoken words would take many years to heal.

During their trip, minor needs turned into major nightmares. There was no money to buy diapers, and the car's air conditioner broke. Finally, Robert and Cindy saw the signs on the highway they had been waiting for: "Welcome to Albuquerque." They hugged and wept for joy. At last! Their long ordeal, they believed, was over.

"Let's go to 12th Street, Northwest, "Cindy said excitedly, "and we'll find Mary. I know where she lives. Look, I've got the last letter she wrote me, and it says the address right here: 1415 12th Street, Northwest."

The family made their way to the address with much anticipation, but there was no house or apartment, just a parking lot. After asking around, they found no one who even knew who Mary was. After tears of bitter disappointment and a few inquiries into the Albuquerque job market, Robert was convinced there were no welding jobs currently available. The entire family piled their way back into the car and cried. The Wilsons just sat there, too tired and drained to do anything other than cry—and wait.

Seven hours later, a police officer asked them if he could help. Hearing their story, he said, "There's only one shelter that will take you at this time of night and let you all stay together, and that's Joy Junction." An hour later, Robert, Cindy, and the children arrived at Joy Junction.

Because of the shelter's structure, Joy Junction is able to help many families like the Wilsons by providing them shelter and keeping their entire family together during such a crisis. Unfortunately, shelters like Joy Junction are still very few and far between. Can you imagine how families like the Wilsons would feel if they had to be split up? What would it do to them? It would separate them when they needed each other's support the most.

I hope you are beginning to understand how important family shelters are and how we, as Christians, are biblically obligated to provide more shelters like this one. I reiterate that what you have just read is a composite of a homeless family. While the Wilsons are a fictional family, I drew from characteristics I have noticed in homeless families over a number of years.

The following are actual case histories. Some time ago, I distributed, in a random, unscientific manner, a questionnaire to the residents staying at Joy Junction. The questions asked for name (optional), family size, highest educational grade reached or any college training received, home state, what work the respondent had been trained to do, and what work they were currently doing.

I then requested details about how they became homeless, why friends and relatives were unable to help them, how they felt about being homeless, how they ended up in Albuquerque, whether they planned on staying, and what they would feel like if their family had to be separated in order to stay in a shelter.

Here are some of their responses. I have changed only their names to protect their privacy.

Jane

Jane obtained her GED in prison and has also completed two years of trade school. Her home state is New Mexico. Jane is qualified to do commercial driving, computer data entry, computer analysis, and other skilled jobs. Jane has been doing all sorts of temporary work but mostly cleaning and general unskilled labor. How did she become homeless?

"At a certain point in my life, I had some trouble with the law over worthless checks. It was an election year, so I was convicted quickly and subjected to the full penalty of the law: forty-two months in the New Mexico Corrections Department.

"During this period of time, I finished high school and entered college. I had high hopes for reintegration into society. Upon leaving prison, I found it difficult (impossible) to find work, because I had to disclose my parole status. I checked out schools and found that I could not use any credits from prison as a base to continue my education. I had to begin over again at an accredited school.

"I finished my training and also my parole. I was still unable to pass checks by prospective employers because of my conviction. I did menial jobs when I could find them. I was promptly fired in most cases if any hint of my criminal record came to light.

"Pretty soon, I could not pay rent anymore. I lived in my car till it was vandalized to the extent that it no longer provided shelter."

Jane continued to tell why her relatives were no longer able to help her.

"When a person has been convicted of a crime, by the time they leave the Department of Corrections, they no longer have supportive families and their 'friends' are often not friends but often other ex-cons worse off than themselves."

Jane described what she feels like being homeless.

"It feels somewhat humiliating, because there are a lot of general misconceptions about homeless people, i.e., that none of them want to work. That they are lazy, and thieves, etc.

"There is a stigma attached to the term 'homeless,' and people do not realize that any kind of disaster could render them in the same position, regardless of careful planning. It is degrading to make people discover this about you, because it alters their opinion [of you] the moment they become aware of the fact."

Many people think that most or all homeless people are transients, who aimlessly float across the country. Jane was born in Mountainair, New Mexico. She talked about a common shelter practice—separating families.

"I am currently not living with my husband, because he is in the Corrections Department, but if we were together, we would prefer living in our car to being separated. To me, homelessness is a temporary living condition that is hard to overcome because of financial setbacks and job search problems. I would not stay in a women's shelter while my husband was forced to stay in the streets, car, or another shelter. I would stay with him until it is possible to rent for ourselves again, regardless of the circumstances."

Jane had an interesting perspective on the need for more family shelters to be built around the United States. "I think there should be more shelters built, but I also feel, because of the immense concern over homelessness, that it is important to make the public, and especially the church congregations, aware that their interaction and help (not financial, necessarily) in counseling, fellowship, and job opportunities is vital to the successful rise of a family from the despair, isolation, hopelessness, and depression of homelessness."

Steve and Maria

Steve and Maria had one child on the way: Maria was seven months pregnant. Steve said he had an associate's degree in English, and, "My wife has a sixth-grade reading level but supposedly graduated high school." Steve's home state was California, and Maria's was New Mexico. Steve said he was trained in sales, cooking, cashiering, a little computer programming, data processing, and typing. Lately, he had been doing a little cooking and cashiering.

In his own words, Steve told how he became homeless: "We tried to make it in California, but I was unable to find a job. The money she [Maria] got from welfare for her pregnancy wasn't enough to live on, so we lost our place."

Steve said that while relatives did what they could, it still was not enough. "Most of my friends were unable to help, because their homes were full or their parents wouldn't allow them to." He painted a graphic picture of the horrors of homelessness. "It's really terrible. I do not know how I am going to take care of my wife and my soon-to-be-born child. I do not know from one day to the next if we are going to have a place to stay or food to eat. I feel absolutely helpless and worthless, because I can't provide for my family."

Steve said if things work out in Albuquerque, "We'll be staying for a while." Asked how he would feel if his family had to be separated to stay in a shelter, Steve responded, "I wouldn't like that at all. My wife has a history of medical problems, and I would be afraid that something would happen. I would sooner sleep on the streets, where I could keep an eye on her, than stay in a shelter, separated, where I couldn't."

Steve stressed the importance of more family shelters being built around the United States: "The number of homeless families is growing, but there is nowhere for them to go. In my hometown in California, there are no shelters for families and few for men and women, other than the battered women's shelter."

Tracy

As I collected case histories and did my questionnaire, every person I asked said they would not stay in a shelter if they had to be separated from their family. Minnesota-born Tracy was no exception. She said it would be too lonely to be separated from her family, and she just would not do it. "I'd sleep when I could and travel when I had to [if she had to be separated], but no shelter."

Tracy had two years of college and was trained in technical-electric assembly. She was receiving Social Security disability and said she became homeless through a drop in her income. Illness caused her to quit working and start receiving Social Security.

"Through Social Security," Tracy said, "my income dropped to half of what I was bringing in per month. I had to move, to compensate for the lack of money, to an apartment which was a lot smaller and cheaper than what I was living in." Tracy still was not making it, so she came to Albuquerque, because friends told her there was cheaper housing and an overall lower cost of living than in Minnesota. "So I saved my money and drove here in two days.

"Homelessness is very depressing. I miss my home and things around me. Just to brush my teeth seems a chore, because I have to dig through everything to get my toothbrush. Then, if there is room at the sink even to get it done. I get angry very easily over little things, because I cannot even have a minute to myself. Everyone needs a little space to call their own."

Tracy said that while she had relatives, they could not help her, because they were on limited incomes. "They're retired, but maintain their homes, as they're paid for. They can't afford to have one more person to feed." She said it would be a blessing for everyone if there were more family shelters around the United States.

David and Karen

David and Karen moved from Big Springs, Texas, to Albuquerque, for entirely different reasons—their eldest daughter's health. David was a high-school graduate, but Karen left school in the tenth grade. They had two daughters. David's home state was Texas, and Karen was a native New Mexican. David said he was willing to do "anything possible" in the construction field.

There were simple reasons for moving to Albuquerque, About his daughter, David said, "We can get more help for her here. She's handicapped with epilepsy, and Texas was overmedicating her." David and Karen said relatives could not help them out in their plight, and they did not have any friends in Albuquerque.

"Homelessness is depressing," David said. "No privacy, but thankfully we have a roof over our heads, meals for my kids, and a place to sleep." Asked if he would separate from his family in order to have a place to stay, David said he would not. "My girls need both of us, and we need them." They agreed that there was a need for more family shelters around the country, "because there are a lot of families that need the help and shelter."

Sam and Deborah

Sam and Deborah did not have any children, and they both graduated from high school. Sam was a truck driver, and Deborah worked in factories and kitchens, but both had been unemployed for a year. They said they became homeless through divorce.

Sam said that neither friends nor relatives were able to help them because, "Neither one of us gets along with our families very well, and most of our friends couldn't help." The couple said it was hard being homeless, but there had been some very nice people who had helped them along the way.

Deborah said that Sam's former employment resulted in their coming to Albuquerque. "Sam used to drive a truck through Albuquerque, and he liked the town, so we decided to move here. Yes, we are planning to stay." Sam and Deborah said they felt it was important that there be more family shelters built around the United States, as many states don't have shelters where the whole family can stay together.

David and Jean

David and Jean were also residents at Joy Junction. David had a ninth-grade education, and Jean was a high school graduate. They are from Texas and have no children. David said he had trained to do landscaping, sprinkler-systems repair, construction, paint and bodywork, and plastering.

Jean recounted how they became homeless: "My husband lost his job in El Paso, because the company went out of business. We lost our apartment through lack of money." She said they stayed with friends for a couple of days, until they made enough money to buy bus tickets to Albuquerque.

"We got in Tuesday and went to the Albuquerque Rescue Mission, and they told us about Joy Junction. We called, and they came and picked us up. The people here are very nice and also very polite and understanding and caring." Jean explained why they could not get any more help than they did from friends. "I didn't want to stay there, because they were into drugs." Their family in El Paso could not help them, because they were already supporting other children.

The couple came to Albuquerque "to stay and get a good job and start a new life here." Jean said, "It's scary and horrible to be homeless, because living out in the streets you could … trust no one out there. People are getting mugged in front of the El Paso Rescue Mission and the Salvation Army. We are very thankful for Joy Junction having us here."

Jean believed there were more job opportunities in Albuquerque than in El Paso, and the couple planned on staying here. "It will take time, but with God's help, we are going to get back on our feet again," they said. She said she believed it was very important that more family shelters be built in the United States to give homeless families with children a safe place to stay.

Ordinary People in Need

Homeless people are not "bums." They are people just like you and me who need a break or a second chance. Have you noticed also that most of those who stay at Joy Junction say they would not stay in a shelter if they had to separate from their loved ones? The sad fact is that there are so few shelters in the country, and in Albuquerque, there is only Joy Junction that makes it possible for an entire homeless family to be provided for physically, spiritually, and emotionally. We have received calls from families in other states who want to come to New Mexico, because they have heard about a family shelter called "Joy Junction," and they would like to stay with us.

There is an untapped mission field out there of homeless, hungry, hurting, and desperate families, waiting for someone to show them the love of Jesus Christ in a tangible way. There are so many homeless families and so few shelters that meet the need.

I assume that the fact you are reading this book and have gotten to this point shows you have a concern and a heart for the homeless and other people in need. Is God continuing to work on your heart even now? As you continue through this book, be very careful. It might result in making a life-changing career decision!

More Homeless Speak

Sara

Sara never planned on a life of drinking. Who does? But it happened to her nonetheless. She told me that in her younger years, she would notice a bedraggled homeless woman and flinch. "We callously called her a 'bag lady' back then," Sara said. "I was appalled at how one could allow oneself to get that way. I pitied her."

Other images bought similar feelings to mind. Like when Sara would see a drunk man stumbling along or lying in a doorway, or a drunk woman carousing in a bar.

But Sara drifted into a life of drinking and drugs very similar to the ones she had not so long ago pitied. She said she cannot really pinpoint a definitive experience that led to her decades of drinking. However, "I'd often find myself drinking and cogitating about all the poor decisions I'd made in the past that were affecting me now, and instead of changing my ways, I became more morose about it as I drank."

Sara recalled some still vivid instances of those alcohol-ridden years. She would wake up in the hospital emergency room with no idea why or how she got there. She would be dragged into a police station in shackles or just fall down drunk at parties. Many times, she would have no idea how long a particular blackout had lasted. Most distressing was what this lifestyle did to her family, Sara said. She would break promises to her daughter or tell her to go across the street to play in the park while she drank in the bar. She even walked away from two long-term relationships, because she knew that to continue them meant getting help for her alcoholism and drug abuse.

Here is a description of what Sara's life was like in the 1960s in southern California, when she was in her teens and twenties: "You couldn't imagine the availability of recreational drugs that were in plentiful supply during the hippie era. LSD wasn't even illegal yet when I started taking it. Pot, acid, mushrooms, and peyote were there for the asking, with the groovy people I hung with to turn on and drop out. Psychedelics were cool. Acid was my favorite. I didn't feel rebellious really, just liberated mentally and artistically."

Sara used drugs for many years, even into her fifties, although alcohol, "became king of the party," as she put it. How did alcohol affect her? "It's an amazing accelerant for burning bridges, or stomping out after an argument to end up in a bar with the old, 'I'll show them,' attitude, or making bar acquaintances for the sole purpose of having rounds bought by others. I thought I was asserting control and being independent and doing what I pleased, regardless of the consequences. It was a way of life, such as it was, with the 'they'll get over it when I sober up attitude.'"

But this description barely scratched the surface of her alcohol-infused life. She went through alcoholic treatment programs four times, usually at the request of others who wanted her to get help. She said, "I knew in my heart and soul that I needed to do something, though I was averse to admitting there was a problem I couldn't handle myself. Getting sober for others was short lived at best, a year here, six months there. With varying lengths of sobriety under my belt, so to speak, I would invariably go retrograde and find myself drinking, drunk, and dazed in short order again and again."

Sara always balked at step two of the Alcoholics Anonymous creed, which is to ask for help from a higher power. "Greater Power? Sure. Sanity? Elusive. I attempted to find the strength in myself to carry on my sobriety. Ha! Obstinate and independent minded, I struggled for years, though I knew in my heart of hearts that there had to be a God. Seeing the mountains, the ocean, and the sky all around us, who could deny the divine maker of the universe? As perverse and insidious as alcohol's grip was on me, my spirituality was always there within. But I had shoved it to the wayside, the proverbial back burner, for the pursuit of the ultimate party!"

As a result, Sara said, God's grace allowed her to flounder, because she was too proud to ask for help. Of course, pride comes before a fall, and even though she was lost, she did not realize how far she had fallen. Among other things, she had lost her home, her jobs, her possessions, her self-respect, and the trust of her loved ones.

Her daughter told her, "Mom, when are you going to get help? I'll help you; I'll take you to treatment—anything! Can't you stop? I don't want your grandkids growing up knowing Gramma only as a drunk! You've fallen down, stumbled, and slurred in front of them enough." Despite that desperate plea, Sara continued drinking for years more. She said, "My daughter's voice, when on yet another of her Mommy rescue missions, resounds in my ear: 'Mom, grow up, the party's over!'" All in all, Sara's drinking lasted forty years.

Finally, all of Sara's options were exhausted, and her daughter suggested she call Joy Junction. "Actually, she called for me, as I was sobering up that morning at her house. Thank God, it was her last rescue mission! That was a little over two years ago. Coming to Joy Junction, I thought I'd hang out a week or two. Alcohol had taken so much from me. I was grateful to have a place to lay my bleary head at night. I felt as though all my guardian angels were heaving great sighs of relief."

While at Joy Junction, Sara was reintroduced to the Bible. Many of the Scriptures she read reminded her of her mother and her home of so many years ago. Sara is now on staff at Joy Junction as part of our maintenance team, and we are so proud of her and everything the Lord has done in her life. Her daughter told her, "Mom, I'm so glad you're at Joy Junction now. I don't have to worry about you anymore."

Sara said, "I thank God for all that Joy Junction has helped me do through the love of God and community. I also praise God that I still have the wherewithal to be able to share this with you and that my daughter never gave up on me. Her love helped guide me when I was too blind to see the way myself."

We are so proud of Sara and all she has allowed the Lord to do in her life. She is an ongoing testimony to the goodness and power of God. Looking at her transformed life demonstrates what the Lord can do in our lives when we turn everything over to him.

Lilly

Lilly (not her real name) is a recent Joy Junction life recovery program graduate. She recalled vividly the embarrassment and humiliation she suffered in years past, when she had to use the bathroom. At one point, pregnant and suffering from a urinary tract infection, Lilly went into a restaurant and asked to use the bathroom. She was not allowed to do so. Lilly was in such dire straits she ended up relieving herself behind a Dumpster in the parking lot.

"It was degrading," Lilly said, "The people looked at me as if I was the scum of the earth. All I wanted to do was use the bathroom. It's not like they couldn't *see* I was pregnant, yet they still treated me like I was scum." She experienced disapproving looks and similar refusals at many other restaurants and businesses.

Lilly said, "It felt as if they were treating me less than human. I felt embarrassed."

The trauma Lilly experienced is multiplied countless times by countless numbers of the most needy among us. It is so important that this story be brought to the attention of as many people as possible. What can you do to help?

Sally, Sarah, and Synthia

Joy Junction operates a faith-based, multistage CIPP program that revolves around the changes necessary for our guests to get back on their feet. Graduating members of Joy Junction's homeless shelter's six-month life recovery program receive their certificates at a very special ceremony. While some smile, others are very nervous. They all work hard to complete their program, and they all deserve their special moment of recognition.

People come to Joy Junction for many reasons. For some residents, it is the difficult economy and the lack of ability to cope with life in our ever-increasingly stressful society. Others struggle with drugs, alcohol, poor money management, poor parenting skills, and mental health issues.

Three of our graduates told us a little bit about their lives and what being in the program meant to them. Pray for all of them and their continued success.

Sally (not her real name) was an abuse and rape victim. Before she came to Joy Junction, she lived with her cousin and tried to find a job. Unable to find employment, she was asked to leave her cousin's apartment and ended up at the shelter. Sally described how she felt on her arrival at

Joy Junction: "When I got here, I was nervous and scared, because I didn't know anyone, and I was alone."

Although she was alone, she felt safe, and she quickly realized she did not want to leave the security of Joy Junction and deal with the uncertainties and dangers lurking on downtown Albuquerque streets. It didn't take Sally long to realize that joining the CIPP would be the right decision for her.

Although the CIPP was sometimes difficult for Sally, and initially she felt that God wasn't there for her, she now feels much differently. Most important, she's gotten closer to the Lord as well as developed better life skills. She said she knows also that if she needs to talk, she can share her heart with our staff as well as directly with the Lord.

She said, "The program has taught me how to handle things better at a job. I also know that everyone here cares and loves me along with God, that I also have a roof over my head and food to eat. It has helped me to feel safe here."

Sally said she is so happy that she finished something she started without having to have someone "push" her through it. "Thank you, guys, for being there for me and helping me through my problems and the negative things I have gone through most of my life."

Sarah (not her real name) also told us her story. Mother to three beautiful children, she and her husband have been at Joy Junction for a little more than a year. Sarah came to Joy Junction because she had never had a real job. Her "employment" had been trafficking drugs. After serving her time, an extended stay with relatives didn't work out for the family, and they were eventually forced to leave.

This was not Sarah's first stay with us, for she recalls being here when she was nine years old, after her mother fled an abusive relationship. She lost her dad due to alcohol when she was eight and had lived on her own since she was fourteen years old. She admitted dabbling with drugs and alcohol even back then, but she said addiction was never a "real" problem.

She did say, though, that she has been "confused" about God for all of her life. When she lost her mother, she blamed God and asked why he would make her suffer. After joining the CIPP and graduating seven months later, Sarah now has a different perspective. She said not only did she learn about the Lord's love for her but, very important for her recovery and self-esteem, she was also able to finish something she started.

She added, "I know God brought me here to strengthen my relationship with my family and get to know him better. I am very grateful for Joy

Junction and what they have taught me. It is not just a homeless shelter; it is more like a family."

Sometimes it takes more than one attempt to successfully complete the CIPP. Synthia (not her real name) first came to Joy Junction with a meth and alcohol addiction. She had also endured and finally left an almost two-decade long abusive relationship.

Synthia completed about half the CIPP her first time around before she left. It wasn't easy for her expanding family. She got pregnant after leaving Joy Junction and, along with her daughter and boyfriend, moved from motel to motel for a while. Eventually, her boyfriend obtained employment, and the family was able to get an apartment, just before the birth of her son.

More problems lay ahead. During her pregnancy and subsequent birth of her son, Synthia was having serious kidney issues, while her boyfriend was having problems with his gallbladder. Synthia had five surgeries on her kidneys, and her boyfriend was also hospitalized. As a result, they ended up behind in their rent and lost the apartment. After this, they came back to Joy Junction and rejoined the program.

Synthia said, "I hadn't finished high school, and I've gone to college a couple of times but never finished anything that I have started. Finally, I finished something—the CIPP. Being on the CIPP and successfully finishing it has brought up my self-esteem and makes me feel good to help people."

Synthia has also been clean from her meth addiction for a couple of years, and that, she said, makes her "feel good." As a CIPP graduate, she is continuing for the moment to serve those individuals in similar circumstances to those she was in not so long ago.

She said, "To give back to the community of the homeless is a great honor, and it makes me appreciate everything Joy Junction has taught me and done for me."

With the Lord's help and the support of his people, Sally, Sarah, and Synthia will continue to succeed. To those who prayerfully and financially support Joy Junction, thank you. Without you, these stories wouldn't be possible.

Samantha and Jack

Samantha (not her real name) was married to a man who abused her. I am glad she left her abuser, because if she had stayed, she might not be alive today. I learned the misery that characterized her first marriage started with emotional and mental abuse.

"He told me I was useless," Samantha said. "I was always being corrected and reprimanded; nothing was ever good enough. Then it turned physical. Being slapped and hit by a man three times my size was more than I could take. The police were no help. When I got the courage to leave, he became completely obsessed and possessive."

After Samantha married Jack (not his real name), her abusive ex-husband tracked her down. "He made our lives a living hell," she said. The couple decided to relocate from the South and move to the West Coast to live in a state where there were more job opportunities. But unexpected events led them to Joy Junction in Albuquerque. Even though this wasn't where they expected to be, Samantha says, "It's a true comfort and a blessing for both of us to be here at Joy Junction, knowing that we are safe and our identity is protected."

Jack took up the story. He said the couple left their former state with, "all our cherished possessions." They sold their furniture and electronics to finance the impending journey. The trip was pretty uneventful until they arrived at a truck stop just west of Amarillo, Texas.

Jack said, "We had spent the night in our van and had been in and out of the truck stop's store a number of times. We ran in once more, just before we were going to leave, and we came out to find our van gone—along with Samantha's purse, which contained all our money, IDs, and debit cards, not to mention all our possessions—pictures, kids' yearbooks, and precious keepsakes from both our families."

Samantha added, "Like a dummy, I had put the keys on the floorboard. Someone must have been watching, because we were only inside for a couple of minutes."

Fortunately, much-needed help was on the way. A Christian family heard about the couple's predicament and offered them a place to stay in their barn, as well as food, in exchange for helping out at their alpaca ranch. The same family, Jack said, also rescued animals from all over the southwest. Jack said they felt so blessed by the kindness of strangers, "yet not surprised at how the Holy Spirit moves."

The family also provided Jack and Samantha clothing, luggage, and personal hygiene items. They stayed with this family for just over two weeks. While they went on a business trip, they were able to drop Jack and Samantha at Joy Junction.

Jack and Samantha said, "The love and acceptance we have found here has been a true blessing from God. As we pray and lift up our need for bus tickets [out West], we know in our hearts that God will provide. [He will help us] both with our immediate needs of shelter and food and also for our transportation needs."

In the meantime, Jack and Samantha have joined Joy Junction's CIPP. Like many others, life has dealt them some hard blows, but they are not buckling under. They feel that what the CIPP has to offer will help strengthen their relationship with the Lord and give them a new beginning, a beginning that will benefit them for many years to come. As Jack said, "If it had not been for the love and assistance of Joy Junction, we do not know what, or where, we'd be."

Without friends who prayerfully and financially support the ongoing ministry of Joy Junction, there would have been no refuge for Jack and Samantha to come and feel the peace and love of the Lord Jesus Christ. Nor would there have been a place to stay and nourishing meals to eat. I continue to be amazed by God's grace and the miraculous transformations and life healings we see at Joy Junction on a daily basis.

Seth

Seth didn't stay at Joy Junction the night I met him. Judging from his condition, I have a suspicion that he probably stayed outside or in an abandoned building somewhere. But I believe he went to bed on a full stomach.

When my friend David and I met Seth, it was on the corner of First and Central, in downtown Albuquerque. We went downtown to get a cup of coffee and a bite to eat after the Saturday evening service at Joy Junction. We had a great time of fellowship and some good food, and were within a few feet of my car when Seth, wobbling along on a cane, entered our lives.

He seemed to recognize me immediately. Slurring his words he said, "You're Jeremy from Joy Junction, right?" I acknowledged I was, and Seth, who was visibly drunk and with the stench of alcohol assaulting me as he spoke, said something to the effect of, "You want to give me some money so I can buy food?"

I let Seth know that we didn't give money, but we would be happy to buy him a meal if he wanted. All I could see across the street was a sushi restaurant (which Seth declined), but then my friend remembered we had just passed a restaurant that sold pizza. David asked him if he wanted pizza, and Seth said no. He did, however, want something to drink. We walked across the busy street, watching Seth carefully to make sure he didn't get run down, and entered the sushi restaurant, where David bought Seth some cold water.

After David handed our new friend the bottle of water, Seth looked around as if considering his options. This time he said he was hungry, and he would like something to eat. The idea of pizza seemed more appealing to him now. We walked the few hundred feet to the pizza restaurant. Seth did not want to sit down inside, and since we were not sure if he would wander off, David stayed outside and talked with him while I went inside to order a couple of slices of pepperoni and cheese pizza.

I came outside the restaurant and saw that Seth was looking carefully at David's college ring, which he had taken off at Seth's request for him to see up close. I tried to engage Seth in some limited conversation, but even that was too much for him to cope with that night, struggling as he was in his addled alcoholic stupor.

I wasn't really sure what we were supposed to do next, but I knew the Lord had this precious man encounter David and I (out of everyone else he could have run into) for a reason. With that in mind, it seemed it would be a good idea to pray. David placed his hand gently on Seth's shoulder. Even that soft but apparently unexpected touch startled Seth enough to make him jump, as if it he had been shocked by a high-voltage electric current. He got up from his chair (with difficulty) as if he was about to leave.

David persuaded him to sit down again, and we prayed a simple prayer of faith for Seth, asking the Lord's blessing and protection for him. After that, we looked directly at him and said we had to go but to stay right where he was until his pizza arrived. He didn't promise, but neither did he move. I was prayerfully optimistic!

I don't know what more we could have done for Seth. The rescue missions downtown were full, and there was no more "room at the inn" at Joy Junction, either. The county jail has not offered "protective custody" for many years. Seth was out of options.

It would have been easy to dismiss Seth as just a drunk, a bum, or a vagrant. The Seths of this world make many people nervous. They are also an embarrassment to some in city government, because they are a visible reminder of a side of our city some want to keep hidden.

Many of us would say, "He needs to get a job and get his act together." Such an attitude enables us to erect a wall of self-righteousness and justify our unwillingness to help. But before judging Seth and writing him off (and hundreds of thousands like him), we should ask what experience he suffered that may have played a major role in him looking to alcohol for solace and comfort. Was he abused, emotionally devastated, raped, abandoned, or made to suffer any one of myriad similar horrors?

Or was Seth someone suffering from mental illness? Perhaps he got lost to the system and could not afford the medication that could calm his troubled mind. Because of a lack of resources, many are reduced to spending their days shuffling along city streets and enduring embarrassed, nervous looks, a few snickers, and the continuous barking of orders to, "Move on."

I hope and pray the Lord brought peace to calm Seth's troubled soul. Whatever we think of the Seths we encounter, they are very precious in God's eyes, and they are people for whom the Lord Jesus Christ shed his blood and died upon the cross of Calvary.

Linda and Jimmy

This is not a story with a happy ending, at least yet. In fact, this tale is still unfolding. But it is one, nonetheless, that needs telling, because it is happening in our city and in cities all over America.

Sitting on the curb by a shopping cart overflowing with belongings, they were hard to miss. I met the engaging, but physically and emotionally worn, Linda and Jimmy on Sunday while at Bullhead Park, located behind the Veterans Hospital in Albuquerque. We were there as part of Joy Junction's new Lifeline of Hope meal outreach.

After we gave them sack lunches (which they ate ravenously), sodas, and blankets, I asked them if they would tell me some of their story. They graciously agreed to a brief interview. I learned that Linda and Jimmy are close friends and provide much-needed support and encouragement to each other. They said they have lived for years on and off at Bullhead Park. I asked Linda to tell me how she feels living there.

"It's not fun," she said, coughing. Linda said while she has been asked to leave by the police on a few occasions, they are, on the whole, pretty kind to her. They even ask her if she and Jimmy are doing okay. That is, as okay as you can be living in a park.

Jimmy told me he has lived at Bullhead Park for five years. Before that, he used to work at a local apartment complex as a groundskeeper. I asked him what happened, and he admitted he likes to drink. He quit his job and went to California and then Texas; he wound up back in Albuquerque. He said he doesn't go to a homeless shelter because it's "too far."

Linda ended up living at Bullhead Park because when she had an apartment and got a disability check, "I had a lot of friends over ... and I got thrown out, and now I'm having a hard time getting another place to live."

When the weather gets down to bone-chilling freezing, Linda says, "We just ... brrr." Jimmy said, "We've got plenty of blankets, but it still gets cold." As he spoke, the thought of my comfortable, thermostat-controlled house on the other side of town flashed in my mind. How grateful I was for the security it offers me on very cold nights.

Linda added, "You just wrap up and do the best you can."

Jimmy said, "Body heat, you know."

I asked Linda and Jimmy what hope they see for the months and years ahead. Linda said, "I'm hoping I can do a little bit better. I get a monthly check, but it ain't enough, and I got kicked out of my apartment, because I was letting all of my homeless friends come over and stay with me. I got kicked out not for nonpayment, because I paid my rent until the third, because I do get a monthly check."

I told Linda it almost sounded as if she was trying to run her own homeless agency. Laughing, she turned to Jimmy and said, "I had a lot of people living there, didn't I? About five people one night."

I asked Linda what she would say to individuals who routinely tell me that people like her want to be homeless. She said, "I think they need to come out here and be homeless for a while. Like I said, I get a little monthly check, but it ain't enough to really go around. The people who say we want to be homeless are crazy. Because it's cold outside."

Jimmy picks up cans to make a living. He said, "I do all right with cans, and people give me money, food, you know ... they help me out. I got my life pretty good, you know." I asked Jimmy whether he would continue to live in Bullhead Park or if he would really like to live in a house. He said he plans to live in an apartment once he gets his ID and Social Security card, which had been lost along with his wallet, but he can't do that right now.

To those who write off Linda and Jimmy as just a couple of bums who choose to live in the part, Linda says, "Just because we're homeless, we're not bums." Jimmy would tell them, "Why not spend a whole week here, just one week, and then you can call me a bum." Linda added, "Try it for one day. Go out picking up cans all day." She said it was not fun.

Linda said, "I'm working on it. I'm gonna get back on my feet. It might take me another month. Thank you all for the sandwich. We were hungry. We were just thinking about what we were going to eat. Thank God, we were so hungry."

Jimmy added, "Yeah, and here you guys come on over."

Linda's and Jimmy's plight touched me deeply. At one point some years ago, I would have quickly dismissed their circumstances as being the result of a series of poor choices. I can no longer do that, but how easy it is to feel justified with such a quick dismissal.

Many would judge Jimmy and Linda while neglecting to find out their story and starting to form a relationship with them. Befriending them without judgment, and getting beyond their external circumstances and appearance, could play a major part in helping them permanently get back on their feet. After all, isn't that what Jesus would do?

Conway

Stepping outside into the early, cold, pre-dawn hours of Thanksgiving Day, I prepared to head over to Joy Junction. I was thinking about Conway, an Albuquerque resident whose home has been a local park for a couple of years. He told me living in a park is sometimes scary.

"You don't know who's going to come up behind you," he told me. "You don't know who's going to come up on top of you, you don't know if the cops are going to come get you, you don't know if someone's going to stab you or beat you, and you don't know what's going to happen. So, a lot of times you have to sedate yourself. You drink to deal with anything that's going to happen."

Conway said it would be tough getting back on his feet again. "You get labeled and then sometimes you get associated with other people. The police officers see you as a bad guy, but you're not the bad guy. You try to take care of yourself, and you try to do what you can to move on, but sometimes it's not that easy."

Without wanting to pry, I asked Conway if he would feel comfortable telling me what caused his home to be a park. He alluded to "something tragic," and added, "You never thought it would happen to you, and it did happen to you. I guess maybe I'm trying to escape the situation, trying to think, 'this couldn't have happened, 'cause this is not me.'"

It was obvious Conway's new life was a dramatic departure from the way he used to live. He said, "It's difficult when you experience a life of having everything you want and then going to have nothing of what you want. It's tough." Conway said that you end up building your own "family" when you live on the streets. And with those people, he said, "You're always going to be safe."

Conway said, "There's a lot of good people who, for whatever reason, end up out here. I think they can be fixed, but a lot of times it has to do with friendship." He said being regarded as a "bum" by some of the people he encounters hurts. "You get a little resentful and sometimes, depending on your lifestyle and what you've been through … I don't know, maybe it's easier not to even try and get back on your feet."

Conway is appreciative of ministries like Joy Junction and others that provide a place to stay, hot, nutritious meals, and an array of other services. But the recovery process is still hard. "You're trying to replace yourself with something different than your present situation, and it's more of a mental thing, so it's real tough sometimes." I offered Conway a place at Joy Junction, but he is not ready to take that step.

One thing is for sure: Conway's healing will be found in a relationship with the Lord Jesus Christ. There is a good chance the Lord could reach out supernaturally to Conway to heal that broken heart, and there is also a good chance God will choose to use one of his children to do so. If God chooses to use us, will we accept the assignment or pass by on the other side of the road?

Joy Junction volunteer coordinator Jonathan Matheny, once homeless himself (along with his wife and children), said, "Either way you look at it, homelessness is not something to fear, scorn, or disdain. It is an opportunity for healing, a chance to help and be more like Jesus by treating our fellow men appropriately. Do unto others …"

James

He didn't know it at the time, but he was about to find out the truth of the Scripture, "Your enemy the devil prowls around like a roaring lion looking for someone to devour" (1 Pet. 5:8). Sometimes the enemy uses those you may least expect, like your coworkers.

James (not his real name) and his family moved to Albuquerque from Reno, Nevada, for a new job in Rio Rancho. Wanting to fit in with his coworkers, James started using crack cocaine and became addicted. After a lot of anguish and turmoil caused by James's drug abuse, he quit his job. Soon, there was no more money. As a result, along with his wife,

Martha (not her real name), and their three children, James came to Joy Junction.

Hoping to permanently conquer what had become a life-controlling and family-threatening addiction, James joined Joy Junction's life recovery program, the CIPP. "My wife told me for a long time to get help, and I figured this was the place to get it. While on the CIPP, I learned more about God and myself than I ever could have on my own."

While James had been doing well, he was about to hit a serious bump in the road. "As I was getting better with my addiction and closer to God, I hit a 'self-destruction relapse' button." James relapsed twice, both times leaving Joy Junction property before succumbing to his old addiction. He said, "That caused me to almost lose my family twice."

When he used drugs, he had no idea what he was doing to his family. "My wife and I have three children. I would spend our money and then tell my kids 'no' about going to the store. I would always put them last, but they never put me last. For almost two years, I did this to my family. My wife would even try to hide money."

By God's grace, James worked through his issues. After we saw the progress he was making, we offered him a staff position at Joy Junction. James accepted, and he worked for us and lived on site for quite a while. When another, higher paying job offer came along, he felt it was time to move on.

Reflecting back on that time in his life, James said, "During my stay at Joy Junction, I received a lot of compassion and a desire to develop a closer relationship to God. The staff here taught me a better way to live with God in my life. After I learned to love my family again, I got a better job. I worked for my family, not for me. I put my notice in and went to work at a tire shop."

Excited about their future, James, Martha, and the kids never dreamed what trials lay ahead. James suffered a massive heart attack. He recalled asking the Lord for his help. After one-year of recuperation, he was able to return to work, but he ended up with a hernia and a nine-month recovery period. As a result, the family got behind on their rent and were evicted. That caused their return to Joy Junction.

Surprisingly, James isn't angry about all the ups and downs he's experienced in life. He said his current stay at Joy Junction has been the most rewarding ever for him and his family, and that is for a very specific reason: "Because we have more love for God, which reflects on to the other people staying here who want that same experience for themselves.

I praise Joy Junction for the reason they're here. Not for the symbol of homelessness, but the symbol of love and of hope of Jesus Christ for all who come here!"

It is such a joy to see James's and Martha's happy, smiling faces at our church services. It is thrilling to report that James has now been drug free for years, and he has never relapsed. I am also so appreciative that when James and Martha had no place to stay, they knew to call Joy Junction. When they are ready and able, we want to see them return to self-sufficiency. Meanwhile, we believe every day they live and serve the Lord while they stay at Joy Junction is a step in that direction.

Janey

Since she was a child, Janey (not her real name) had prayed for a baby boy. The Lord fulfilled the desire of Janey's heart. But about a month later, the baby's father left. Janey said he couldn't handle the attention being lavished on his new son, Taylor (not his real name). However, Dad did come by weekly and spent about a half hour with his son.

Those visits decreased and then stopped entirely. When Taylor was somewhere between three and four years old, his dad would tell him he would come and pick him up for the weekend. She said, "Taylor would get his overnight bag and sit on the curb and wait for his father, who would never show up. After a while, he would come in with tears and ask me why, and it would crush my heart." As that same scenario continued, Janey said, resentment and anger followed.

Janey recalled that when Taylor was four, she met a man who was a chef. They started dating, and both Janey and Taylor fell in love with him. Her son's affection, and the fact that the three of them went camping and fishing together, thrilled Janey. She was delighted that the man she had chosen to be in her life loved her son as his own.

There was a side to this man, however, that Janey didn't know. It didn't surface until they had both gotten a job at a local bar. At first "fun and exciting," Janey's life quickly became a nightmare. The man she thought loved her was drunk 24/7. Black eyes and "a busted head" became the norm for Janey.

One night, it was especially bad. "As we were walking, he turned around and pushed me in the chest, and I flew backward. I cracked my head wide open. I heard my son's blood-curdling scream and ran to him. I just couldn't imagine what he felt like, seeing my face and clothes drenched in blood. I just held him as he cried."

Janey left this man, but more trauma was on the horizon. Initially comforting, the trauma took the form of a male friend Janey had been supporting—until she caught him lying, cheating, and stealing. Although Janey told him to leave, he began stalking her, placing unwanted calls, and even going to her place of employment. Desperate, Janey moved. That wasn't enough, though, as he still found her. At that point, he started abusing Taylor emotionally and Janey physically.

Janey recalled a terrifying incident in the middle of the night, when he broke into her apartment. He wanted to use the phone. As she had to get up at 4:00 AM, Janey told him to hurry up. "He threw the phone at me, and it hit me in the temple. All I felt was warm fluid rushing down my face, and I heard my son running into the room. Fed up with me getting hit all the time, and abused verbally, emotionally, and physically, he started hitting, screaming, and crying."

On another occasion, this human nightmare again broke into her apartment. He said he wanted to talk to her. Janey said, "I wanted nothing to do with him. I was so afraid. He grabbed me by my hair, turned me to face him, and punched me in my right eye. To this day, I can't see really well out of it, as it is still a little blurry. My son and another friend spending the night ran into the room, and there it was again, my son angry and terrified."

Although law enforcement was called, nothing came of it. The nightmare continued. "A couple of weeks later, I woke up to pain and about three hundred pounds of pressure on top of me. He had taped plastic gloves on his hands and was ripping me up inside. I came to find out he had raped another woman shortly before. Needless to say, I didn't press charges."

While things settled down for a while, it was too little too late for her son, who, by this time, was a very angry middle-schooler, and who, unknown to his mother, had joined a gang. At this point, her little boy was no longer her little boy. He had so much anger and was so out of control they couldn't talk. Janey prayed that moving to a new house might help Taylor.

Although she still had her job at a fast-food restaurant, Janey said by this time she was a hard alcoholic. "The whiskey with my beer, come home and relax, and I didn't go anywhere without my son." As the months went on, Janey said she became close to a man who lived just across the street from her and Taylor. Initially, she said, David (not his real name) was gentle, kind, caring, and giving. Her son became good friends with him.

Eventually, David moved into their home. She remembered, "It was wonderful. The feeling in our home was very warm, and it felt blessed. The only thing that was uncomfortable was he was so jealous of everything and anything." Janey said she didn't know at first that David had a bad cocaine problem. When she found out and they talked about it, he told her he was doing an eight-ball a day.

"I went, 'Wow,'" Janey said. "I couldn't believe it. But it made sense. When he was drinking beer and snorting coke, he would become extremely jealous and intimidating." The situation escalated when Janey discovered they had about one hundred dollars less cash than she had estimated. She asked David what happened with the missing money. His answer was not what she expected. "He slapped me so hard my ear rang. I found myself lying back, with his hand around my throat. I could not breathe. For some reason, he stopped. I played it cool to be able to get out."

Janey walked down the stairs to her neighbor, who was cooking breakfast. "I wanted to tell her what was going on. But, of course, I knew he would come and see what was up." David did just that, and all Janey remembers about what happened next is a blur. When she came to, she was in her house, and the paramedics were stumbling around looking for a light switch.

She had received a terrible beating from the man she planned on marrying in six days. "I am pretty sure I was in total shock. To this day, I do not remember a thing, and my ear still hurts me badly."

After Janey's traumatic beating and emergency room trip, Taylor told her more of what had happened. It was Taylor who called the police. He told her that after the beating, David told him, "'You better go check on your mom. I think I might have killed her.'"

And in fact, it is amazing Janey is still alive. She attributes that to the grace of God. She said that following the incident, "My son found part of my skull in the kitchen, crime scene and all. No child should have to go through that at any age, and for so many years." Thankfully, David is no longer a problem to her or Taylor.

It was at this point that Janey and Taylor lost contact for a while. They were both on the streets, but not together. Janey was still drinking heavily, and Taylor, understandably angry, was struggling with a gang mentality. Janey would quite often come into Joy Junction on an overnight basis and leave the next morning.

She said, "Before my son and I came to Joy Junction together, I came alone, here and there. I couldn't find him, and he couldn't find me. It was a living nightmare. I would close my eyes and picture him shot or stabbed to death—24/7." Finally, they reestablished contact, and the two of them began coming into Joy Junction together. However, because Janey and Taylor were staying at that point at Joy Junction on a nightly basis, their beds were not guaranteed. On one particularly busy night for Joy Junction, they called in too late.

She said, poignantly, "We ended up behind a McDonald's Dumpster downtown. Most of the time, we were together on the streets, scared and hungry. We hustled to get what we needed." It is terrifying to think what could have happened to them. Janey and Taylor disappeared for a while, but resurfaced a few months later. Joy Junction volunteer coordinator Jonathan Matheny said, "When they came back, Taylor had added some pounds and was definitely more grown up. You could tell, though, that they had been living on the streets."

It wasn't long after this that Janey asked Jesus into her life. Janey said, "By God's will day by day we will get stronger. Taylor is my life, and with the Lord Jesus Christ, we now have a life." She is now one of the program members most of the others respect. Watching this transformation in both of them, and the resulting changes in the family unit, has been interesting and gratifying.

Thank God, he had his mighty hand of protection over Janey, both during and after her awful abuse. I believe the Lord will continue healing the emotional scars with which Janey and Taylor are still dealing. And thank God for allowing us to keep the Joy Junction doors open, so we can be there for the many other Janeys and Taylors who are out there on the streets of Albuquerque and need our help.

Elly

The journey to Joy Junction for Elly (not her real name) began fifty-nine years ago, with a grandfather who sexually abused all the girls in the family. As the song says, it was a long and winding road.

The abuse had profound effects on Elly as she grew up. When she went through puberty, "acting out" with boys and men became a way of life. Elly got pregnant and initially planned on going to El Paso for an abortion. But her "moral code" was pro-life, and so she gave the baby up for adoption.

Elly had strict guidelines for prospective adoptive parents. They had to be Christian, involved with the community, and have a military background. "I wanted my child to be safe," she said. "God, I believe, was my strength and salvation in this effort. He put me on a path where my well-intentioned goal was met. Through prayer, he gave me the strength and wisdom to find the right help as well as locate a nice family."

Elly came to Albuquerque and started working in hotels, something she did for twenty-seven years. She progressed from being a front desk clerk to a reservation and sales manager. But Elly was beginning a downhill emotional slide. "Depression had become a continuing problem, as well as lack of trust in authority figures. I was married for seven years, and depression and anxiety led to divorce. I became increasingly isolated in my life." She thought of ending her life.

After almost three decades of working in hotels, Elly decided a change was in order when a new company took over the hotel where she worked. She got a new job and began working at a country club. Elly said that went well, until, after eight years, sexual harassment became an issue, dredging up old, painful, and buried memories from the past. She realized the need to face these issues and began to deal with them. As she did so, the Lord intervened. That, Elly said, "helped me to erase part of the past and start to understand God's grace."

Elly's life took another difficult turn when her mother passed away. That, she said, led to more running and a change of jobs. At that point, she said, her son contacted her. She said that while there was a, "honeymoon period, not all tales are fairy tales." She said, "I do not believe God wanted me involved in his life, long term. He did, however, want my son to know who I was. But this is when I began to understand the dangers of trying to live up to other people's expectations. I came home again."

Elly now battled chronic depression. As a result of cuts in mental health services, the assistance she had been relying on was no longer there for her. She ended up homeless in the middle of the night and arrived at Joy Junction at about 4:30 AM. This was her first experience of homelessness, a challenging and sometimes terrifying experience for anyone. Her experience was a good one: "Everyone was very nice and helpful."

When she learned of Joy Junction's CIPP Life Recovery Program, she joined. She thought it could help her successfully face the issues she had battled for so long. With assistance from the shelter and outside medical professionals, Elly began working on the roots of depression and anxiety.

She said, "With the power of faith and Jesus as my Savior, I have conquered the persistent depression and running away from pain or hurt. The Lord is still teaching me to stand and accept the blessings and trials he uses to make me strong. I no longer wish to end my life. I feel that God will use me as a tool to glorify him. I can still have my feelings hurt, but the depression is no longer dark and damaging ... Joy Junction did care, and through my ups and downs in the program, they have continued to care. I have changed. I am not perfect, but I am continuing to change. I am born again and more joyful in life and thankful for life."

Joy Junction assistant resident services manager Lisa Woodward says, "Even though she has graduated from the program, she still continues to help us by handing out the linens every night. Elly just can't rest unless she knows everyone has a nice area to sleep. She is part of the reason that our evenings here at Joy Junction go so well. Her gentle spirit and giving heart puts our overnight guests at ease."

Elly expects nothing and gives everything. She will tell you what a blessing Joy Junction has been to her, but she has done a lot of blessing on her side, blessing us and people who are in need of our help.

Dwayne

I don't hold much stock in coincidences, but I am a firm believer in divinely arranged meetings. With that in mind, I regularly ask the Lord to direct my day in such a way that I will be open to where he wants me to go and open to whomever he wants me to meet. Doing so takes a lot of frustration out of difficult days and replaces it with an excitement about the next experience for me on God's agenda.

While at the Albuquerque Convention Center for our annual Pre-Thanksgiving Day Feast, I just "happened" to be introduced to Dwayne. He was there as a volunteer, helping serve hundreds of hungry people. But not so long ago, Dwayne was himself homeless and staying at Joy Junction. Here is some of his story.

Formerly homeless on the streets of California, Dwayne ended up in Albuquerque and at Joy Junction. As a result of his homelessness and other issues, he was in despair. "I was hopeless when I first got there, and Joy Junction gave me the tools I needed, such as Bible study and ... a little bit of hope."

Did he know Jesus? "I knew him before, but I got more intimate with him there, because I got to see that I just wasn't the only one needing help.

There were more people like me. I didn't feel quite as alone. Because there's other people, as I looked around, that were in the same situation I'm in."

Dwayne said that the Bible study and the mentoring by some of our staff gave him hope and were the things that helped him the most during his stay at Joy Junction. It's been my experience that many of our guests feel pretty hopeless when they arrive at Joy Junction. I think it is a combination of being without a home and the emotionally and physically debilitating situations that landed them in that sad predicament. I was so glad to hear that our staff had encouraged him.

He didn't want to say what issues specifically landed him at Joy Junction, and I never want to press people to share anything they are not comfortable sharing. However, Dwayne was willing to say "hard times" in his life resulted in his homelessness. "I come from a family of nine," he said, "and we didn't have much, you know, all my life. I was in foster homes and group homes, and foster homes and boys' homes, and I just had a hard time."

Good news was on the horizon. Since leaving Joy Junction, Dwayne now works at a local hotel, has a studio apartment, and attends a church where he also volunteers. "I'm just giving back, because the Lord has blessed me so much."

I asked Dwayne what advice he would have for someone maybe in the depths of despair and perhaps wondering if he or she could come to Joy Junction or enroll in a recovery program.

Without hesitating, he said no one should stay in despair because of the existence of Joy Junction and many other programs. "And don't give up, because there's a living God out there. He loves you, no matter if your family doesn't, if your brother doesn't, if your teacher doesn't. Jesus loves you so much."

Dwayne added, "I was hopeless all my life, because nobody ever loved me. I come from the projects in Los Angeles, South Central. There was no love in those projects, just drugs, alcohol, and all that stuff. But you know what? I know now that God loves me. He sent his Son, Jesus Christ, to die for me. You can't get that kind of love anywhere on this earth. There's nothing else like it. You might search and search all around the world, trying to find the love in people and materialistic things, but there's no love like the love of Jesus Christ."

He encourages volunteers and donors to keep helping out, adding that to do so, "makes you feel wonderful inside, and plus, we're doing the Lord's work. And that's what it's all about. Give because there's so many people out there that are in need, especially at Joy Junction. They take care of hundreds of women and children, so we need to give to Joy Junction."

That's what we are all about, being used as vessels, so God's restorative love can be poured out spiritually and physically upon those in need.

David

Tall and weather-beaten, with soulful eyes and a prominent moustache, David was a hard person to miss. I met him at a citywide Crusade for the Homeless, where a number of relief agencies were gathered for the day as a sort of a "one-stop shop" for the homeless. Services offered included haircuts, food, clothing, and an array of information to make the lives of the homeless and near-homeless a little easier.

David stopped by our booth, and I asked him to tell me some of his story. He said he has a home, and he is grateful for it. But it is difficult to live, as the assistance check that pays his rent is the only thing that is guaranteed. For David, everything else is a mass of uncertainty, "Not knowing from month to month whether I'm going to be able to pay my utilities and keep those on. And supply myself with food. Sometimes I can get assistance, and other times not."

It is very difficult not knowing where your next meal is going to come from. "Especially when you have health problems and health issues, and there are some foods that you can't really eat, because it'll make your health issues worse."

I asked David if he thought that people he encounters really understand the plight faced by those in his condition. He said the majority of them don't. He added, "They ask you questions. You start telling them the truth about something, and they'll turn around and walk away." He said, "It kinda makes me feel useless. Like I don't have a place anymore in this world, in this economy. I used to have a very good job, and it's very difficult these days with the economy and with jobs that have been outsourced to other countries. Especially manufacturing, which is what I was doing for over twenty years."

The Crusade for the Homeless event is very important to people like David. "Today, I'm here looking for clothes for the winter. If it wasn't for something like this and other places like it, there wouldn't be anything."

How would David respond to those who say that if he wanted, he could do more? He said, "Those are people that don't really understand, because not everybody on the streets or close to being without a home are addicted people. There are people like me that have gotten caught up in this in this economy, too." He hopes they won't dismiss everyone they see on the streets with a backpack as being addicts and unable to get a job.

I echo David's words, but I would expand on them to say we are also obligated to show the love of Jesus to addicts. It is so easy for us to label people, make off-the-cuff judgmental statements, and say (maybe a tad smugly), "If that was me, I wouldn't be in that position." The person about whom we are commenting is not us, and there but for the grace of God go you and I. Many times, we have no idea about what led the addict (who we sometimes blithely dismiss and depersonalize as "that junkie") to end up in their predicament.

I am not defending a person's use of illegal drugs. Absolutely not. But prayerfully consider circumstances such as abuse, rejection, rape, or mental illness that may have resulted in, or contributed to, their difficult position. The next time someone asks you for help, would you prayerfully consider your specific role as a Good Samaritan for the needy? What you decide could potentially determine the physical and spiritual destiny of a homeless or needy person in Albuquerque, or in whichever city you live.

If you are like me, I know you do not want to make anyone feel useless and without a place in the world.

Jim

The emotionally and physically worn man was sitting in his van with a sign in the window reading, "Homeless vet needs work." As I looked at him, I wondered what he had experienced. His face suggested he was tired and perhaps somewhat desperate. Beyond that, there wasn't that much more visibly apparent. He appeared to exhibit a quite understandable guard.

The van was parked outside a Whole Foods market, a few miles from Albuquerque's downtown. As I walked over to the van to see if I could help, a small dog growled and barked protectively. I introduced myself and asked the occupant whether I could help and if he would tell me his story. His name was Jim.

Jim told me he came to Albuquerque during the winter, en route to Long Beach, California, and he ended up getting stuck in Albuquerque. More specifically, he had car problems and ran out of money. And with a job awaiting him in Kansas City, he was anxious to be on his way.

I asked Jim how receptive people were to his plight, and he said they had been pretty nice, but I inferred he had experienced a pretty difficult time in obtaining employment. In fact, he said, getting a job can be easier said than done. "Not everybody has a pristine past. Some people have a checkered past. They made mistakes in their past before, and just because you go in front of a court and they give you a sentence, it doesn't stop there. It follows you. So, a lot of times you fill out an application, and you don't tell them about your past. Then once they get on the computer, they find out about it, or you tell them about it, and you don't get a job. So, it's kind of a catch-22."

Shannon was Jim's dog. "I was camped out by the American Legion on Lomas. I sleep with the doors open, and I woke up one morning, and she was in my driver's seat. I tried to get her to move, and she bit me. We have been together ever since. Yeah, she bites me every day, but she's my buddy."

Jim told me he thinks using some of the stimulus money to help the homeless would be great thing to do, put more people to work who would otherwise be a drain on society I asked him where he would spend that night. He said probably by the American Legion on Lomas. He felt that location is safe because of the close presence of the Legion. In addition to that, there are very few people there, and he felt safe sleeping with the doors open.

What would it be like sleeping outside in what would be such potentially dangerous conditions? What if the weather went from cold to freezing? Would Jim survive the night? What if bugs started crawling over his body? Would he even be able to sleep? Even though he believes he will be safe, what if he were harassed? Would he make it out alive? Would his adrenaline keep him going? Would "fight or flight" kick in?

A posttraumatic stress disorder makes it difficult for Jim to stay at homeless shelters, as that usually means being around and getting along with a lot of other people. He said while he would take donations to help him along the way, he was also willing to work. I bought Jim some gas and some food to help him on his way. I prayed and wished him Godspeed.

My mind was in overdrive as I drove home that night. What has gone wrong with our country when someone like Jim, a veteran, slowly and perilously makes his way from city to city? Would he ever make it to his new job in Kansas City? I knew I would make it to my final destination. I knew the comforts that awaited me when I arrived home. But what about Jim? What would it take to help get him get to his destination? And how long would that take?

I only know the answers can be found in the hands of God and in those he prompted to help Jim. (Kathy Sotelo contributed to this story.)

Sally

Sally (not her real name) enjoyed a good childhood. She was raised in a Christian home and attended Christian schools. But all that was to change when she turned fifteen. Sally said, "My innocence was taken away by a rape that ended up being an unwanted pregnancy. Being an adopted child, I put my daughter up for adoption to Christian parents. The pain was too great for me to handle."

Reaction of Christians to the incident hurt Sally. She also began questioning how the Lord could allow one of his children to be harmed in such a manner. As a result, she started running from her family and other loved ones, and for years, she kept running. And as she ran from the Lord, she wound up in the arms of the enemy.

She said, "I ran to drugs, and this led to men who were abusive mentally, physically, and sexually. It seemed like I could not get away from this type of lifestyle." Sally said she finally decided to settle down, get married, and raise a family, thinking her life would change. But it didn't. There was always some kind of abuse from her husband. "I left my husband and three children, returning to my old lifestyle in the dark world of alcohol, drugs, and bikers." The second man Sally married was a biker, and once again, she entered into an abusive relationship. She became his "property." The second marriage soon ended in a violent divorce, and Sally was homeless for a time.

Sally's next relationship turned out to be more broken promises and ultimately, another broken relationship. It ended when she was again addicted to drugs and, as she put it, tired of being "broken."

She wanted to find out who she was really destined to be. She knew the answer in her heart but felt she had strayed from that place. In an attempt to fix the damage, Sally found herself at the women's division of a gospel mission. She was addicted to pain pills, crack, and marijuana. A staff member suggested she sign up for the mission's rehab program, called Family Hope Discipleship, and Sally did not hesitate. "I wanted change. I needed to let go and let God do his work in me. About one month later, at a huge church, I accepted Christ back into my life," and two weeks after that, she was re-baptized in one of the nearby lakes with about eighty other people. "Wow! What an amazing, warm feeling came over me when I came up from the water. I knew the Spirit was in me."

Sally did well until she fell in love with a man from the men's discipleship program. After eight months, the two of them were asked to leave. She and her boyfriend did very well for a while, but that was about to change. She said, "Soon, he began to drink, and things started to go down real fast from there." Not long after, Sally's boyfriend was diagnosed with third-stage, small cell, lung cancer. She said, "My faith soared during this time, despite his illness. I quit my job to take care of him full time. He had become paralyzed, and his speech was slurred. God answered our prayers during this time. Our best friend finally told him, 'You should marry Sally. She has gone through so much for you.'"

The two of them got married, and their church raised enough money for his ex-wife and daughter to fly in from Grants, New Mexico, for the wedding. After ten years, he would see his only daughter. "A miracle," Sally said. She continued, "Just 168 hours later, my husband died in his sleep. I never lost faith during this whole time, even though I was mad at God for taking him from me."

Sally said in the last three weeks of his life, God brought them back to the gospel mission to be around the friends and teachers they had in rehab. She stayed there for eight months.

Sally and her teenage daughter then went to live with her oldest daughter. She stayed single and never dated for sixteen months. Sally texted an old friend the words, "Happy New Year," and a friendship between her and that old friend (Albert—not his real name) started to bloom.

She lost her job and could not save her house. Due to stress, she found herself in the hospital, while the courts put a twenty-four hour quit notice on the house. She lost everything. Sally was homeless again. That resulted in Sally and Albert staying with friends for a few weeks.

Meanwhile, Albert decided to turn himself in for an old DUI in a nearby county. Sally returned to the mission once again, leaving every morning to go to work, while her teenage daughter was going to her friend's house and running the streets. After Albert was released, their troubles increased. They stayed in a rundown hotel in Kalamazoo for about a month. As a result of some bad associations, they received death threats. Sally said, "The threats kept coming, and I started having nightmares of Albert being shot in front of me and dying in my arms." Despite the threats, Sally said their faith kept them strong, and they grew closer. Albert's uncle lived in Tijeras, New Mexico, and he told them to, "Come on out." They loaded up their car with all their belongings and headed west. Things went well for a while.

While there, Albert spent his mornings chopping wood and talking to God. Sally spent her mornings reading Psalms and Proverbs and then they would both write to God. "I really felt closer to God being in the mountains."

But they left Albert's uncle's place and came to Joy Junction. "Since being here, we have told people our story and shared with them what God has done with us. We have tried every day to serve God in all we have done here. Though we have our ups and downs, we do not lose our focus on God."

Where would Sally and Albert have gone without Joy Junction? Sally said, "We would have had nowhere to go without Joy Junction; home was not an option. To me, this is a safe haven for myself and for people who are broken in any area of their lives. Here they can find healing. No matter why I'm here, God has been with me. He has never left me, and he never will." Sally added, "I feel more comfortable, and my walk is getting stronger every day. My heart is turning into a servant's heart, with no questions of why."

Sally and Albert have always stepped up to help other members of the Joy Junction community in need. They do this with a nonjudgmental, humble attitude. What a blessing it is for us to be involved with them and in the lives of all the guests the Lord brings to Joy Junction.

Raymond

Grateful for a food box, a sack lunch, blankets, and coffee, Raymond's eyes were moist as he told me his story of ending up homeless on Albuquerque's West Mesa. Raymond used to drive a truck, until the fateful day he received a call and learned that his wife and son had been killed by a drunk driver.

"I went home. My wife was dead on the scene. My son died two hours later. I couldn't sit home—too many memories." After traveling around devastated for about two-and-a-half years, Raymond settled on Albuquerque. He had been through the city in his driving days and liked it. His inner pain is always ever-present, and he is still hurting badly. I can't even imagine what he experiences as the dawning of each cold day brings more tear-wracked memories.

Raymond's story reminds me of my friend Randy Stonehill's song "Christmas at Denny's." It's the story of a man whose daughter was killed. Just like Raymond, this man couldn't stay home either, and he started traveling. One Christmas, he ends up at a Denny's restaurant. The lyric says, "And I'm dreaming about a silent night, holy night—when things were all right. And I'm dreaming about how my life could have been if only, if only, if only. But somewhere down the road I gave up that fight. Merry Christmas. It's Christmas at Denny's tonight."

Raymond recalled the day he came to Albuquerque. A friend who used to help him load and unload trucks when he was driving told him about a makeshift campsite and that they could camp together. I asked Raymond what life had been like for him since he got to Albuquerque and whether he was ever jumped or hassled. He said no; it was just hard being able to weather the cold living conditions. To those who are upset they don't have more in this life, Raymond says, "Come and try to live the way I've been having to live."

Raymond said he gets through life by taking it one day at a time. Albuquerque's residents have been treating him okay, and he ekes out a living by loading and unloading trucks. "It's hard, the way people look at you, but I try to stay clean. I mind my own business. I don't mess with nobody. I go to work; come back; go to bed [and] stay to myself."

Raymond has a message for people who judge him. "Don't judge a book by its cover. Everybody's out here for a certain reason. All of them have different reasons. I don't do drugs; I don't drink. I try to work [and] just get by." Raymond's faith has helped him weather the last few years. He says that without Jesus, he couldn't have made it during this terrible time. "I never lost faith. I read the Bible every day. I pray every day." He is optimistic about the future, and he would like to get a house or an apartment. He hopes people will pray for him.

There are so many people like Raymond all around Albuquerque and all across America and the world—people who have experienced emotionally debilitating tragedies in their lives. Some decide to travel to be as far away as they can from their place of pain, while others try numbing their anguish through alcohol and drugs. Like the individual in "Christmas at Denny's," they have perhaps come to believe, "Life's made of cruel circumstance. Fate plays the tune and we dance—dance 'til we drop in the dust and we're gone and the world just goes on."

Every day at Joy Junction and around Albuquerque, with our donors' help, we are reaching out to precious broken, hurting, hungry, and homeless people by offering a warm place to stay, meals, hygiene kits, sleeping bags, blankets, underwear, and Bibles. The Lord can move anyone from despair, hopelessness, and addiction to new life in Jesus Christ. That is the best Christmas gift of all!

Ace

With his turquoise top hat, dark glasses, and otherwise overall distinctive appearance, Ace is a hard person to miss. We caught up with him recently outside a McDonald's on Albuquerque's West Mesa, while Kathy Sotelo and I were driving the shelter's Lifeline of Hope food wagon, which was donated to us by Summit Electric's Vic Jury.

After offering Ace coffee, juice, a sack lunch, and potato soup, he told me he was a Vietnam veteran, who is also known as "Top Hat." He has been on the road for many months, and the experience, "has been difficult in a couple of spots … I was almost beaten to death in Truth or Consequences, New Mexico, over something that I'll never know was said, because the girl who told the guy was drunk. She doesn't remember what she said, and he came and got me while I was asleep. I had to be air-evacuated to El Paso."

Following his hospital stay, Ace said he walked from El Paso to Las Cruces, a long and difficult walk for anyone. For Ace, it was even more so. "It took me four days. I have a cane, and I had a stroke last year. I've also had a heart attack, and I've been in seven motorcycle wrecks."

I asked Ace what having a sack lunch meant to him. Did it brighten his day a bit? He answered effusively, "It does. This little bit of what might seem like nothing to somebody is a lot to me. It's my sustenance." Ace told us that this is what he would like people to know about him: "I'm not a bad person. I don't sit on the corner and beg just to get drunk. I sit out there and fly my sign that says, 'Traveling, Broke, Hungry,' because that's what I am. I'm traveling, I'm broke, and most of the time, I am hungry, because most of the time we don't get enough to eat out here. A lot of people think people come by and give you food all the time, money, clothes. It doesn't happen like that. Things happen, like what happened to me … you get beat up and get sent to a hospital and have to stay there for six days."

Ace spent some time in prison. When he got out, he was homeless and had only forty cents in his pocket. He was understandably panicked, so much so, in fact, that, "They had to drag me out of the prison cell to get me out of there." Things didn't get much better at the parole office,

Ace explained. "I told the parole officer, 'You know what? You can send me back right now.' That's how bad it was, because I could not get a job anywhere. I've got a first-degree attempted murder conviction behind me, and I didn't even kill anybody, but that's what it says on the Internet. First-degree murder. And then people scroll up, and they see it's attempted murder and that I didn't kill anybody."

What hopes does Ace have for the future? He has set his sights on Alabama, where he has a few friends and hopes to land a job. "Not a lot of friends, but I have a few, and then—if I work two years—I'll be able to retire. If I can get two years of honest work, if I get a paycheck, I can retire."

Ace says he is a praying man, and he admits to having a personal relationship with Jesus Christ as his Lord and Savior. He reads God's Word and prays daily, and he says he would not have been able to make it without him. Ace said he would like Christians who read this little story to pray for him.

I asked Ace if he had anything to say to those individuals who just write him off as a "bum." "I'd tell them, you have no idea what I've gone through. Try coming out here for three days and trading places with me. Let me have your car, your job, your house, and you come out here and live under a bridge for three days and find out how easy it is. It's not."

If we dismiss people like Ace and fail to make even a small attempt to get to know them, we are missing a bright treasure the Lord chose for whatever reason to bring across our path. If we do something to bless them, somewhere along the way we may also get an unexpected blessing as well.

Thomas

Even die-hard chili lovers may not be so grateful if all they got for Christmas was a bowl of chili. But Thomas was delighted. Homeless, he sat outside on a wind-chilled Christmas Eve outside a fast-food restaurant on Albuquerque's 98th Street. We were dispensing some Christmas cheer from our Lifeline of Hope food wagon. Among other things, we were giving chili, soup, sack lunches, coffee, soft drinks, blankets, and personal hygiene kits.

The wind whipped through my bones as I stood there talking to Thomas. I asked him how the chili made him feel. Thomas replied, "It makes me feel great. It makes me feel very happy. No one else has given me anything for Christmas. I'm just happy you guys are here."

He told me something about his plight. He had been living in a shed with an electric heater close to the restaurant for about six weeks. Before that, he had been living on the streets. Thomas described the difficulties of living outside. "Not good," he said. "It was pretty cold in the winter. I didn't have no blankets or anything. Sometimes, all I had was my jacket to cover myself. It was pretty cold at night, and it was pretty cold in the mornings. I'd get up in the mornings and wonder what I was going to make my breakfast with. Sometimes, I'd go over to one of the shelters over there, and they were all filled up, and they'd have no room to put me up for the night. So, I had to sleep on the street."

What caused Thomas to become homeless? He said the deaths of his whole family precipitated his descent into homelessness just two years before. "I have no one. I used to have my mother to go to. She'd put me up for the night, for the evening, or I'd go to one of my brothers. They're all gone … my aunts, my uncles, my whole family's gone. My grandmother's gone, my grandfather's gone, my cousins, they're all gone. They all passed away."

Thomas said it's hard to get through each day. "Sometimes, I come over here [to the fast-food restaurant] in the morning and drink me a cup of coffee. If I'm lucky, somebody will ask me, 'Have you eaten yet?' They'll buy me maybe a hamburger or something to eat in the morning. But in the afternoon, you've got to try to make a little bit of change or something. Then I get me a loaf of bread or something or a little bag of bologna to take home."

He said his faith helped him make it through each day. "I pray every night and every morning when I wake up. I thank the good Lord for helping me make it through the night and helping me make it through the day. I pray to him every day." Thomas's hopes for the New Year are very modest and practical. His doctor wants to operate on his knee. "If they operate on my knee, then hopefully I can find a little janitorial work, as a custodian or something, that doesn't have heavy lifting. Hopefully, then I'll get a place to live."

But Thomas had more medical troubles than just his knee. He had what looked like serious frostbite on the back of his right hand and right index finger. He promised me he would get some medical attention immediately following the Christmas holidays.

To those of our donors who made our Christmas Eve trip of cheer possible, Thomas has this to say: "Just never lose hope; keep on praying, and Jesus will come through one way or another. The people at Joy Junction—they're beautiful. They come out here and feed you, and whenever you're feeling down, they help you the best way they know how."

Thomas's optimism is absolutely phenomenal. Thomas, who doesn't have a place to stay, was encouraging us to have hope and faith. What a lesson for those of us who have so much and still find ourselves wanting more.

Shelly

Here's another one of those "coincidences" that I believe are really divine appointments. While leaving a diner on Central (Route 66), close to some of Albuquerque's homeless hot spots, after a late working lunch with Joy Junction outreach coordinator, Kathy Sotelo, we were stopped by a well-dressed woman. Shelly (not her real name) apologized for what she called an "intrusion" and asked me if I was Jeremy Reynalds from the homeless shelter. When I told her I was, she nervously asked me if we could possibly buy her a meal. I quickly said yes. She was obviously embarrassed and close to tears.

Shelly told us she had been employed by a local corporation but had been laid off and was unable to find a new job. She had run through all her savings and didn't know what to do. She said she hadn't eaten at all the day we met her.

I asked Shelley if she still had a place to stay. She said she paid her rent and telephone bill three months in advance and was determined not to live on the streets. However, eating was a different matter. Like too many people in these hard economic days in America, she had to make a choice between paying the rent or having food to eat.

Kathy gave her numbers for some local resources, and I asked her if we could pray for her. She graciously agreed, so we joined hands, and for just a brief moment, we turned that diner into a holy place. When we opened our eyes, Shelly's eyes were moist, and she hugged us both. What was the "chance" of Shelly passing the diner at the exact moment we were coming out? I believe it was a divinely arranged meeting.

Route 66 is where the Lord Jesus Christ, his love, presence, and Spirit, are very much alive and active.

Jamie

The worst part of being homeless is, "When you have to go without food. And when it's just so cold that you can't even bear it, and you don't have enough to wrap up in, and you're losing feeling in your body parts because you're so cold." This is what Jamie told me. She is a missionary pastor's daughter and didn't plan to be virtually homeless, living with her husband on the West Mesa in Albuquerque, New Mexico. But that is how she started 2010.

I met Jamie recently while on an outreach with the Joy Junction Lifeline of Hope food wagon. She told me how appreciative she was of the supplies we had given her and her husband. She called the unexpected gifts "wonderful."

Jamie's life is very difficult due to ongoing pain, a number of surgeries, and a delayed disability assessment. While living in Chicago and working in the medical field, she dislocated her shoulders, tore up her hand, hit her nose, and had to have reconstructive sinus and hand surgery. Now in Albuquerque as a result of her husband's employment, Jamie is undergoing a series of operations.

After Jamie's husband left his job, he began traveling and looking for employment. Ultimately, he found work in Albuquerque, but it hasn't been at all easy. There are a lot of barriers to moving into an apartment or a house that people don't necessarily think about, Jamie said. "I don't even know my way around Albuquerque. I don't know the good places or the bad ones. How am I going to feel like I'm safe to go off and get an apartment when I don't even know the area?"

Fortunately, she has been able to communicate. "My family's bought me a cell phone, and they pay for it so that I can at least get all my doctors' calls. Between that, you know, and them helping me, that's all I get. My unemployment's all gone, and they wouldn't even let me have an extension. They told me I didn't make enough to get an extension."

Jamie said the people of Albuquerque have treated her wonderfully. "So much more wonderful than Chicago, where I'm from. I think that's one thing that keeps me out here." To the people who have helped her, such as her husband's employer, she says, "Thank you to everybody that's pulled together during the times when I needed it. I didn't have a vehicle when I went in for surgery, so my husband's boss he let him take me to surgery in the service truck. He picked me up in the service truck and gets my medicine in the service truck. There are good people out here."

Jamie is also grateful for the Joy Junction donors, whose kindness and generosity allows us to keep the Lifeline of Hope on the road. She said if it wasn't for the Lifeline, she would have to wait another month before being able to buy desperately needed supplies. Not having the needed food and supplies is the most difficult thing about being homeless. And at that point, Jamie said, "I feel like I'm alone ... and that nobody cares." But I reminded her, "We care for you, Jesus cares for you, and a lot of generous donors around town care for you as well."

I asked Jamie what hopes she has for the upcoming year. She said she wants to make it through the remainder of her six surgeries and get her disability. "I don't want to be pushed away by the courts any longer because of my age. I'm hurt, and I can't work ever again, even if the surgeries do work."

Jamie said her relationship with Jesus enabled her to get through the last year. She said that without him, "I wouldn't be here. I would have already committed suicide. I can guarantee you that. I have been through such a hard last fifteen months that if it wasn't for the Lord, I would have just said, 'Forget it.'" She encourages everyone who reads her story to believe in God. She said, "If you do, he'll bring you the good people, and that means really believing in God when you're down and out, crying to him. Don't cry to your mom. You really, really have to 100 percent believe, and people will come to you. They will be there to help."

Jamie is one of the "flock" God allows us to touch. It is such a great opportunity to share the love of Jesus Christ tangibly with those who are outside the walls of Joy Junction. Our friends and donors make it possible.

Charles

Traveling the streets of Albuquerque on Joy Junction's Lifeline of Hope meal wagon is an adventure I wouldn't miss. It provides an opportunity to share the spiritual and physical love of Jesus with people the Lord chooses to put in our way. It is such a blessing to share food and essential supplies to worried and discouraged people.

Some of these people were involuntarily displaced from an apartment complex that had been closed by the city as substandard. We passed a man with a sign, sitting on the corner of Menaul and Carlisle. He had eyes of heartfelt desperation. It was as if they bore into our souls and compelled us to stop. We pulled into a parking lot, introduced ourselves, and asked the man if he was hungry. He said he was, so we gave him a sack lunch and a bottle of vitamin water. He asked for another lunch and water for his friend, which we happily gave. We gave another sack lunch to a man who asked for an extra meal for his friend, "who can't get up and come over here." Again, we were happy to oblige. We have found it a common occurrence that many of the homeless are very concerned for their friends and that there is an intense camaraderie between those in need.

Then there's Charles, who we met at another location where we feed people. He told me that the Lifeline helps a lot. "Because when I don't got nothing, they always come help me right here. Always," he said.

Charles told me a bit of his story, and he had some pretty good advice about the perils of drinking. He said, "I used to drink hard liquor every day—vodka, whiskey, anything I could get. It almost caused me to lose my family and everything. My wife told me to choose the alcohol or choose my family. I choose my family. I still drink a bit every now and then, but it's nothing like being an alcoholic. At least I'm doing better. I'm getting better at it, and I'm still with my wife for thirty years."

Faith is how Charles has gotten through all the trials in his life: "Faith. Faith in my Lord Jesus Christ, and my wife being on my side. She keeps my best part of me. She makes a difference in me doing better." Charles had experienced some tough love from his wife, of whom he spoke so admiringly. She told him, "'You either want me and the kids, or you want to live by yourself and be homeless.' I didn't want to be homeless; I love my wife and my kids." As a result, Charles said, he decided to put his wife and family ahead of alcohol. He continued, "I put them first from now on in my life because God blessed me … and gave me the strength to do so."

What would Charles say to those thinking of experimenting with alcohol or drugs? "That ain't a good thing; that's not a good thing. You need to recognize it's okay to drink a little bit occasionally, but not to be a drunk. Never be a drunk."

I asked Charles what he sees ahead. He said, "God blessing everybody through my Lord Jesus Christ. Keep your faith in the Lord Jesus Christ, and you'll be all right." Charles, I couldn't say it better. Thanks for brightening our day when we see you in your part of Albuquerque. I pray you keep serving the Lord and grow in his grace and love.

A Slice of Life at Joy Junction

Have you ever wondered about life behind the scenes at a homeless shelter? I don't mean what you get to see on those special "open house" days, when the shelter puts its proverbial best foot forward. I am talking about typical everyday life.

In early 2002, I spent some time observing a slice of life at Joy Junction, and I have written about this in my book *Homeless Culture and the Media*. For continuity of the story, I have condensed the observation times into a couple of days, when they were in fact longer.

A Sunday Afternoon

It is 3:20 on a relatively calm Sunday afternoon in the main building of Joy Junction. A pregnant guest, holding a baby, is distraught about the recent abandonment of five children at Joy Junction; the kids ended up being placed in foster care. She says, "I just want to go out and find that woman. But my husband says, 'Maybe she was suicidal, so perhaps the kids are in a better place.'" I ponder briefly their vastly different reactions to the abandonment.

A man with physical and mental problems staggers into the office and says, "I hate Channel 4," Someone asks him why, and he replies, "Because they always cut out."

Just as the Channel 4–hater is staggering out of the office, a Joy Junction staffer comes in. He is casually dressed in a plaid shirt with a blue undershirt and blue jeans, with hair sticking up. He asks the shelter pastor, "That girl you had at the movies. Was she eighteen?"

"No, she was in her mid-fifties," responds the pastor.

"Okay, just trying to scare you," says the Joy Junction parking lot attendant. That's typical humor at Joy Junction. I've heard that humor like this is a coping mechanism that often shows up in environments like ours.

A few minutes later, I hear a snippet of a sad conversation drifting out of a neighboring office. "He drinks too much, and he's already hit her."

It is now 4:30, and dinner is well under way. Most people are sitting and eating their evening meal, but about a dozen or so are still standing in the serving line. There is not much audible conversation going on from my fairly unobtrusive listening post a few feet away. Just a few laughs here and there.

I can only see one person not eating, an elderly black woman with graying hair, sitting quietly on a couch. Her vacant stare into midair personifies the stereotypical image many people have of the homeless.

A Well-Ordered Atmosphere

The overall atmosphere behind the scenes at Joy Junction resembles a busy, well-ordered, and well-structured beehive. While it appears (to me, anyway) to be a comforting, reassuring environment, I wonder how many of the scores of people I can see eating dinner are as comfortable with it as I am. Maybe my comfort level is due at least in part to my being the director and because I've been here so long. Also, I am not homeless; they are.

By 5:10, supper is over, and all the tables have been stacked to one side to make way for the upcoming church service. As a faith-based ministry, church services and Bible studies form a core part of Joy Junction's mission.

I hear another snatch of conversation coming out of an office. Someone says, "All you had to do was answer the question." Another person says, "Tough it out." The first individual responds, "I'm tired."

A couple of minutes later, two tall men begin their after-dinner chores of methodically sweeping and mopping the floor prior to the chairs being put back down for church. Daily chores are required as a condition for staying at the shelter. Continued refusal to do chores will eventually result in the individual being asked to leave. It's all about trying to help our guests be responsible and transition back into the real world.

The black woman is still sitting in the same place. The only difference is that she now has a soft-covered Bible balanced on her lap. There are about a dozen people sitting on the couches that line the perimeter of the building. They are all just looking.

Later, a kitchen worker drops off some meals for the workers on an upcoming shift. He is a troubled but affable young man, who needs some positive male role models in his life. I ask him if he's behaving. He says, "Yeah, I was just dropping off lunches. See, I've stacked them nice and neat." He knows who I am, and he is anxious to please.

The kitchen worker disappears from sight, but then a man comes by and stops at the office right in front of my listening post. I ask him how he's doing. He says, "Not so good." I ask him why, and he replies that because he has broken up with his spouse, his stay at Joy Junction has now reverted to overnight status. He's disappointed and says, "I had a lot of plans. I had a lot I could do for this place. See these three couches? That's what I used to do for my business. I used to fix them." I utter condolences, saying, "Yeah, that's what happens."

He responds, "Rules are rules," and walks off. This is the man who has been accused by his wife of hitting her. Even though I've now worked with the homeless for over twenty years and think there is nothing left to surprise me, some things still do. This man is apparently more concerned about his inability to fix the shelter's couches than he is about his relationship with his wife.

People continue to sit.

At 5:35, with the chores completed, the sound service is in the final stages of set up, and the chairs are being put back on the floor for the 6:00 church service.

At 5:40, the band is practicing. A handful of people are sitting in the brightly colored orange and yellow chairs, waiting for the service to begin. A smiling African-American woman waves to me and points proudly to the baby she has cradled in her lap. The pastor is making some last minute adjustments to the sound system, and a number of people are sitting around on couches.

It's now 6:00, and guests are singing, "Sing a joyful song unto the Lord, praise the Lord with gladness because he alone is God."

There is a small amount of clapping going on to accompany the singing. Seventeen people are standing up, about 15 percent of the entire crowd. While most of those singing don't have a home, they still want to sing and worship the Lord. It is spiritual hope in the midst of physical despair. I realize that a similar scene is duplicated in hundreds of gospel rescue missions across the country.

While the singing is under way, a man supported by a walker at the back of the building stands, looking on. Just behind him in the building entrance is a shopping cart piled high with clean bed linens ready to be put away. There is a stark contrast between the normal church service at the front of the building and a normal homeless scene at the back.

Monday Morning

At 7:55, I am back at my vantage point in the office of Joy Junction's main building. It is very quiet, with just a couple of people sitting around on chairs.

A woman approaches and says, "I was in bed for thirty days with the flu. My doctor years ago in Arkansas gave me a little blue pill, which had no side effects. I had to take it every day. It was just an allergy tablet. It's allergies. I was just born with that reaction. Some of the people here really don't care. Their brains still race. I just wanna get rid of these sinus sniffles. It's been an infection."

She stops for a moment, and I look across the building, where a man is doing his morning chores, slowly and methodically mopping the floor. Chores are always on the agenda at a shelter the size of ours.

The woman continues talking and says, "Spanish people, they talk so fast, amigo, amigo. Four years of it. I beg their pardon. You think they talk slow. They don't."

She suddenly switches gears and blurts out, "You ever been down to 'La Jumbo Fish,' crawfish pie? Why is it so important to remember the names of songs these days?"

The woman wanders off momentarily but returns quickly with a purposeful walk and says, "Did they ever cure whiplash? I was in a vehicle accident in east Texas. I was a passenger and impacted by an eighteen-wheeler. What do you have to do to get a neck brace? Go in the ER?" She puts her hand on the back of her neck and wanders off again.

I realize that while she is apparently seriously mentally ill, I have nonetheless heard much worse during my years spent working with New Mexico's homeless.

A Quiet Interlude

At 9:40, it is still very quiet. A couple of boys are walking around aimlessly. One of them is swinging a pair of socks. Four people are sitting at the table, talking. A lady is sitting on a couch, apparently engrossed in something, although it may be nothing. I hear snippets of conversation from a neighboring office. A voice says, "Michael is going to be upset when he gets home."

Someone responds, "I seem to have no eyesight when I first wake up. I just can't find it." I love Joy Junction humor. My staff says a lot of it is my fault.

I am startled out of my brief reverie when an unknown guest appears in front of me and says, "Hi Jeremy. I didn't know you were Jeremy." She walks off without saying anything else.

There are now six people in the multipurpose room. A woman is sitting on the couch with her suitcase in front of her.

At 1:00 PM, the suitcase lady is still sitting on the couch. An elderly looking woman, who I suspect is much younger than she looks, comes to the office door, looks at me, but talks to herself. She then puts her hand on her stomach and moves away.

It is quiet at 3:35. I can see five people.

At 4:15, a woman calls and asks if she and her three children can come to the shelter. She and her husband stayed with us some years ago. They committed their lives to the Lord, and we thought they were doing well. I learn that her husband quit his job, against the advice of his pastor and wife, and instead of looking for another job, he has been reading the Bible and spending all his time consumed in Bible prophecy.

The wife says the situation has become too much for her to handle, and when she told her husband to get a job, he starting hitting her. Not surprisingly, she left. As the woman is checking into the shelter, I hear her gratefully exclaim, "Thank God that at least we've got a place to stay!" "Where?" asks the youngest of her three children. "Right here," says Mom, pointing to a couch before they were given a room. "Weird," says the little girl, clutching a donated stuffed animal. "Very weird." Out of the mouth of babes.

It is 5:07, and supper is being held up briefly as all the volunteers coming to serve are not here yet. There are about twenty-five people sitting around, some at tables and some on couches.

Dinnertime

At 5:22, everyone is quietly seated at tables, waiting to be served by the volunteers who have now all arrived. The exception to the quiet is a baby crying in its mother's arms.

It is 8:10, and the building is full of people getting ready to go to bed. People are lying on mattresses and couches all around the building.

At 8:20, a young child is running around. I hear someone asking for a toothbrush. Our driver comes in, clutching a donation of eight dozen maple donuts—a staple for shelters. He asks for a key to the kitchen.

A couple of minutes later, a former guest thanks me for helping her out again. She is in Albuquerque only for the night so she can bail her husband out of jail for public drunkenness. She says, "I miss this place; that's why I'm volunteering tonight." She doesn't tell me just exactly what it is she is volunteering to do.

At 8:55, a woman comes into the office to talk to the women's counselor, who is doing double duty answering the telephones. The woman has been written up for being "disruptive" during the previous night's church service, and she is very annoyed. She says she wasn't at all disruptive but had been laughing at a funny comment made by the pastor.

At 8:58, the quiet hum has been interrupted by a loudly crying child.

At 9:01, the lights should be out, but things are running a little late. Most people are now lying on their beds, talking or reading. I see one man sitting on his mattress, fiddling with a roll of toilet paper, and a woman sitting on her mattress, drearily combing out her hair.

It is now 9:04, and the lights are turned out in the multipurpose building. Lights are turned out in common areas at 9:00 and at 10:00 in private rooms. It is almost the end of another day at Joy Junction.

God in the Details: Everyday Evidence Around Joy Junction

Baseball Bat–Toting Business Owner Chases Away Area Homeless; God Has Other Plans

Pointing to a small baseball bat positioned close to him on the counter, the businessman said he used it to threaten any homeless people coming in his store he perceived as being troublesome.

I could scarcely believe what I was hearing. Let me explain. Joy Junction's Kathy Sotelo and I were on our usual Friday outreach in Joy Junction's Lifeline of Hope food wagon. During one of our stops, we met Steve (not his real name), a man we'd been helping, who asked us if we would stop by an area liquor store he said had been experiencing problems with the homeless, prostitutes, and drug addicts.

We said we would be glad to. We've visited many places where we have left our business cards, which display an 800 number people can call any time of the day or night for the homeless to get a ride to Joy Junction. We parked by the heavily barred and fortified store and made our way into what could be described as an alcoholic's paradise. A buzzer alerted store employees to our entrance.

Kathy spoke first to the individual at the counter. She introduced us and tried to give the man, who turned out to be the business owner, our cards and a Joy Junction brochure. She explained our van service to Joy

Junction and how that could help him assist individuals hanging around his store in need of shelter and other assistance.

Without hesitation, the store owner told us he did not have a problem with the homeless. He said he would just, "take a baseball bat to 'em."

As we exited the store in complete shock, Kathy said, "His helping the people in need around here wouldn't be good for business." Without her saying any more, I knew what she meant. Like her, I suspected that this angry man was only too willing to serve the homeless when they had money to give him for the alcohol that would feed their life-controlling addiction. But when they were out of cash and every pore of their body still cried out for alcohol, they were out of luck. This individual was not even willing to call Joy Junction.

My mind started whirling, trying to anticipate some of the questions I knew would be asked if I told this story. I suspected the main one would be, "This man is a businessman trying to make an honest living. People don't have to drink, right?"

Wrong! Obviously, the initial choice was theirs, but who knows what circumstances these precious souls were navigating that caused them to drown their sorrows in a blurry alcoholic haze? And it didn't take very long before that initial bad choice (and who among us hasn't made a series of bad choices?) became a life-controlling addiction.

Kathy and I got back in the Lifeline of Hope wagon, and I turned the key. Nothing happened. I tried again, but all we heard was a click. I guessed it was an ignition problem, or maybe it was the battery or alternator. "Oh, well," I told Kathy, "the Lord has a reason for this." Admittedly, at that point I had no idea what it was. We called Robert Batrez, our staff mechanic at Joy Junction. He said he would be there as soon as he could, so we settled back to wait.

We were sitting in the food wagon when Steve approached us, and he was concerned when we couldn't get the wagon to start. As we waited for Robert to come to our assistance, I told Steve about our experience in the liquor store. He said, "He [the store owner] gets them addicted and then profits from their addictions."

Robert arrived and got under to the hood to work out why the Lifeline of Hope wouldn't start. Nothing seemed to work until Steve leaned on the food wagon. Call it a miracle or divine intervention, but as soon as he touched the truck, it started! We were once again shocked! What was it about Steve? As soon as the Lifeline was running, Steve, who knew the area, rounded up a variety of people in need, and we prayed with some of them and provided chili, soup, sack lunches, and personal hygiene kits. We fed about thirty people, precious souls who would have otherwise gone to bed that night with hunger pains gnawing at their stomachs.

I was trying to understand what had occurred when the Lord assured me the incident was not about Steve. Rather, it was all about Jesus! He wanted us to encourage some discouraged folk in this terribly economically depressed part of Albuquerque. He used Steve and a temporarily disabled Lifeline of Hope truck to communicate his will to us.

And he uses our supporters and donors, who make it possible to accomplish Joy Junction's ongoing ministry of compassion.

A Heartwarming Christmas Tale

The day before Christmas Eve was an even busier one than usual for Joy Junction homeless shelter staff. Our mission—which is home to as many as three hundred people, including about eighty children—was abuzz with pre-Christmas excitement. The youngsters were very excited, like all children at this season. They were able to forget, at least for a while, their homelessness and anxiously anticipate a multitude of gifts made possible by generous donors. The volunteers unload bags of "Santa's treasures," and the children follow their parents pleading to, "just open one present today." Parents mumble that they have no idea where they will put it all.

However, the children's attention was diverted by small snowflakes falling. They came running to Joy Junction assistant resident services manager Lisa Woodward, asking her, "Can you call Dr. Reynalds? Please, Lees" (the children's affectionate name for her). Lisa was curious why the youngsters wanted her to call me. She tried explaining that I was very busy.

The kids insisted. "Ask him if we can build a snowman." "Does he like snowball fights?" "Will he let Kitchen Mike make us snow ice cream?" Lisa laughed and promised them she would e-mail their requests to my ever-active BlackBerry and return with an answer should we actually get enough snow to scoop up.

This was not what the kids wanted to hear. Lisa said, "Slightly annoyed with my apparent lack of being able to prioritize, they wandered off with a parting comment, 'Lees, you better remember. We are gonna ask him. He likes us.'" She watched the children make their way to a Christmas activity and reminded them about the true meaning of Christmas and why we give gifts. She was touched when she heard the kids talk about how the Lord would understand their dilemma and phone the good Dr. Reynalds.

Lisa said, "I'm an adult, and I remember flashes of my Christmases prior to Joy Junction. But I had never felt love or the true spirit of Christmas until I came here." Lisa, who lives on-site, said, "Someday I will live in a dwelling away from the loving land of Joy Junction. Who knew that this ground could be so blessed or beautiful? But I hope God will call Dr. Reynalds every year and remind him to invite me home for the holidays."

I appreciate the tireless efforts of Lisa and the rest of our staff. Working at Joy Junction is so much more than a job. It is a calling. We must thank our Lord for his faithfulness, and we must thank our donors for supporting us in this calling. Without them, we could not share the love of Jesus with the ever-increasing number of those in need.

The Disappearing Diapers: A Higher Street Value than Cocaine

During the Thanksgiving and Christmas seasons, Joy Junction homeless shelter is blessed with an outpouring of donations of toys, food, clothing, personal hygiene kits, and more.

One Christmas season, we had an organization donate cases and cases of diapers. While diapers may seem a pretty mundane gift to most of us, it is hard to appreciate their value until they are needed and not available. As a result, the families staying at Joy Junction felt as if Christmas Day had arrived early.

As things settled down (at least until the next kindhearted group of generous donors came by), Joy Junction assistant resident services manager Lisa Woodward told me she learned that a few of the shelter's single residents had taken several cases of the donated diapers. Quite understandably, she was more than a little curious and started an immediate search. We shelter between sixty to eighty children nightly with their parents, so diapers donated to Joy Junction are a precious commodity.

Lisa found out that a few of the individuals who had taken the diapers had children living off-site with family members or friends. While she was not thrilled to learn they had taken the diapers without going through the proper channels, she did understand. After all, how must these mothers feel when told by their children's caregivers that diapers are a badly needed but perhaps financially unattainable item?

But Lisa found out something else that floored her. She asked one of the residents why she had two bundles of diapers. The woman asked

Lisa if she worked for Joy Junction and if she was not aware of some of the informational releases put out by the shelter. Lisa said, "I stated I was fairly sure I was aware of most of the releases, but in this age of Facebook and Twitter, maybe I was not aware of everything." The resident told Lisa that her boss (me) was aware that there are minimal toilet facilities in downtown Albuquerque for the homeless, and that situation puts the homeless in a humiliating dilemma. She said that because of the lack of toilets, the homeless have to disgrace themselves by urinating and defecating behind Dumpsters and any other place with some privacy. It is doubly bad for females, as they must disrobe to do either.

This resident told Lisa that when she and other homeless individuals could not make it to a day shelter or Joy Junction, they could use the diapers in their jeans and then discard the waste with some dignity. Lisa said, "She stated that, at this point, diapers had a better street value than cocaine. I was stopped in my tracks. I have been homeless, and I have worked within the gates of Joy Junction for a little over four years. But I had never heard this. I apologized to the resident for questioning her and returned to my office very humbled."

The lack of restrooms is a big problem. However, the homeless have learned to be creative. These residents said the downtown Albuquerque library and the Alvarado Transportation Center were their first and second choices, respectively. One individual said you have to be "sneaky" when using the Greyhound terminal. He only uses it when he has enough time and money to pretend he is getting a snack or looking at schedules. Even then, he said, once you leave, make sure you disappear, and do not hang out in front.

Some homeless hop over fences on construction sites and use the portable toilets there, or at other times, "They will just find a spot." Some Joy Junction guests say when they ask for directions to a restroom, many times they are either ignored or receive hateful responses. One person was told, "If you had a home, you would know where the bathroom is." A comment like this is so hateful it defies description.

At Joy Junction, we remember the plight of those who have no home—and no bathroom—and we always ask the Lord what we can do to help.

AN INCREDIBLE JOURNEY

Not long ago, in the inaugural edition of Joy Junction's *Good News Gazette*, we mentioned a desire to run a lunch wagon that would be filled with coffee, soup, sandwiches, and other food with which we could bless the homeless. The plan was for the wagon to visit areas frequented by the homeless and provide a lifeline in the form of food, drink, and prayer. This lifeline of hope would say, "someone cares," in a tangible fashion to those using its services, and it might even save a life—or more.

A few days later, I received an e-mail from a local businessman and a very dear friend of Joy Junction. He said that he had gone online and found something on Ebay that may work for us. I took a look and was immediately excited. The vehicle looked like it was everything we needed to make our vision a reality.

However, the vehicle was in Florida's West Palm Beach. I thought and prayed and sensed that the Lord wanted me to personally go and pick up the vehicle. I mentioned this to the donor, who immediately responded that if I was sure I wanted to do this, he would pay for my air ticket. What a wonderful blessing!

A few days later, along with Rich Gonzales, an employee from Joy Junction's corporate office who kindly offered to come along with me, we set off.

Those three days were truly a whirlwind of activity but also provided an opportunity for me to reflect on the Lord's goodness—both personally and to Joy Junction.

Day 1: The Journey Begins

Sleep eluded me for much of Monday night, as I lay there tossing and turning, waiting for the alarm to go at 4:45 AM, signaling it was time to get up and catch the 7:10 plane for Florida.

I stumbled out of bed, took two aspirin to ward off the painful rumblings of an approaching headache, forsook my usual chai latte, and turned on the shower.

After a relatively deserted road and a much quicker than usual trip to the airport, I arrived at a packed airline ticket counter, where I met Rich.

There was a quick trip through security, and then time for a quick stop for chai (and a piece of ham and green chili quiche). The lady serving me the chai looked at me and said, "Oh, I didn't think you'd have time to travel."

A little taken aback, I answered, "I'm on the way to pick up a donation for Joy Junction—a lunch wagon."

"Oh," she answered. That was it, other than a comment that my quiche would be at the microwave. Oh, the joys of being known!

We made our way to the line for the plane. The adventure was beginning. Our plan was to get to West Palm Beach to pick up the lunch wagon and drive north to Tallahassee before we stopped for the night.

"How far is that from West Palm Beach?" I asked Rich. "Five or six hours," he said quite cheerily, without even blinking the proverbial eye. Oh, the joys of youth!

Boarding the plane, I told an ever cheery Southwest flight attendant I was hoping for lots of jokes.

"Maybe singing," he said with a smile.

A few minutes later, we were airborne for the first leg of our journey, which would take us through Houston and Tampa on our way to West Palm Beach.

The flight was smooth and uneventful, but just as we were nearing its conclusion and I was thinking the flight attendant had let me down on his promise of singing, he burst into song, singing something like, "We love you, you love us, we're much faster than a bus. Marry one of us, and you'll fly free."

I love Southwest Airlines humor! It continued just prior to the next leg of the flight, with one of the crew asking people to hurry up and get all the formalities disposed of so we could take off. He said his wife had just called, and his mother-in-law was getting through security. He wanted the plane in the air before she made it, he said. Most of the passengers laughed.

The Houston–Tampa leg was pretty smooth, and I passed the time by reading a captivating but equally horrifying book by Nick Reding titled *Methland: The Death and Life of an American Small Town.* I recommend it—the book is horrifying but a real eye-opener.

After a quick layover in Tampa and time to take care of some e-mails and phone calls, we boarded another plane for West Palm Beach.

Making my way up the aisle, I couldn't help but hear a one-sided portion of a conversation I was trying hard not to overhear.

Speaking on his cell phone rather loudly, a man was saying, "I'm fifty-two; I don't do drugs, and I don't want kids."

Hmm, I wondered. *Now we've got that taken care of, tell me how you really feel?* I wondered about the other half of that conversation.

The flight from Tampa to West Palm Beach was short and uneventful, and about forty-five minutes or so later, we touched down. Even walking through the air-conditioned airport, the humidity was apparent. While I love mountains and the ocean, humidity is definitely not for me.

Walking outside the airport, where we were met by a dealership employee who gave us a ride to the truck, I was assaulted by even worse humidity.

We arrived at the dealership a few minutes later and saw the lunch wagon. It was beautiful. A few minutes later, we were introduced to the general manager, a man not shy about sharing his faith.

He asked us about Joy Junction and how I began the shelter over two decades ago. He listened attentively as I told him. As I shared with him what the lunch truck would be used for, he seemed delighted. He initially believed, I think, that we would be selling food as a profit-making enterprise. His mouth dropped when I told him what we had in mind.

After signing all the papers necessary to transfer ownership of the lunch truck to Joy Junction, we were on our way. We prayed, ask for the Lord's blessing, and Rich started driving.

Tuned into a variety of country stations (each of which seemed to fade out of range quickly) to help ensure we stayed alert and awake, we pulled about two hours later into a services area with some relatively healthy food. Rich had a wrap, and I somehow ended up with another piece of ham quiche—but minus the green chili. This wasn't New Mexico.

We finished eating and made our way out to what the dealership staff had called our "747" lunch mobile. I agree. It is beautiful!

On the road again, and another couple of hours till Tallahassee. I offered to drive, but Rich offered to take the wheel again—for which I was admittedly grateful. It gave me the opportunity to write again. We kept driving!

Even while sitting in the 747 and rolling toward our hotel, ideas were beginning to swirl in my mind about how we could best bless the homeless with our new acquisition. We already had a staff member who was very interested in being involved in the lunch truck operation. How exciting!

We continued driving, and I kept on answering e- mails and writing. I also checked on some of the early Albuquerque municipal election results by going to Facebook. My life without Facebook and BlackBerry? Did I even have one?

As we drew in to about fifty miles of our hotel. I felt grimy, my legs were aching, my back hurt a bit, and I just wanted rest. How grateful I was for a motel room, a clean bed, and a place to stay.

It made me think of why we were doing this cross-country jaunt in the first place—to make living easier and perhaps save the life of someone by giving them life-sustaining water or coffee and some hot, nutritious, and encouraging food.

How thankful I was for this wonderful donor who had purchased this vehicle, and for the Lord who continues to sustain this amazing ministry!

A few minutes later, we pulled into our motel and checked in. I thanked the Lord for his goodness and collapsed into bed!

Day 2: The Incredible Journey Continues

It was day two of our marathon trek in the 747 lunch wagon before we hit Dallas.

Note to the TSA folks. If you unscrew liquids in my suitcase, would you please screw the cap back on so they don't spill all over my suitcase? Thanks!

It was 9:30 am in Florida—7:30 back home—and time to get on the road in the 747.

As I stepped out of the hotel, it was so humid that my glasses fogged up. This was so just not me. I couldn't wait for Albuquerque!

However, a chai and a sausage piadini would have to suffice for now! They did, and as I made my way back through the lunch wagon to the parking lot, it was such a relief not to wander directionally challenged around the parking lot in search of my little Pontiac Vibe. It would be next to impossible to miss this beautiful vehicle.

After asking the Lord's blessing on the day and our travel, we took off! Rich was happy to drive for a while, so while he did, I e-mailed and took care of "JJ" business from the BlackBerry—my international mobile office!

As I did so, I was listening to the words of the song "Live Like You're Dying." Yes, it's country, and while it may not have been written with that intent in mind, what a biblical theme. How much of the way we live would we change if we knew we only had a short time to live? I think there might be some significant changes.

We had a basically uneventful morning and pulled into a Chick–fil-A for a quick lunch. It was good, quick, and cheap. We then made our way over to Jackson, Mississippi, where the 747 needed feeding.

Pulling into a gas station with heavily barred windows, my attempts to pay at the pump were met with a computer-generated message telling me to see the attendant. I did just that, but when I offered him a credit card, he said somewhat tersely, "We don't take no credit cards." We didn't stop to inquire further. We just thanked him and went a few hundred feet across the street to a station that did.

Then we set out again. Next stop was for coffee and a couple of other small purchases. I used my VISA debit card and was very surprised when it was denied. A call a few minutes later to my credit union revealed that the credit function of the debit card had been uniformly disabled for all members in about six states due to data that had been compromised somewhere and somehow earlier this year.

Fortunately, I had an alternative method of payment. While I later learned the debit function still worked, it took a call to the credit union to find that out. Another on-the-road adventure.

We plowed (well, drove!) on. We were driving 120 west to Dallas, so somewhere west of Shreveport and about 170 miles east of Dallas, we stopped for supper. It was fast food, because we didn't want to stray too far off the highway, and as a friend told me, "Fine dining off the highway is an oxymoron!" How true that is.

I had buffalo wings with honey mustard sauce, a small fries and a coffee—the smallest cup of coffee I had ever seen. It looked like it contained about six ounces, and that's being generous! It made me laugh though.

A few minutes later, we were on the way. Dallas, here we come! What a whirlwind trip this was. As usual, my BlackBerry kept me in touch with everything and everyone.

Close to our hotel and very tired, it was an encouragement to see the Soulman's Barbeque Restaurant with a "Jesus is Lord" sign.

A few minutes later, with the help of the GPS on the BlackBerry, we pulled into our hotel. Rich and I checked in and headed off to our respective rooms.

I thanked the Lord for yet another day to serve him and collapsed into bed.

Day 3: The Incredible Journey Concludes

On our final day, I knew we needed to do two things: pray and visit Starbucks.

While talking to the barista in Starbucks, I told her that I was on the way home to Albuquerque. Another employee overheard me and said she loved Hatch green chili. She'd never been to New Mexico, but friends regularly sent her chili.

I left with my chai, happy that she'd been reminded about New Mexico and hoping that maybe I had, with the Lord's help, made her day maybe a little better.

The day passed pretty uneventfully, with Rich and I sharing the driving. I e-mailed prolifically when not driving. Running Joy Junction is a job that never ends, and it is definitely not boring.

Late afternoon we arrived at Amarillo. It would be hard not to pay a visit to the Big Texan, home of the free seventy-two-ounce steak (make that more like a roast) if you devour the gargantuan delight and sides in an hour or less.

I'd been there a number of times, but Rich had never visited. He had a (much smaller than seventy-two ounces) steak, while I settled on a heart-stopping, artery-clogging chicken fried steak. Both the food and the service were excellent.

Coming out, we were assaulted by bone-chilling temperatures, which made me thank the Lord for the safety of a warm truck (our 747food truck) and the promise later of a warm and safe house and a comfortable bed in which to rest.

I was unaware of the homeless situation in Amarillo, but I breathed a quick prayer for the Lord's blessing and protection for those homeless souls who, for whatever reason, would have no place to stay that night.

We "fed" the 747 and started off on the last leg of our long and tiring, but nonetheless fulfilling, journey.

A short while later, we were in New Mexico—with a food truck—a very tangible lifeline for the homeless. It was so good to be home again and enjoy the beautiful sunset as we got closer to Albuquerque. I so much appreciate New Mexico, where I have spent more than half of my life.

Hope and Help for the Hungry in Downtown Albuquerque and Beyond

A largely deserted lot in downtown Albuquerque that backs onto railroad tracks took on new life and hope for a while last Sunday.

It was there that about fifty homeless people enjoyed a sack lunch, a beverage, and the offer of a blanket from Joy Junction, New Mexico's largest emergency homeless shelter.

Providing a Sunday meal downtown was a new venture for Joy Junction, located about five miles from downtown, in Albuquerque's South Valley. While we serve more than ten thousand meals each month at our 4500 Second Street Southwest location, we had never before served meals off-site. But when I learned that there was a lack of resources downtown on Sunday for the city's growing homeless population, it seemed a natural thing to do.

After all, I figured, it's rather ironic that with Sunday being dubbed the Lord's Day, it was instead a day of lack for the city's poor and homeless rather than a time of bounty and provision.

Wanting to make sure we did everything right, we checked on the appropriate city requirements, and talked to the owner of the lot at First and Iron, asking whether he would be willing to allow us to hold the event there. He graciously agreed.

We started preparing. Our kitchen manager at Joy Junction, along with his crew, put together some great sack lunches. Then last Sunday, at 1 PM, our crew headed over to First and Iron.

We took one hundred fifty lunches, but I wasn't really sure about the size of the need and how many people would turn up. We set up shop, and within a few minutes, a line of people had formed. They were all hungry, extremely well behaved, and very grateful.

We served about one hundred meals to our fifty or so guests. That was because a number of people asked us if they could take another sack lunch. In some cases, it was to feed a hungry friend; for others, it was an assurance they would have something to eat that evening. How tragic that any of us have to wonder where our next meal is going to come from.

Many of those we served were understandably reticent to share the circumstances that had led to their plight. However, one man told local media he had been traveling the country, looking for work, but had run out of money and gas, and his unemployment check hadn't arrived. However, he said, at least he now had a full belly, something for which he was very grateful.

Joy Junction Outreach Coordinator Kathy Sotelo said the event touched her deeply.

"Taking part in such a wonderful event was so heartwarming. Knowing that we made a difference of that kind is unlike anything else I've ever experienced."

Kathy said as she saw the weary and sometimes emotionally and physically weighed down people take a sack lunch, she was grateful to have had a moment to chat with them.

She said, "Hearing some of their stories made me feel so much more connected."

Joy Junction Volunteer Coordinator Jonathan Matheny was equally impacted.

He said, "Probably the most moving sight was the line of homeless individuals sitting on the curb, devouring their lunch, drinking their coffee or juice, and carefully protecting their newly received blankets. They had their own little personal space, staying in their comfort zones, making sure not to waste any crumb of food or drop of liquid."

Jonathan said he began to think about the solidarity shared by our lunchtime friends. He said although there was a variety of backgrounds represented there, something special happened.

"While they began their meals as loners," Jonathan said, "they opened up and started to share stories. They began to introduce each other and exchange ideas of their individual migratory habits. [They talked about] where to go for food, who was not being nice to the homeless in downtown, and invariably, comments about Joy Junction always trying to help."

With the Lord's continued help, we will continue to keep serving Albuquerque's hungry—at Joy Junction, downtown and beyond.

Summit Electric Supply's generous donation of the Lifeline of Hope has helped us dramatically expand that initial outreach.

The Lifeline can, quite literally, make the difference between life and death to someone hungry, cold (or dehydrated), and frightened.

It launched its mission Sunday, November 8 2009, at 1 PM at the corner of First and Iron and then made its way to a number of other locations. It was stocked to serve about one hundred fifty on its launch. Now we typically feed as many as three hundred meals on a typical Sunday at various homeless "hot spots" throughout the city, and hundreds more during the other days of the week we serve.

I am very excited about this new outreach, something so needed in this difficult economy, but I'm counting on you to provide financial and volunteer support. That will allow our successful continuance and expansion. Will you help us?

Be Encouraged!

Jesus said, "'The poor you will always have with you'" (Matt. 26:11). That is not an economic indictment but a call to Christian service.

According to Scripture, we are all engaged in spiritual battle. "For our struggle is not against flesh and blood, but against the rulers, against the authorities, against the powers of this dark world and against the spiritual forces of evil in the heavenly realms. Therefore put on the full armor of God, so that when the day of evil comes, you may be able to stand your ground, and after you have done everything, to stand" (Eph. 6:12–13). This spiritual battle, along with our own predilection to sin (Romans 3:23 says, "For all have sinned and fall short of the glory of God"), explains the source of human greed and underscores the truth of Jesus' gospel. When faced with unrelenting human poverty, we have a choice to make in our own hearts. We can feel overwhelmed, or we can act on that feeling by doing God's will to provide for those in need, even though it may seem to us at times like we are taking one step forward and two steps back. That is why the very best advice I can give is to be encouraged!

Remember that at the end of long spiritual struggle, either on a personal level or in the bigger scheme of things, and by God's grace, we ultimately win! When we are slugging it out on a day-to-day basis, we sometimes lose sight of the fact that the battle is already won. We only need to be found faithful until that grand culmination of human history in the clouds.

The apostle Paul said, "For God did not appoint us to suffer wrath but to receive salvation through our Lord Jesus Christ. He died for us so that, whether we are awake or asleep, we may live together with him. Therefore encourage one another and build each other up, just as in fact you are doing" (1 Thess. 5:9–11). How could we not be encouraged with good news like that?

We are always going to have hurting, broken, spiritually needy, and financially devastated people who need the love of Jesus Christ shared with them. You are the person God has chosen to do just that.

As this book draws to a close, let me summarize some of the "know-how" I have gained as the director of a homeless shelter for the past nearly thirty years. If you need a quick word of encouragement in the future, come back to this chapter!

1. Know Your Calling

Don't start a homeless ministry if there is any doubt in your mind that God has called you into this work. If you are sure of your calling before you begin, you will always have the assurance you need when times of trial come. And make no mistake about it: trials will come, and you will want to throw your hands up in exasperation or frustration. But like all things, that too will pass if you have the assurance beforehand that you are walking along the path God has chosen for you.

There is a passage in Luke we don't hear preached from the pulpit very often, but it is important for anyone thinking about the demanding work of homeless ministry. In chapter 9, there are men who say they are ready to follow the Lord. However, when Jesus bids each one in turn to "'Follow me,'" they each come up with an excuse for not doing so. One has to bury his father, and another needs to say good-bye to his family. Jesus had a stern warning for those who voiced a false calling. He said (in Luke 9:62), "'No one who puts his hand to the plow and looks back is fit for service in the kingdom of God.'"

With that warning in mind, let me say that it is a wonderful thing to pray about starting a homeless ministry. Enlist support. Explore the possibilities. But don't actually begin unless you are prepared to go the distance with Jesus, even when the times get tough. If you have a genuine call, you will not be able to fall away, even though you may sometimes feel you want to. If God has called you, you can be assured you will finish well.

2. Know Your Mission

When you incorporate as a nonprofit corporation, you must formulate a mission statement. That says in a sentence or two what you are all about. It is the reason for your existence. Hold yourself to that statement, because it will help you stay right on track.

Besides the important corporate statement, there will be an inner light guiding you if you know your mission. I suggest that you select a Bible verse that encapsulates your vision. It doesn't matter if it comes from Genesis, Revelation, or any biblical book in between. But it should be one that summarizes your mission for the Lord. It could be as broad as Matthew 28:19 and 20, or as narrow in scope as Matthew 13:8. It may be a verse that embraces the whole world, like John 3:16, or it may be something very personal, such as 1 Thessalonians 2:8.

I encourage you to use the verse you select as your motto. Put it on the wall in your office, memorize it, and share its meaning with others in private conversations and public gatherings. It is good to have a Scripture verse that states your mission; it will inspire you, and it will inspire others.

3. Know You Are in Spiritual Work

If you need to see tangible results from your work each day, get a job as a bricklayer, not as a director of a homeless shelter. Ministry is intangible work. It is not as if you start a particular task and finish a few hours or a few days later. You do not. It is work in which you are investing in the life of a person, the full effect of which might not be seen for many years. In most cases, you will not see the tangible results of what you accomplish. Occasional blessings will leap out at you, but they are memorable precisely because they are so rare.

Homeless ministry is doing the work of a shepherd. The wayward sheep you are caring for today will need the same care tomorrow and the day after that. The shepherd model is very different from the teacher model. Teachers generally offer information, see it internalized in the lives of their students, and then see some progress in their lives as a result. Teachers can measure mastery, but shepherds cannot. If you know the true nature of shelter work as you begin, this should not discourage you.

I do not want to minimize the importance of the training you will, I hope, offer your residents. Training is an important building block for homeless people, whether it is spiritual or practical in nature. But seeing yourself as a shepherd, with all its risks and lack of clear resolution, is a better model for the minister to the homeless.

The primary goal of every shepherd is to feed the sheep, not to please them. People-pleasing is a political activity far removed from ministry, and the more you get tangled up in it, the less effective you will be in your work.

You will feed the sheep physically and spiritually. You can have some tangible sense of accomplishment by keeping track of meals served, but dishing out spiritual food is different. Sheep can be disagreeable, ungrateful, exasperating animals.

The reality is, you can only direct the sheep along the proper path as an "overseer"; you cannot change their essential nature—only God can do that. I believe this was the point the apostle Peter was making when he said, "Be shepherds of God's flock that is under your care, serving as overseers—not because you must, but because you are willing, as God wants you to be; not greedy for money, but eager to serve; not lording it over those entrusted to you, but being examples to the flock" (1 Pet. 5:2).

If you are a good example to the flock, you are fulfilling God's call in your life. That is true success in any spiritual ministry.

4. Know Your Limits

A friend of mine recently told me about a car accident he was in. A drunk driver rammed him from the back, and it seemed like the inside of his car exploded. He got out of the car after the dust cleared, and bystanders asked him if he was okay. He said he was fine, not noticing he was bleeding profusely from the head. The ambulance took him to the hospital, and after they bandaged him, he left. He made it out to the parking lot before he collapsed, and they had to bring him back inside.

My friend simply did not know his limits. He said, "I was in a daze from the accident; I have no idea why those doctors listened to me when I told them I was okay."

We are all in the same boat when it comes to knowing our limits. We think we know, but we don't, and that is why it is so important to have a spouse or close friend monitor us as we serve the Lord. When they see burnout approaching, we need to have the wisdom to listen to them and take a break.

Although there is always going to be that overwhelming need, there is only one of you. Remember that you are limited by the resources with which God entrusts you. As great as the need seems, it is still more important to be obedient to God. God is more impressed by your obedience to him than by the scale of what you do.

5. Know How to Nourish Yourself Spiritually

If you are operating your shelter for the homeless in the power of the Holy Spirit, all is well. But if you are trying to run it in your own strength, your work will burn like the wood, hay, and stubble that the apostle Paul describes in the third chapter of 1 Corinthians. The difference between running a shelter in the flesh and running it in the Spirit is determined by your own personal spiritual life. That is why I strongly encourage you to know how to nourish yourself spiritually.

The first rule in this regard is simply never allow yourself to get so busy that you don't spend time with the Lord. You will get faint in body if you do not eat, and you will become faint spiritually if you don't spend time feasting in the Word of God.

You can nourish yourself spiritually by reading the Bible devotionally, by praying often, and by sitting in the presence of the Lord, praising and enjoying him.

One of the pitfalls you are likely to encounter is studying the Bible to prepare messages or lessons but not taking the time to read it to nourish your own soul. I encourage you to learn this distinction early in your ministry to the homeless. The tendency is to think we must feed others to feed ourselves, but the opposite is true. It is essential that we spend time in the Word each day.

Too often prayer becomes nothing more than a recitation of needs. There is nothing wrong with asking God to meet our needs, of course, as our Lord wants to hear the desires of our heart (even though he has the power to change those desires to those more in keeping with his will for your life). But at the same time, we need to be mindful that prayer is something of gigantic dimensions. We pray for the poor because they are all around us. We pray for our needs because we are needy. We pray for bread because we are hungry. At the same time, we need to expand our prayer horizons and remember other things going on in this world, whether it be politics or overseas missions. It is a matter of getting out of the box.

I have often wondered what God would do if those around the world who are homeless started praying for each other.

Big prayer will nourish you spiritually. And as you pray, don't forget to praise God for his many blessings. We serve a wonderful God!

Two important ideas about spiritual nourishment are that you will be a spiritual leader to the homeless and your staff, and you will be a spiritual leader in your home. These are important responsibilities you must embrace.

When it comes to your staff, you must always be the one to take them back to first principles. Inevitably, they will get caught up in the mundane tasks and lose sight of the greater mission. You can be a godly example by always reminding them of their mission, keeping your own emotions in check when a crisis arises, and by frequently encouraging them. Lead your staff in group devotions on a set schedule.

When it comes to your family, you cannot neglect them spiritually for the sake of your work at the shelter. You need to take the time to have family devotions, to go to church together as a family, to take part in church fellowship activities as a couple, and in the special events in which your children may be involved.

The devil has one big lie he keeps using over and over to destroy families. The lie he will put in your mind is this: "I am too busy to spend time with my wife and children now, but I will spend more time with them later, when I am able." You will discover that you will only become increasingly more busy if you allow it to happen, and your family will drift away from you in such a subtle way you will not realize it until it is too late. Sadly, you will never be able to capture time lost; it is best to make the most of every moment with them.

6. Know There Will Never Be Enough Money

We all know that the Lord owns the cattle on a thousand hills, and he has the resources to pay our bills. Then why do they sometimes not get paid? The problem is not with the Lord, for he is already on record as saying he wants to abundantly bless all his children (John 10:10). The problem is with other people who do not obediently give to the Lord's work. They are the ones who shut down the Lord's supply lines. In order to keep those lines open and flowing, get before audiences as much as you can. That is why I place such an emphasis on working with the media and the community.

That kind of vision will keep you growing and on target. But do not get ahead of the Lord by spending money you don't have and can't get. Remember, every vision you have to expand your ministry will be confirmed by a godly man or woman with a desire from the Lord and the resources to help you. If they do not appear, it is just a personal dream and not a vision from God. There is misery enough in ministry without money misery. I always liked the equation Charles Dickens gave: "Annual income twenty pounds, annual expenditure nineteen six, result happiness. Annual income twenty pounds, annual expenditure twenty pounds ought and six, result misery."

The key is to make sure your vision is not bigger than your income. If you already know you are doing God's will by operating a shelter, there is no magic in your decision-making process; you must raise money before it becomes due or curtail the service you are offering, painful as that may be. The long and short of this is realizing there will never be enough money, so be careful with the money you have.

7. Know That People Are Making Progress Whether You See It or Not

Many shelter directors see some of the same people come back in the same desperate predicament year after year. This is especially disturbing, as you know what it takes for these individuals to get back on their feet again. You believe they know what they need to do, but for whatever reason, they are not doing what is necessary to get back into mainstream community life.

There was a man at our facility named Mike, who had been an alcoholic for most of his fifty-three years. He had plans to return to college so he could learn to restore classic cars. He said, "I know I have to get my life together, and this is something I really want to do. If I had the education, I could get a job if one came along." I would not want to demean Mike in any way or limit what God could do in his life. But sadly, Mike is in a loop, and he has been at this very same place in his life scores of times before. In times past, he found his way back to the bottle, then entered recovery, and then imagined big plans for the future.

When you work with people like Mike, you can sometimes doubt that they are making any progress. But the reality is, they are making progress in their own way, and we need to thank God for that. The fact that Mike has any hope for the future at all is a great blessing. He could have died in a drunken stupor many times, but he continues to move forward. His bouts of drunkenness become less frequent, and his days of hopeful thoughts more frequent. In our perspective, that may be growing at a snail's pace. But for someone like Mike, that is real, measurable progress.

The simple fact is that as long as God's Spirit is working in the lives of people, progress is being made. We like to measure progress by our own standards, but that is not the way it works. Our role is to show compassion, and it is God's work to bring change into the hearts and lives of individuals.

8. Know You Cannot Reach Everyone, but Jesus Can

As you know, at Joy Junction we do not wait for the homeless to come to us. We go out on the streets of Albuquerque with our bus or van and pick them up. We are fulfilling the biblical mandate that Jesus expressed in Luke 14:23 where he said, "'Go out to the roads and country lanes and make them come in, so that my house will be full.'" Yet, at the same time, I know that each night there are homeless people sleeping on the streets, people we cannot reach.

The simple fact is that even when some needy people do come under our care, we sometimes cannot reach them. Sometimes, they have deteriorated so much either physically or mentally that there is little we can do for them except direct them to outside medical help.

Have we failed because we could not inspire them with the life-changing message of the gospel? No, of course not. We must simply trust God as he works out his will in the lives of individuals in ways beyond our understanding. Our role is to show compassion and then to leave the results to God.

I understand how difficult this can be. We all want to do great deeds for God, but the spiritual reality is that things work the other way around: God is in the process of doing great things in and through us. When God does great things through us, he uses them to point to him. We are not doing it; God is doing it. And that is why it is so important to yield. If we want to do the job right, we must fall back on that old cliché, "The best ability is availability." Being totally available to God can produce wonderful things.

A New Theme Song for Joy Junction

Country star and Joy Junction friend Rockie Lynne wrote and recorded this wonderful song for Joy Junction. We are so grateful and encourage you to contact Rockie through his Web site at www.rockielynne.com to express your appreciation for his kindness to Joy Junction. I loved the song the moment I heard it.

"Hand Up"

There's a lady standing in an unemployment line
She's got a baby in her arms and two tagging along behind
Man says the wage that you make can't pay for your day care
Ma'am you'd be better off on welfare
She don't need a hand out
She needs a hand up
Some solid ground where she can stand up
Fallin' down's been rocky and rough enough
She don't need a hand out she needs a hand up

He's got a bottle hidden in a bag that's brown
It's not enough to swim in but it's enough to drown
He don't need a lecture or a Sermon on the Mount
He just needs a place to lay his head
While he's trying to lay that bottle down
He don't need a hand out
He needs a hand up
Like a ray of sunshine in the pouring rain
Joy Junction is an amazing place

(Instrumental)

They don't need a hand out they need a hand up
Some solid ground where they can stand up
Fallin' down's been rocky and rough enough
They don't need a hand out
They need a hand up

Written by Rockie Lynne
(c) Carolina Blue Sky Music (BMI)

My benediction for you is that you have complete faith in God as you seek to serve the homeless in his name. God has a special blessing for you, and it is found in Psalm 112:

Blessed is the man who fears the LORD,
who finds great delight in his commands ...
He has scattered abroad his gifts to the poor,
his righteousness endures forever;
his horne will be lifted high in honor (1, 9).

LaVergne, TN USA
13 September 2010
196883LV00001B/2/P